Student Companion to
Tennessee
WILLIAMS

Student Companion to

Tennessee WILLIAMS

Nancy M. Tischler

Student Companions to Classic Writers

Greenwood Press
Westport, Connecticut • London

Library of Congress Cataloging-in-Publication Data

Tischler, Nancy Marie Patterson.
　　Student companion to Tennessee Williams / Nancy M. Tischler.
　　　　p.　cm.—(Student companions to classic writers, ISSN 1522–7979)
　　Includes bibliographical references and index.
　　ISBN 0–313–31238–9 (alk. paper)
　　1. Williams, Tennessee, 1911–1983—Criticism and interpretation.　2. Williams,
Tennessee, 1911–1983—Examinations—Study guides.　I. Title.　II. Series.
　　PS3545.I5365　Z853　2000
　　812′.54—dc21　　　　00–025147

British Library Cataloguing in Publication Data is available.

Library of Congress Catalog Card Number: 00–025147
ISBN: 0–313–31238–9
ISSN: 1522–7979

First published in 2000

Greenwood Press, 88 Post Road West, Westport, CT 06881
An imprint of Greenwood Publishing Group, Inc.
www.greenwood.com

Printed in the United States of America

The paper used in this book complies with the
Permanent Paper Standard issued by the National
Information Standards Organization (Z39.48–1984).

10　9　8　7　6　5　4　3　2　1

For
Allean Hale, Al Devlin, and the late Lyle Leverich.
Good scholars and good friends.

Contents

Series Foreword

This series has been designed to meet the needs of students and general readers for accessible literary criticism on the American and world writers most frequently studied and read in the secondary school, community college, and four-year college classrooms. Unlike other works of literary criticism that are written for the specialist and graduate student, or that feature a variety of reprinted scholarly essays on sometimes obscure aspects of the writer's work, the Student Companions to Classic Writers series is carefully crafted to examine each writer's major works fully and in a systematic way, at the level of the non-specialist and general reader. The objective is to enable the reader to gain a deeper understanding of the work and to apply critical thinking skills to the act of reading. The proven format for the volumes in this series was developed by an advisory board of teachers and librarians for a successful series published by Greenwood Press, Critical Companions to Popular Contemporary Writers. Responding to their request for easy-to-use and yet challenging literary criticism for students and adult library patrons, Greenwood Press developed a systematic format that is not intimidating but helps the reader to develop the ability to analyze literature.

How does this work? Each volume in the Student Companions to Classic Writers series is written by a subject specialist, an academic who understands students' needs for basic and yet challenging examination of the writer's canon. Each volume begins with a biographical chapter, drawn from published sources, biographies, and autobiographies, that relates the writer's life to his or her work. The next chapter examines the writer's literary heritage, tracing the literary influences of other writers on that writer and explaining and discussing the literary genres into which the writer's work falls. Each of the following chapters examines a major work by the writer, those works most frequently read and studied by high school and college students. Depending on the writer's canon, generally between four and eight major works are examined, each in an individual chapter. The discussion of each work is organized into separate sections on plot development, character development, and major themes. Literary devices and style, narrative point of view, and historical setting are also discussed in turn if pertinent to the work. Each chapter concludes with an alternate critical perspective from which to read the work, such as a psychological or feminist criticism. The critical theory is defined briefly in easy, comprehensible language for the student. Looking at the literature from the point of view of a particular critical approach will help the reader to understand and apply critical theory to the act of reading and analyzing literature.

Of particular value in each volume is the bibliography, which includes a complete bibliography of the writer's works, a selected bibliography of biographical and critical works suitable for students, and lists of reviews of each work examined in the companion, all of which will be helpful to readers, teachers, and librarians who would like to consult additional sources.

As a source of literary criticism for the student or for the general reader, this series will help the reader to gain understanding of the writer's work and skill in critical reading.

1

The Life of Tennessee Williams

Tennessee Williams, or Thomas Lanier Williams, was born in Mississippi. He assumed the name "Tennessee" after college, when he decided to become a professional writer. By that time, he had rejected his early lyrical poetry and gothic tales for a new type of literary image. He was afraid that the name of his collateral ancestor, Sidney Lanier (a nineteenth-century Southern poet) would sound too precious for the popular playwright he planned to become.

The Tennessee Williams known to the public was largely his own creation: The birth date he used much of his professional life was incorrect. He was actually born in 1911 but lied about his age so as to appear young enough to enter a contest for young playwrights. His devil-may-care attitude, bringing him fame and fortune as a playwright of sexuality and violence, really was a rebellion against his Puritan upbringing. Deep down, he was an intensely serious writer who saw his creativity as a gift and writing as a vocation.

EARLY YEARS

Williams was born in an Episcopal rectory, in Columbus, Mississippi. In his early years, he was pampered by his grandfather, his grandmother, his mother, and his sister Rose. Walter Dakin, his grandfather, was an Episcopal priest who moved around the South ministering to a number of small congregations. The Delta country, around Clarksdale, Mississippi, where Williams spent his childhood, was to become his fictional "Two Rivers County." The heat, the storms, the floods of that region, the division into social classes, the colorful imagery and rhythms of the speech were to shape his setting and dialogue. Many of the people in that town were to provide the names and details of the characters he later used in his plays and stories: families like the Cutreres, Bobos, Wingfields, and first names like Brick, Blanche, and Baby Doll.

No characters were to be more important to Williams than the members of his own family, whom he immortalized in his plays. His mother, Edwina Dakin Williams, became the model for his antiquated Southern belles and overprotective mothers. Tom had been critically ill as a child, giving his mother an excuse for hovering over him and providing him with a lifelong concern for his health. His father, Cornelius Coffin Williams, considered by Edwina and the children a frightening and alien male presence, was only occasionally in their home. He was the powerful, swaggering bully who became Big Daddy and Stanley Kowalski. Tom's beloved sister, Rose, who was close to his age and his favorite playmate as a child, turned into a fragile, lost young woman—Laura of *The Glass Menagerie*. The grandfather who sheltered the mother and her children in the early years and in later years became his famous grandson's favorite companion, was immortalized as Nonno in *The Night of the Iguana*—the oldest living, practicing poet.

When Tom was seven years old, his domineering father took on a new importance to him by suddenly moving the family from the rectory in Clarksdale to an apartment in St. Louis, Missouri. Cornelius had been promoted to an important position in the central offices of the International Shoe Company after years of traveling from place to place as a "drummer" (the term used at the time for a traveling salesman) for Red Goose Shoes. He thought this would be the beginning of a grand career. For a while, this appeared to be the case; Cornelius was genial and smart, a real man's man. He loved to drink and play cards with the men. One fateful night in 1936, the game turned violent; a fight ensued, and a companion bit off Cornelius's ear. The ear was surgically reattached and the family tried to keep the story quiet, but this was the end of Cornelius's rise in the International Shoe Company (Leverich 1995, 191–92). Even so, he was far more prosperous than most heads of families during the Depression. He always had a job and was able to find work with his company for Tom whenever he needed help. For all of his boisterous ways and failure to understand this effeminate son, Tom's father was a source of financial support for the writer until he reached his mid-thirties. The relationship was strained; the father did not understand why Tom could not be like him, but he never stopped worrying about him and defending him (See "The Man in the Overstuffed Chair," in *Tennessee Williams: Collected Stories* 1985).

Tom found the big city of St. Louis crowded, dirty, and unfriendly. Other children laughed at his Southern accent and made fun of his "sissy" tastes, driving him into an even closer relationship with Rose. His mother hated her reduced status as one of many matrons in the city, no longer the honored daughter of the respected Episcopal priest. (In small towns, the clergy ranked with the lawyers and doctors as the resident intellectuals. Their families were considered upper class, even though they may have been comparatively poor.) She undertook to rectify this social fall by striving for a better neighborhood and for increased prestige through taking an active role in the Daughters of the American Revolution (DAR). Her unhappiness was undoubtedly communicated to the children, making them even more desolate. When Dakin, Tom's baby brother, was born and became the center of attention, the older children found themselves even more isolated. Neither Tom nor Rose did very well in school.

To help Tom recover his health and improve his grades, the family sent him back for an extended visit to Clarksdale, where he enjoyed the total attention of his grandparents. The letters from that period, 1920, reveal a child delighted with his life and proud to be writing home to Rose and "King Dakin." After a year and a half, he returned to St. Louis, where he gradually discovered that he could compensate for his misery at home through his satisfaction in writing. From his early teens, he won prizes for his poetry and his stories, even getting some of them published. His mother kept scrapbooks of his accomplishments, demonstrating her pride in his success. (These remarkable scrapbooks are part of the collection at the Harry Ransom Humanities Research Center at the University of Texas, Austin.) His father, on the other hand, preferred Dakin, who proved to be a good student and more of a "regular" guy.

In 1928, while he was in high school, Tom had an adventure that was to color his life. He took a trip to Europe, by way of New York City, with a tour group his grandfather was guiding. Their brief stopover in New York city allowed Tom to see Broadway, his first taste of big-time theatre. The romance of the ship passage and the travels through Europe gave fresh meaning to many of his readings, and encouraged him to adopt a lifelong love of travel (*Memoirs* 1975, 19–23).

In the meantime, Rose was finding little success either in her studies or with boyfriends. She had a series of "nervous" disorders, which her mother at first considered physical. The family tried a number of strategies—sending her to visit relatives, shipping her off to a girls' school in the Delta, and finally taking her to a series of doctors and clinics. Gradually it became obvious that her problems were psychologically based. She would focus her attention obsessively on food or clothes or boyfriends; she became increasingly withdrawn and peculiar. She finally slipped into schizophrenia, a condition that eventually forced the family to institutionalize her. Tom visited her occasionally, but his journals—the diaries he began to keep—reveal that he was horrified at the transformation in his sister. His mother did not encourage his visits, fearing that he would follow her example. Several years later, in 1943, when Rose had a frontal lobotomy that disabled her permanently, Tom felt particularly guilty. This operation, which was used to "cure" shell-shocked soldiers in the war, involved cutting into the brain, leaving the patient calm, but permanently limited (Leverich, 224–25, 480–82). Rose had been his soulmate from childhood, his best friend and his most imaginative playmate. He had not been able to help her at her time of crisis; in addition, he was too busy with his own affairs. Furthermore, he made his first great success out of writing her story. In his mind, her fall was closely tied to his rise.

EDUCATION AND APPRENTICESHIP

On graduation from high school in 1929, Tom entered the University of Missouri at Columbia, a college famous for its journalism program. He enjoyed his writing classes, the French and literature, but hated to get up in time for ROTC (Reserve Officers' Training Corps), which was required of the men at the university. He found he did not like writing the assigned pieces for journalism classes—reports on the egg market, obituaries, etc. He preferred creative writing and tried his hand at a few short plays. He was invited to join a fraternity and discovered quickly that he enjoyed parties and drinking.

When his grades testified to his poor study practices, especially his neglect of his military obligation, his angry father cut off his funding, brought him home to St. Louis, and settled him into a dreary clerical job at Continental Shoes. This was in the middle of the painful period of Rose's decline, before her institutionalization and surgery. The family was worried about her, the mother and father were involved in constant warfare, and Dakin was the designated favorite. Tom had never been so unhappy.

For the next few years, he lived at home, wrote every night, and went to the movies. Like the hero of *The Glass Menagerie*, he was determined to escape from this trap. Luckily for the young man, there were others in St. Louis, which he later renamed "St. Pollution," who shared his artistic interests. He found a band of poets who spent their evenings writing lyric poetry. But even more important, he found a small theatre group in St. Louis, called The Mummers, who were producing plays. He joined them, wrote for them, and was delighted to see his work become flesh. For the most part, they were talented amateurs, but they gave him a chance to discover what was to become the love of his life ("Something Wild . . . ," in *Where I Live* 1978, 7–14).

His grandparents, seeing how miserable Tom was at home, encouraged him to go back to college. At first, he tried classes at Washington University, which was located nearby. Although his grades were uneven, his grandparents agreed to sponsor his entry into the theatre program at the University of Iowa, which had a renowned faculty and remarkable facilities. In these final years of college at Iowa, he learned a great deal about acting, stage management, and writing. He also came to know a number of professional theatre people and understand the business of theatre. Though he had been an avid reader all of his life, it was here that he did much of his reading of plays.

THE EARLY TENNESSEE WILLIAMS

When he finally graduated from the University of Iowa in the summer of 1938, Tom Williams found himself faced with another challenge—the need for a job. This was the middle of the Depression, and Tom realized that he would be wise to return to the shoe factory in St. Louis, a safe place to settle. He also realized that such safety was tantamount to death. Determined to use his newly acquired skills in playwriting, he sought work elsewhere—first in Chicago, then in New Orleans. At that time, the Federal Writers' Project was sponsoring young playwrights, but that program was coming to an end.

On his way from St. Louis to New Orleans, Tom stopped by to see his grandparents, who now had retired and were living in Memphis, Tennessee. While there, he put a few of his short plays in the mail, sending them to a contest for young writers sponsored by the Group Theatre, pretending that he was only 23 years old (though he was actually 27), and calling himself, for the first time "Tennessee." He thought the Memphis postmark would keep the judges from discovering his true age and identity.

He then spent a few weeks in New Orleans, where he discovered Bohemia. This amoral life of the Vieux Carré, the old and arty section of the city, full of lively conversation and colorful characters was the existence for which he knew in his heart he had been born. He stayed only a couple of months, but he knew this was his spiritual home. He would be back. Then, with a new friend, Jim Parrott, he headed west. The two penniless young men had little more than Jim's car—a Ford V-8—and Jim's clarinet-playing to get them to California, sleeping under the stars, taking any job that would provide money for gas and food, and finally settling on a squab ranch near Los Angeles run by Jim's uncle.

They were still there when Tom heard that "Tennessee Williams" had won a prize in the Group Theatre Contest. The award letter and the $100 were followed by an offer by a New York agent, Audrey Wood, to help him with his career. Williams spent the money on a bicycle trip he and Jim took to Mexico along the Camino Real, the coastal highway. On his way back to Los Angeles, he discovered an artists' colony at Laguna Beach. He and Jim rented a cabin in a nearby canyon for a time. Then he began to portray himself as a vagabond poet in letters to Audrey Wood and old friends. He was reinventing himself, transforming timid Tom Williams into dashing Tennessee.

By the summer of 1938, he had run out of money and was ready to return home. His family sent him bus fare to St. Louis, to which he traveled by way of Taos, New Mexico. He had grown increasingly interested in the life and work of D. H. Lawrence and wanted to meet his widow, Frieda Lawrence, and discover something of the countryside that Lawrence loved. Although the play he had in mind at the time was never fully realized, D. H. Lawrence was to remain a major influence on his work. This poet-novelist, whose works touched on many of Williams' concerns, wrote movingly of his own childhood, his love-hate relationship with his mother and father, his tormented love affairs, and his critique of the modern world, sexuality, and humdrum conformity. Williams thought the man to be a true prophet. In Taos, he was welcomed by Lawrence's widow and the community of true believers who still clustered about her.

Williams, now "Tennessee," stopped briefly in St. Louis, and then joined one of his poet friends who was heading to New York. He wanted to meet Audrey Wood and the members of the famous Group Theatre, who had invited him to come north. He also wanted to see something of professional theatre, realizing that to be a success he had to conquer Broadway. He discovered Audrey to be exactly the guide he needed. For the next several years, Audrey was to be his fairy godmother, finding him grants and jobs, helping him to survive during the many years of forced apprenticeship between his arrival in New York and his final success with *The Glass Menagerie*.

THE ROAD TO BROADWAY

Between the time when the penniless young man stepped into the dazzling world of New York theatre and the moment he took his first bows, he had several frustrating years and one devastating failure.

At first it looked as if he had an idea for just the right play to interest professional producers and directors. It was called *Battle of Angels* and used some of his vagabond experiences, his Delta background, and his enthusiasm for D. H. Lawrence's philosophy of sexuality. (Lawrence—and Williams—thought we had lost touch with our primitive roots and rich sexual nature, becoming sterile and conformist. Both authors attributed much of this to the influence of repressive Puritanism.) Williams called his hero Valentine Xavier, making him a bit like blues musicians he had seen in Clarksdale (the home of the blues), something like Rudolph Valentino (the current movie idol), with a touch of Vachel Lindsay (a popular poet of the period), a good bit of Christ imagery, and a fair helping of Tom/Tennessee Williams. This curious loner wanders into a small Southern town and turns the place upside down. The play, which was produced by the prestigious Theatre Guild, opened in Boston in December 1940. It provoked outrage there and quickly closed, without moving on to Broadway.

The young playwright, shocked and discouraged, resumed his frantic travels, looking for a place to recuperate, to rewrite his failed play, and to rediscover his courage and creativity. He soon located that haven in Key West, Florida. There he found a friendly welcome, warm weather, and beaches for his favorite form of exercise and relief—swimming. In those days—just before World War II—Key West was inexpensive and raffish. Later, when he had made his fortune, he bought a small cottage there, which became his real home.

By the time he retreated to Key West in 1941, he had acknowledged to himself that he was gay and had gathered a cluster of homosexual friends, but he chose to keep this recognition a secret from his family. In New Orleans, Provincetown, New York, and Key West, he found communities of like-minded companions, with whom he sometimes stayed and frequently corresponded. His sexual orientation was not to become an openly stated part of his plays for a number of years, but it was apparent in early poems and short stories (which he asked his publisher to refrain from marketing in the St. Louis region). His brother was probably the first member of the family to realize that Tennessee was gay; later his grandfather lived with Williams and his partner, clearly understanding their relationship. But the mother and father never acknowledged that they had a homosexual son. In that era, and in that culture, such an admission would have been shocking. The conflicted need to proclaim his truth and the embarrassment he knew it would bring his family caused Tennessee Williams to lead a double life for many years. The devices and pretenses involved may well have contributed to insights and subtleties in his plays. He knew what it was to play different parts for different audiences.

The next few years saw Williams becoming a compulsive traveler, going from Key West to the Georgia coast, then to St. Louis, then to New York, to Mexico, to New Orleans, and then to Provincetown and back to New York. This mad journey continued for the rest of his life, even after he had his cottage in Key West and his apartment in New Orleans. The obligatory pilgrimage always included New York, the center of his professional life, and St. Louis, the core of his family life. At first, before he was a success, he settled into places where the living was cheap, the moral oversight minimal, the weather warm, and the swimming superb. Tracing his itinerary is a biographer's nightmare. He left behind him along the way a tell-tale trail of unpaid debts, lost laundry, misplaced manuscripts, pawned possessions, and damaged furnishings.

In the meantime, his artistic life was remarkably disciplined: he woke early, had his coffee, settled down to his typewriter, and typed steadily for hours. He once said that he was not so much a writer as a compulsive typist. (Any Williams scholar becomes amazed at the constant shifts in type fonts as he wore out one typewriter after another.) When he had exhausted his creative urge for the day, he went for a long swim, a relaxed meal (if money and food and friends were available) and spent the remainder of the day drinking and socializing. In the late hours, when everyone had left, he usually found he was not yet sleepy. It was then that he read the latest books and plays and wrote countless letters—usually on hotel stationery. When the insomnia tormented him late into the night, he would try to force sleep by using heavier and heavier doses of sleeping pills, added to the increased intake of alcohol, which drugged him into an uneasy rest. No matter how late the party ran that night or how chaotic his room, he would rise early the next morning, get his coffee, and begin once again pounding away on his typewriter. If his typewriter was at the pawnbrokers, he would borrow a friend's. If his friends had none to offer, or if he had already hocked theirs, he wrote in pencil. Nothing could stop his writing.

He passed thirty and still was not earning a living with his writing: he existed on handouts from his concerned mother, his sympathetic grandparents, and his outraged father. His grandmother, who made a few dollars teaching music, would stitch a five-dollar bill into a letter. To wheedle a few dollars from his mother, Williams would pretend he was coming home and needed bus fare. He worked at a variety of jobs, rarely for more than a month—as a clerk in a hotel, as an usher at a movie theatre, as a teletype operator for the War Department. Occasionally, he won grants from the Rockefeller Foundation or other groups that Audrey discovered for him. She also found a way to sell a few stories, options on plays, etc. She said that she saw her role as keeping him alive until he was a success. It was a long wait.

In 1943, frustrated with her efforts to find him a production on Broadway, Audrey won Williams a job at Metro-Goldwyn-Mayer writing dialogue for the popular stars of the era. He tried to write scenes for *The Pink Bedroom* and other potboilers, but his heart was not in this work. He preferred to spend his time on the Santa Monica beach or in his room, writing a play about his family—a gentle drama that had been taking form in his mind over the years.

At one point, he thought of making this tale, sometimes called "The Front Porch Girl," sometimes "The Gentleman Caller," the story of Rose's sad efforts at attracting young men. At another, he saw it as his mother's efforts at reestablishing her position in society by becoming the regent of the local chapter of the DAR. His sister's decline into madness and her hideous surgery in 1943 had focused his attention increasingly on her tragedy. He remembered the old apartment in St. Louis that had been such a nightmare for the family, the unhappiness and the sense of poverty, the love and frustration of the cluster of refugees from the South, and his own need to escape this tender trap.

He drafted and submitted the idea for the play to MGM. They rejected it and suspended him. He took the money he had saved during the months working in California, went to Mexico, and completed work on *The Glass Menagerie*. Audrey, when she read it, was delighted. She knew she had in her hands a masterpiece—and a success.

SUCCESS AT LAST

The Glass Menagerie opened in Chicago, in midwinter, at the end of 1944. At first, the crowds were modest, largely because of the miserable weather. Then a local critic, Claudia Cassidy, began to scold local theatregoers for ignoring this work of genius. Within a few weeks, the box-office increased, and it became clear that Tennessee Williams was a success. From Chicago, the play moved on to New York, where the 34-year-old author had 24 curtain calls on opening night. It ran for 561 performances and won the New York Drama Critics' Circle Award for Best Play and the Donaldson and Sidney Howard Memorial awards.

At this remarkable moment in Tennessee Williams' life, the war was drawing to a close, and he was positioned to be the outstanding dramatist of postwar America. Even before *Menagerie* was translated into a successful Hollywood film, Williams was at work on more plays: the first a coauthored play based on a D. H. Lawrence short story, *You Touched Me!* (1945) which was not well received. The second, however, was a smash hit, *A Streetcar Named Desire* (1947). This powerful production, his first collaboration with the brilliant director Elia Kazan, once again won the author the New York Drama Critics' Circle Award and the Donaldson award. This time, he also won the Pulitzer Prize. When it was made into a film in 1951, this classic confronted the standards of decency current among the filmmakers at the time, becoming a landmark as the first "adult film."

No one could doubt his success, but Williams found that fame was not so thrilling as he had expected. He discovered that much of the excitement in his life had been based on his struggle to reach the top. Suddenly, he looked around, finding he was King of the Mountain, and the moment proved disappointing. (See his comments in "On a Streetcar Named Success," in *Where I Live* 1978, 15–22.) He found himself indifferent, cynical, and isolated. Since his college days, he had been a heavy drinker from time to time. That self-destructive pattern now deepened. His insomnia also intensified, leading him to taking more and more pills to ensure a good night's sleep, leaving him groggy in the morning. This he rectified by drinking cup after cup of strong coffee, which probably completed the vicious circle of destruction by increasing his insomnia. All of his life he had been a hypochondriac. This concern for his own health escalated over time; his letters frequently note that he is in ill health or does not expect to live long. He was sure he would die young—right up to his death at 72.

His life grew frenzied with a flurry of new plays, travel, films, and fresh contacts with old friends and new lovers. One joyous experience in those busy years was the reacquaintance with Frank Merlo. They became lovers for the next dozen years. Frankie kept Williams' life more orderly than would otherwise have been the case, gave him advice, planned his travels, helped with meals, and saved him from loneliness.

Not every work, even in these glory days, was met with critical acclaim. Another Southern play, *Summer and Smoke* (1948) premiered in a small theatre in Dallas, at almost the same time as *Streetcar*, but was delayed to give *Streetcar* the spotlight. It was not quite so powerful, but was professionally staged by Margo Jones, who was his dear friend and loyal supporter. The play received thoughtful reviews and had fair run on Broadway when it finally got there in 1952. Williams took it back and revised it, returning with a new script which he called *The Eccentricities of a Nightingale* in 1964. In the meantime, it was made into a film in 1961, and later a television play. It never achieved the level of success of *Menagerie* or *Streetcar*.

He experimented with different forms, including a novel about his experiences in Rome, called *The Roman Spring of Mrs. Stone*. The story, while revealing his genuine pleasure in this ancient city and his love of its people, also drew an ironic contrast to the decadent American expatriates who settled there. He himself loved to spend as much time as possible in Rome. The stream-of-consciousness novel was made into a beautiful film with Vivien Leigh and Warren Beatty, but attracted little praise (Yacowar 1977, 84–91). He tried a comedy to relieve the tragic pattern he had established, *The Rose Tattoo*. It celebrated the joy he found in his love for Frank Merlo, a Sicilian-American. In it, Williams used his experiences visiting Frankie's family in Sicily and his genuine delight with Mediterranean manners and mores. Again it was a modest success on Broadway, when it opened in 1951, winning only the Tony award. After all his early triumphs, this seemed a comedown. It too was immediately turned into a movie, which was filmed in his neighborhood in Key West (Yacowar 25–31). He continued to publish short stories and poems. His old friend Jay Laughlin, owner of New Directions Press, brought out the individual poems in his annual collections and published two separate volumes of his poetry, as well as several collections of his short stories, but never to the general acclaim that he received from his plays.

Williams' greatest disappointment in those days was the failure in 1953 of an experimental piece called *Camino Real*. He thought it his most poetic and interesting play and was horrified at the audience response. As the chapter on this play explains, it was ahead of its time in many ways. Only recently have directors rediscovered this wildly surrealistic play, producing it in small theatres in Williamstown and Hartford to enthusiastic response. In this effort, Williams found that he was too avant-garde for popular theatre. The audience found it confusing and excessively symbolic, giving no real credit for the brilliant production. He began to suspect that, if he wrote about the things that interested him most deeply, he would never again know full blown success on Broadway.

Suddenly, his luck changed. *Cat on a Hot Tin Roof* opened March 24, 1955, winning the Drama Critics' Award, the Donaldson, and the Pulitzer. Not only did he triumph, proving that there are some second acts in American success stories, but he did it his own way. For the first time, he confronted his relationship with his father, who by now was an old man, lonely and divorced. In a guarded manner, he also began to speak out about homosexuality. Unfortunately, a quarrel with Elia Kazan about the third act of the play, which he made public, briefly alienated this talented director, who had been a vital element in his career.

The following year, he once again worked with Kazan, this time on a film version of some early plays, in a work which continued their confrontation with the censors. *Baby Doll* was condemned by leaders in the Catholic Church, and was considered a shockingly explicit sexual film in 1956. By modern standards, it a funny and comparatively innocent play about frustrated sexuality which turns into gentle love. It would hardly be considered daring today.

The next year, he tried again to win success for his beloved *Battle of Angels*, this time revising it as *Orpheus Descending*. He thought it might have more luck if the religion involved were pagan Greek instead of Puritanical Christian. He was wrong. It failed once again.

His father died that year, and Williams began to see stress lines forming in his relationship with Frankie. Both of them were increasingly promiscuous and cruel to one another. Williams began to accuse Frankie of not loving him. He also thought Frankie was becoming a drug addict. Williams' own chaotic life was growing more frenzied, his relationships laced with paranoia. He believed everyone was stealing from him. The two old friends grew increasingly alienated, finally separating, each thinking the other was the culprit.

From the time that Rose's problems developed, Tennessee was always afraid that he, like his beloved Rose, would end up mad. He tried psychoanalysis, but found that he needed his anxiety if he was to preserve his creativity. The experience of psychotherapy became the basis for his fullest exploration of his sister's illness. *Suddenly Last Summer*, which he wrote at the time, and produced with another short play as *Garden District*, was the painful chronicle of a family pressing a woman to have a frontal lobotomy rather than facing a hateful truth.

The absent hero-poet, named Sebastian, bears considerable resemblance to Williams and the friends he collected in Europe. Sebastian is his cruelest example of the gay aesthete who uses other people, usually children, as if they are articles on the menu, not human beings. Broadway was clearly unprepared for this shocking play. For the first time, he decided to experiment with off-Broadway. Even there, without the enormous expenses of a full-scale production, the plays were a failure. (His old advocate, Brooks Atkinson, praised it, but others saw it as "too nervous to make a dramatic statement," settling instead for a "sensual wallop" [Crandell 1996, 166]). Once again a film version proved quite successful some years later, perhaps because of a young, voluptuous Liz Taylor, who appeared in a revealing swimsuit.

By now, his old plays were becoming new films, Broadway productions were being replicated in London and Paris. His works were translated into dozens of languages, known all around the world. In spite of a series of failures with his new plays, Tennessee Williams continued to be an artistic and financial success. He was on his way to becoming a millionaire.

In 1959, *Sweet Bird of Youth* revealed for all to see the decadent Mr. Williams. Portraying himself as one of the sad old actresses he had come to know over the years, he exposed his alcoholism, drug use, and his pathetic reliance on young predators. He had lost many of the key stabilizing forces in his life. Kazan rarely found time to direct his work; Frankie was no longer waiting for him at home; and he even managed to break with Audrey Wood, his faithful agent. He continued to see his mother, his grandfather, and his sister; but his day-to-day relationships were increasingly unstable.

The Night of the Iguana, his last great success, opened at the end of 1961. It displayed the full sense of his alienation from other people, his weariness with life, and his sense that he was abandoned even by God. By then, he had known an unprecedented run of good luck: When he was preparing to produce or cast a show, he attracted the finest talent the world had to offer, actresses loved the parts he wrote for them; actors found their reputations made by a small part in a Williams play; the best directors and designers found scope for their own creativity by signing on to one of his productions.

Tennessee Williams had one of the longest sustained careers in theatre history. In addition to winning the prizes already mentioned, he also was elected to membership in the American Academy of Arts and Letters. He was able to help his family, who had for so long been such staunch supporters of him. He had provided his mother with the means to free herself from Cornelius. He spent a fortune on his sister, providing her with the best care that he could find. He invited his grandfather, now a widower, to join him in his home in New Orleans or Key West, to travel with him from time to time.

He was able to indulge his hunger for motion by traveling all over the world, from Europe to the South Pacific. He was wined and dined by the artistic and political leaders of the world. Yet he was deep down a sad, lost man.

THE LAST ACT: DECLINE AND FALL

It started with some bad reviews, occasional failures. *Camino Real* puzzled many critics and playgoers. *Suddenly Last Summer* shocked them. They tended to think most of his works in the 1950s inferior to his earlier masterpieces. Williams grew nervous about opening his plays on Broadway, risking expensive failures. He began to alienate some of his best allies, forcing him to rely on lesser talents.

In 1955, just before the opening of *Cat on a Hot Tin Roof*, his grandfather died—a great loss to Williams. By the 1960s, Williams was drinking more than before. His use of pills had become an addiction. He became involved with a doctor who injected him with amphetamines, under the ruse of giving him vitamins. His behavior became more and more erratic. After driving Frank Merlo away, he discovered that his old lover had lung cancer, Williams was haunted by his own cruelty as he tried to reconcile with him in 1963, when Frankie was on his deathbed.

He had lost a number of dear friends by now, and thought of himself as an old crocodile, surviving while everyone else died. When he looked in the mirror, he didn't see how anyone could love this old man. He began to quarrel with his theatrical associates, growing more thin-skinned about negative criticism. His plays were gradually changing, as theatrical tastes were shifting. He found no market on Broadway for the new plays he was writing. Audiences, still in love with his early plays, wanted more of the same, and could not understand his gradual transformation into a more abstract, experimental writer. His mood grew darker, and his use of a wide range of drugs and alcohol drove him deeper into paranoia. In his autobiography, he described the 1960s as his "lost decade" (*Memoirs*, 202–27).

Finally in 1969, responding to alarms about Tennessee's health and mental condition, his brother, Dakin, put him into the mental ward of the hospital in St. Louis. Williams later described this abrupt withdrawal from drugs and alcohol as a near-death experience. Dakin insists that he saved his brother's life. He also converted him—briefly—to Roman Catholicism.

The years after this traumatic event, the 1990s, found a chastened Williams trying to reconstruct his life and his reputation. Ironically, the confessional mode he adopted right after his hospitalization and brief conversion to Catholicism, went a long way toward destroying his image. An interview on television with David Frost, in 1970, ended with a snicker and a confession, "I've covered the waterfront" (Devlin 1986, 146). In that interview, he also identified with Sebastian's problems in *Suddenly Last Summer*. Then in *Small Craft Warnings*, originally named *Confessional*, he openly—for the first time on the stage—expressed his views on homosexuality. *Memoirs* and *Moise and the World of Reason*, both embarrassing revelations of his own outrageous behavior, also contributed to his continuing fall from popularity.

He wrote a number of short plays over that final decade of his life, a couple of books of short stories, a novel, and a few longer plays. The one on which he staked everything was called *Out Cry* or *The Two-Character Play*. A nightmare for the stage, this curious piece was never a success in any of the many versions he drafted. Other failures clouded those last years—the play he based on the life of Zelda and F. Scott Fitzgerald (*Clothes for a Summer Hotel*), the one that tells of his first love affair, in the summer of 1941 (*Something Cloudy, Something Clear*), or the one which presents an apocalyptic urban jungle (*The Red Devil Battery Sign*). Based on his early plays and a handful of the later pieces, critics continued to cite him as one of America's finest playwrights; but they also continued to sneer at his later works. He had become his own toughest competition.

The final act for Tennessee Williams was—like his own title—a *Slapstick Tragedy*. He raced from country to country, often surrounded by a coterie of "artistic" young people who were using him for their own aggrandizement. He gave drunken, incoherent interviews that further damaged his stature. Even his death in 1983, proved to be both grotesquely comic and pathetic. He choked on a bottle cap lodged in his larynx, at a hotel in New York, with his secretary in another room. This final scene itself became the source of curiosity and confusion. The coroner's verdict of accidental death by choking has been challenged, the funeral was contrary to his wishes. (He had asked to be buried at sea.) And he was finally laid to rest beside his mother in the city he despised—St. Louis. Since then, the grave has been vandalized, and Dakin has continually pursued a suspicion that Tennessee was murdered before he could change his will.

His fortune was inherited by his sister Rose, who survived him by several years and was eventually buried at his side. Harvard University was the delighted recipient of his papers—all of those many versions of plays and poems, letters and essays. (Many of his papers were earlier contributed to the Harry Ransom Humanities Research Center in Austin, Texas, and some bought by Columbia University.) After the death of Rose, the University of the South at Sewanee received the bulk of his estate—to be used in the cultivation of the talent of young creative writers. At the end, he remembered how hard it is for a young artist to survive long enough to taste success in America. Above all, he loved the world of literature and considered his real family to be those who gave their lives in the pursuit of beauty.

2

Literary Heritage

A SOUTHERNER AND A DRAMATIST

Tennessee Williams was steeped in the culture of the Mississippi Delta—a region with a long history and a peculiar culture. The American South had developed a strong literary tradition in the early years of the twentieth century. Beginning with the poets and philosophers of the Fugitive Group at Vanderbilt University (Robert Penn Warren, Cleanth Brooks, Allan Tate, and others), the Southern Renaissance was to mark the beginning of a unique tradition. While rejecting much of the mythology of the South as a *Gone with the Wind* culture, full of lovely ladies, handsome gentlemen, and contented slaves, these Fugitives still cherished the best part of the Southern heritage. The qualities of courtly manners, traditional Christian faith and moral values, lyrical and colorful speech, and a strong sense of place and of history were to mark this new movement.

The most interesting offshoot of this literary tradition was to be the Mississippi prose writers—like William Faulkner and Eudora Welty. They used the geography, the history, the traditions, the habits, and the people of this region to write a host of tales. Their novels and short stories range in tone from grim to comic, in character from wealthy landowners to ex-slaves and poor whites. The stories have delighted audiences all over the world, including Tennessee Williams.

While sharing their love of the folk of the Delta, where he was born, Williams had little interest in the literary forms these other Southerners had selected. The novel just did not match his talents. He did try the form, as well as the short story, but gradually he came to understand that his genius lay with drama. For him, though he was a talented prose writer, short stories most often proved to be merely the rough drafts out of which his plays were to develop.

Prior to the success of Tennessee Williams, the South had not been a regular part of the theatrical scene. The real center of American theatre was in cities, particularly in New York. Southerners rarely wrote plays that would appeal to New York audiences. There were some exceptions: Just before Williams hit Broadway, *Green Pastures*, a review that derived from Roark Bradford's comic rendition of Black sermons, introduced Southern religion to urban audiences. Poor white Southerners had been objects of condescension in Erskine Caldwell's *God's Little Acre*, which also went from novel to play. And the far more serious and theatrical Lillian Hellman was beginning to develop her richer analysis of the castes and classes of the South in The *Little Foxes* and *Another Part of the Forest*. Hellman was only partially a Southerner, having been raised in New York as well as New Orleans, and having been educated in the North. One of the first plays that Williams saw when he had his first professional visit to New York in 1939 was *The Little Foxes* (Leverich 1995, 328). Shortly afterwards, he began to talk of a "Southern trilogy." His view of the South, however, was far more sensitive and complex than Hellman's. Williams wanted to portray the South in a more subjective way than Hellman had, bringing out the full range of Southern speech and manners, the way that the writers of the Irish Renaissance had done for the folk of Ireland.

Another play he saw during that same visit, *Juno and the Paycock*, written by the Irishman Sean O'Casey, inspired the young writer even more powerfully than Hellman's. O'Casey captured the charm of Irish speech, the blend of comedy and tragedy in the Irish temperament. Williams said of his experience at this play that he carried the whole audience with his laughter—a notorious braying sound. In O'Casey, Williams found a voice that was akin to his own sense of the South. Other authors of the Irish Renaissance, like Synge, also appealed to him, as did writers from other countries. Lorca, a Spanish writer of poetic force, was to become a major inspiration. In each of them, he caught a hint of the poetry that lingers in speech. He wanted to capture in his plays this same natural lyricism, a lyricism he felt he had inherited from his famous kinsman Sidney Lanier, the nineteenth-century Southern poet. In doing this, he also tried to reveal the color of Southern speech, the comic imagery, the exaggeration, the rich religious context, and the delightful rhythms. He took notes on phrases that he heard, noted even the pauses, rhythms, and repetitions in an effort to capture the distinctive language of his region. He also used characters from all classes, treating most of them with respect, more in the tradition of his fellow Mississippi writers than in the Caldwell pattern. He was also capable of drawing on another early Southerner, Edgar Allan Poe, for Gothic ideas and symbolism, and a contemporary friend, Carson McCullers, for grotesques. Everything that Williams saw or heard became grist for his creative mill.

GENERAL LITERARY TASTES

Tennessee Williams was an avid reader, in love with books from his earliest youth when he spent many happy hours reading the books in his grandfather's well-stocked library. Much of this was religious material, including the lives of the saints; the symbols and rituals of the church became a natural part of his life and thought. There were also books of poetry, as well as Shakespeare's plays, from which he absorbed ideas and the language. He enjoyed quoting them in his letters, frequently with a comic twist.

Such reading became the habit of a lifetime. He frequently told his parents or friends what he was currently reading and apparently spent hours every evening reading himself to sleep. His letters testify to his changing tastes, from the early study of literary biography and correspondence to the later study of novels and plays. He mentions, for instance, reading the letters of Van Gogh, D. H. Lawrence, and Katherine Mansfield among others. From these documents, he discovered something of the temperament of the artist and the struggles of the artistic life. In some ways, he shaped his own journals and letters on these famous models, indicating to some of his correspondents that they were to save his letters, apparently hoping to use them later. He went back over his journals in preparation for the writing of his *Memoirs*, enjoying the phrasing he had originally used to express his feelings.

Of all the books of poetry, his favorites were the English Romantics, the French Symbolists, and a handful of modern Americans. He considered himself a Romantic and deliberately lived and wrote according to Romantic ideals. He certainly thought of "The Artist" in much of the same way as Shelley and Wordsworth had; and he recognized in much of his behavior a strong kinship to Lord Byron. In addition to their biographies, Williams had also read most of their poetry, committing much of it to memory. Like them, he saw the artist as a special person, with a gift from God. The normal laws of behavior, the normal path of life were unsuitable for these romantic rebels. He loved their extravagance, their mad behavior, as well as their delight in delicate and ethereal imagery.

He seemed to agree with Shelley's theory of poetry as well as the poet. He too thought that the poets were the "unacknowledged legislators of the world," somehow alert to values and problems to which average human beings were blind. This quivering sensitivity made the poet a particularly vulnerable and lonely person, destined to know more of both joy and sorrow than the normal person. Williams identified with Wordsworth's notions of the development of the poet, his mystic moments, his use of these revelations translated into the language of the common man, recollected in tranquillity (Roudané 1997, 147–66).

The French Symbolists, known for poetic, dream-like imagery, gave him much of his tone. Williams especially admired Baudelaire. Many of his friends in the early 1940s were involved in Surrealist publications, especially VIEW magazine, but he found their ideas never quite matched his own. Nonetheless, certain qualities of Surrealism and "magic realism" do occur in his stories, especially those of his later years as he moved toward increasingly abstract expression. Characters become quite fantastic; it is difficult to separate the actuality from the dream. Even an early story ends with a miraculous lifting of a poor woman into a whirlwind; another has the hero riding off on the back of a dolphin; and a late play shows a "bird girl" fighting other very aggressive birds for fish on Colcaloony Key. Williams was inclined to believe in miracles, mystic events, and mystery. His experimentation with drugs might well have contributed to this tendency as drugs and alcohol led to the more imaginative moments experienced by Coleridge, Poe, and Baudelaire, as well as their gradual artistic decline.

It was the American poets who determined his style: he loved Emily Dickinson's precise and simple phrasing, Walt Whitman's free verse and command of American vernacular. In his "Gold Tooth Blues" and other rollicking "Mountain" ballads, Williams caught the delightful rhythms of country and Western music. His "Heavenly Grass"—the song that Val Xavier sings—is particularly lovely. A number of his poems have been set to music; he had an especially rich collaboration with Paul Bowles, who provided the musical setting for "Blue Mountain Ballads" and background music for *The Glass Menagerie*.

He drew many of his titles and dedications from literary sources, from D. H. Lawrence, Milton, Blake, and his all-time favorite, Hart Crane, whose slender book of poems he said he always carried with him. In a paper on Williams' epigraphs presented at the New Orleans Tennessee Williams Festival, March 2000, Christine Ford listed twelve of his plays that carry epigraphs, all poetic, from the following poets: E. E. Cummings, Sappho, Hart Crane, Arthur Rimbaud, Ranier Maria Rilke, St. John Perse, Dante, Dylan Thomas, Emily Dickinson, and W. B. Yeats. Having seen how central these poems were to the plays, she went through the files at the Harry Ransom Research Center, where she found 41 unpublished epigraphs. This artist was clearly inspired by poetry.

He once said that his early success had been in lyric poetry, and he was well on his way to becoming a minor lyric poet in the style of Sara Teasdale (a St.

Louis poet) when he discovered the theatre (*Where I Live* 1978, 1–6). This discovery transformed his life.

DRAMA AND THEATRE

Williams discovered that he had a natural flair for theatre. Drama is a particularly difficult form of writing, requiring that the author forego most of the narrative explanations of background and action, forcing the characters to present their own histories and hint at their own motivation through their words and actions. Although Williams was to use narrators occasionally and never quite abandoned expository monologues, he gradually developed the ability to build characters with fully developed backgrounds through dialogue and silence, gesture, action, and inaction, visual signs and symbols—a subtle and complex clustering of signals to which we all can respond.

For him, the written words on the page were not enough. He had to see his plays produced. He loved the collaborative experience of the theatre, with the involvement of the playwright, the director, the actors, the scenery, lighting, and costume design. He visualized an entire stage at once and often described details that were vivid in his own imagination. Luckily for him, the twentieth century had developed technology to match his demands, allowing him to experiment with sound effects and lighting in imaginative ways. Williams required special kinds of scenery, acting, and directing to be effective. He often attended the rehearsals of his plays, taking time to explain his ideas more fully and to adapt his script to the particular talents of the collaborators he had assembled.

Williams was fully aware of the whole path of Western (and later Eastern) theatre, from the Greeks to the present. In his wide reading and constant theatregoing, and in his university studies, he read and considered the Greek classics, the Roman plays, the medieval folk drama, Shakespeare and the other Elizabethans, the Jacobeans, the neoclassical comedies of the Restoration and the eighteenth century, and the rich flowering of European drama and opera in the nineteenth and twentieth century. He never stopped learning and experimenting: in the 1960s, he became interested in Absurdist drama. Absurd writers tend to believe in nothing—neither man's dignity nor God's existence—hence the term "nihilism." Though he rejected its nihilism, he was involved in introducing Samuel Beckett's *Waiting for Godot* to the American public. By the middle of his career, he was increasingly charmed by the formal structure of the Japanese and Chinese theatres. He traveled to Asia and saw a number of Noh and Kabuki productions, thereby adding to his repertoire of devices.

He used a great deal of this vast background, taking a phrase from one play, an image from another, a bit of setting from still another. The echoes of other playwrights and other theatre traditions constantly enrich his works. Somehow, he managed to make all of this his very own—both American and Southern.

AMERICAN THEATRE

Theatre in America had a long history, but the nineteenth century was marked primarily by productions imported from England. Traveling companies brought Shakespeare to small and large theatres all over the country. (It was a Shakespearean actor who assassinated Abraham Lincoln.) A few Americans tried their hands at writing plays that captured the flavor of the new world, but with limited success. Especially in New York, which became the center of theatre for America, the real respect was reserved for foreign imports. The really popular American plays were the melodramas, hastily written plays that presented savage villains and perfect heroes and heroines, often in violent conflicts, with the good always triumphing over the evil. Audiences traditionally booed and hissed the evil, usually mustached, villain of the piece.

Toward the end of the nineteenth century, America was treated to the fresh new serious kind of theatre: the realistic drama of Ibsen and Strindberg, and later the lively intellectual plays of George Bernard Shaw. Henrik Ibsen (1828–1906), the master of the well-made play, was to use contemporary Norway as the scene of powerful stories. He risked speaking openly of liberated women, corrupt public officials, and venereal disease. Equally shocking was another Scandinavian, August Strindberg (1849–1912), who saw men and women as continually at war, mothers and wives as castrators of the men in their lives, and dreams as mirrors of reality. Shaw, an Englishman (1856–1950), who had reviewed these new playwrights, used the wave of fresh interest in theatre as the vehicle for ideas, introducing socialism, Darwinian survival, German philosopher Nietzsche's idea of Superman, and a host of other concepts that he explored with an abundance of wit. Of even more importance to Williams was a Russian writer, Anton Chekhov (1860–1904), who developed a more open-ended impressionistic theatre, breaking from fourth-wall realism (which assumed the front of the stage to be a fourth wall allowing the audience to look into actual living rooms, etc.) to discover a psychological truth in his gentle meditations on the decline of the old aristocratic class in Russia.

These new writers with their acceptance of the nineteenth century's most shocking and thrilling ideas were to excite young writers into trying to apply these same ideas to American life. By the early days of the twentieth century, a new ferment was apparent in American culture. The impact of European thinkers such as Charles Darwin, Karl Marx, and Sigmund Freud had transformed many traditional views of the human condition and the world itself. World War I destroyed the idealism and certainty in absolutes previously marking American thought. The new American cynicism demanded expression.

It was at this time that a handful of people began a small theatre movement in Greenwich Village, New York City and in Provincetown, Massachusetts, which introduced new playwrights in creative productions. At the same time, university faculty were beginning to teach young college students about these new voices, encouraging a fresh creativity. Among the most important of these was Professor George Pierce Baker at Harvard, whose theatre program was a model for many that were to follow.

The most impressive of their discoveries was the young Eugene O'Neill, who became a regular with the Washington Square Players and the Provincetown Players. His earliest plays, which these companies produced, were simple one-acts that caught the mood of the New England waterfront and the mixture of ethnic groups who lived there. He expanded over time to full-sized plays and finally to trilogies (clusters of three plays following the pattern of Greek drama). From 1914 until his death, O'Neill was to produce a wide variety of creative plays—full of symbolism, masks, and music; he discovered tragic subjects in farmers, sailors, middle-class families, and Blacks. He broke down the old assumptions of the "proper" materials for tragedy, discovering greatness in the everyday people of America. His plays toured the country, influencing the new wave of dramatists of the 1920s and 1930s, including the young Tom Williams (who wrote to his grandfather about the amazing use of masks in one play he saw).

The excitement of the new American theatre infected actors, directors, scene designers, and other artists who increasingly clustered in companies to produce plays of their favorite playwrights. One of the most famous of these, in the 1930s, was the Group Theatre, whose favorite playwrights were Clifford Odets and William Saroyan—both of whom chose to work with lower-class characters—boxers, factory workers, homeless drifters. For a decade, this vibrant group encouraged a new kind of acting, both realistic and stylized on occasion, developing many talents who would eventually move on to careers on Broadway and in Hollywood. This was the organization that launched Williams by presenting him an award for a cluster of one-act plays he submitted to its contest in 1938.

By this time, the South had become a center of literary activity. Traveling players had always come through cities like St. Louis. Small theatre groups had begun to spring up, without money or formal background in theatre craft but with plenty of zeal. Young Tom Williams had seen his first play, *Bombay, Cairo, Shanghai!,* produced in a garden in Memphis. His next was an opener for an

Odets production in St. Louis. He described the thrill of hearing his own words spoken and seeing the response of an audience to his admittedly bad plays (*Where I Live* 12). He realized at that moment he needed the "anarchy" of the theatre to survive. He fell in love with theatre people who refused to conform to social norms and wear nice three-piece suits, but preferred to shout, to break things, to fight, and to grow their hair long (*Where I Live* 14).

Like his hero in *The Glass Menagerie*, Tom Wingfield, he also fell in love with the movies, the quintessential American form. He spent his youth in St. Louis, a great moviegoing city, where he and Rose went as often as possible to the latest movies. Several critics have written at length on Tennessee Williams and films, demonstrating conclusively that he used the ideas and techniques of the cinema and had considerable impact on the development of the film industry in America. He worked at MGM that fateful year when he was really writing *The Glass Menagerie* and later saw most of his important plays transformed into films, oversaw their development, fought with the censors, and even wrote one script directly for the movies. *Baby Doll*, based on an early pair of short plays, was a film script from the beginning. It is easy to see that many of his characters have ties to contemporary movies. He even used the resonance of other films in making his own. The most obvious example of this was to use Vivien Leigh, who as a young actress had starred as the famous Southern heroine Scarlett O'Hara and as a middle-aged one became his own Blanche DuBois. The unspoken contrast lent power to the later film, emphasizing the deteriorating values of the modern South. Like a filmmaker, Williams used musical background for enhancement of emotional scenes. Maurice. Yacowar mentions that Williams' early writing reveals his particular devotion to film. He planned *Stairs to the Roof* (1941) as either a film or a play and dedicated a couple of his early sketches to popular actors of the day. Even his ideas for a "new, plastic theatre," which he described in the introduction to *The Glass Menagerie*, may have derived in part from the elasticity of filmic creations.

Williams' worldwide fame derives in large part from his numerous films that are available and regularly shown on every continent. Students have used his movies to study English in countries as far apart as Germany and China. Scholars from Japan who come to study in America already know many of the works of Tennessee Williams.

WILLIAMS' THEATRICAL VOICE

Tennessee Williams did have a distinctive style, but not a single, consistent voice. He changed over time, moving with the American culture, trying to lead his audience into a variety of poetic styles, responding to criticism, shaping his plays to fit his immediate concerns and to the times. At first, Williams wrote about the Artist, basing *Battle of Angels* on the lonely artistic vagabond figure, a sexual rebel, in the conservative South. He drew this partially from his own wanderings, but even more from his reading. He used the Delta for his setting, but the characters were exaggerated to the point of stereotypes: chattering church ladies, crude local men and the obligatory brutal sheriff, sex-starved housewives, etc. He did capture something of the language and mood of the South, but the play expressed more of the spirit of D. H. Lawrence than of Tennessee Williams.

When *The Glass Menagerie* scored such a success, Williams realized that he had discovered a treasure in his own family and his own experiences. For the next few years, he wrote of his mother, the superannuated Southern belle; his father, the brute male; his sister, the lost innocent; and himself, the lonely poetic misfit. Eventually, he added his grandfather and his brother to the mix. Later, he began to use the actors he met, tracing their triumphs and failures. Each of these voices was distinctly different, carefully observed, richly developed.

Gradually, he began to introduce his sexual orientation as a topic, moving to a more and more overt expression of homosexuality. He also explored his personal religious concerns, his sense of God's silence and cruelty. He never stopped portraying himself in some form as the core figure in his plays, even when in the mask of an aging actress. He intermingled personal experience with the people he came to know along the way, seeing the grotesques of the world as his favorites. From beginning to end, he was the "Laureate of the Lost," increasingly aware of a pitiful clownishness in the human condition. His challenge was to bring poetry to the grubby folk who are outsiders, those who missed out on the Century of Progress.

He continued to talk about the artist, his life, his alienation, and his torments. Because of his own struggle to survive, his heartfelt descriptions of marginal peoples had an authenticity to them. He often pictured people in a trapped or terminal situation, fighting for their lives against insurmountable odds. He loved underdogs—Bohemians, misfits, prostitutes, alcoholics, and street people. He especially loved those who were relics of a lost civilization, cherishing a vanished pattern of genteel behavior and idealism. His especial sympathy went out to those who continued to hunger for love, for security, or just rest for the night.

His early voice was more realistic and traditional in form, moving to more creative and symbolic plays as he matured in his talent. Knowing that plays like *Camino Real* did not appeal to the public, he moved back and forth from his old realistic form to increasingly abstract plays. After his near-death experience in 1969, he turned almost exclusively to confessional and abstract works. He thought more about his own conflicts, his sense of shame, his loss of critical acclaim, his fear of madness, his awareness of old age and death. These final plays, never popular, were nonetheless fascinating works, especially *Out Cry* or *The Two-Character Play*, a play in which the whole theatrical experience decons-tructs before our eyes.

The plays that had earlier traced the young poet searching for Truth, now became chronicles of the old artist, facing death. He increasingly pictured the failed and dissipated hero, author of his own anguish. As he approached his fi-nal days, he contemplated the immortality of art, the mortality of the artist. He also meditated on the mysteries that we know as silence—the incomplete thoughts, the absence of expression, the stilled voice of God. Several of his last plays are records of this struggle to express the ineffable.

All through his life, he wrestled with his faith, bringing a transcendent di-mension to most of his plays. From his first "battle" with the angels of darkness to his late horror at God's silence, he sought moments of grace, often finding these in human communication rather than in meditation or prayer. Although considered by many an immoral, even a pornographic artist, his most obscene gestures are often a groping for human community—not really for sexual expe-rience. As he said in one of his earliest plays, "We're all of us locked up tight in-side our own bodies. Sentenced—you might say—to solitary confinement inside our own skins" (*Theatre, Vol. 1*, 50). His anguish is palpable. It appar-ently echoed the hunger that many moderns also felt.

Few playwrights in history have written for a longer period in so many styles derived from so many sources for such a wide audience with such a range of success and failure.

INFLUENCE ON OTHERS

Tennessee Williams never forgot how long it took him to climb to the top, and he was always willing to reach out to help others in their climb. When he read Carson McCullers' novel *A Member of the Wedding*, he was convinced that she could turn it into a good play. He invited her to stay with him for a while as she worked on it. He was equally generous with William Inge, who was a thea-tre critic for a St. Louis newspaper when they first met. Williams was undoubt-edly an influence on the characterization of *Come Back, Little Sheba*, the family portrait in *Dark at the Top of the Stairs*, and the celebration of pagan sexuality in *Picnic*. His willingness to encourage young writers continued all through his long career. At the end, he left the remainder of his fortune to the University of the South at Sewanee for the encouragement of creative literature.

His influence has proven pervasive, his voice and his characters have entered the culture in such a thorough manner that it is virtually impossible to isolate individual authors who have responded to him. Obviously Edward Albee benefited from Williams' work: his *Who's Afraid of Virginia Woolf?* picks up on the tortured relationship of Maggie the Cat and Brick, carrying the wit and cruelty of that marriage even further. His *Tiny Alice* echoes the offbeat religious ideas and the curious sacramental sense of Williams' later plays.

Even such well-established playwrights as Lillian Hellman appear to have been touched by Williams' work: Her *Toys in the Attic* is more like Williams than like her own earlier plays.

Certainly, his gradual opening up of the topic of his own sexuality has proven enormously influential in the development of gay theatre. Tony Kushner's *Angels in America* is particularly derivative of Williams, mocking him at times, while paying tribute to his influence by the use of his characters, his phrasing, even his angels, and many of his ideas.

Satires on Williams have been popular from the beginning, a comment on his pervasive influence on American culture. From Arnold Kopit's *Oh Dad, Poor Dad, Mama's Hung You in the Closet and I'm Feeling So Sad* to modern spoofs, which are common on television and in advertisements, we have come to recognize certain lines from *Streetcar* and other plays. Blanche's final lines—"I've always depended on the kindness of strangers" (*Theatre, Vol. 1,* 418)—is one of the most commonly quoted lines of all time. So is Stanley's plaintive cry, "Stella!" It is even echoed in ads. At the annual festival for Tennessee Williams fans, held in the spring in New Orleans, a highlight is the "Stella!!!" yelling contest. In addition, everyone knows how Stanley clears the table.

As a culture, we recognize Tennessee Williams' voice. We see his influence even as far afield as Britain, with the Angry Young Writers, and Australia, with *Summer of the Seventeenth Doll,* in which the tangled domestic portraits and the idiomatic language, range from lyric to gutter. Like the writers of the Irish Renaissance, Tennessee Williams encouraged a variety of authors to discover the riches of their regional speech, to turn it into an instrument of discovery. He also taught them to express the full range of human emotion, and the complexity of it, revealed in the speech, the silences, and the laughter. He encouraged others to consider "Plastic theatre," the techniques of film, the "presentational" devices of Oriental theatre. For him, there were no limits to creative expression. Few authors have found such power in an intermingling of comedy and tragedy, the heroic and the grotesque—as expansive in its scope as Shakespeare. His films have carried his influence even further afield than his plays, taking them to all corners of the world. Tennessee Williams has become a part of popular culture.

3

The Glass Menagerie
(1945)

BACKGROUND

Tennessee Williams had searched diligently for the key to success. He knew in his heart he was a genius and he knew that he was ideally prepared for the theatre, but he couldn't find the right story to tell. At first he tried to write about prisoners in Pennsylvania and coal miners in Kentucky. Although ignored in 1938, when it was written, one of them has since become an international success. *Not about Nightingales*, which dealt with horrible slaughter of prisoners in a "hot box," was a hit in both London and New York in 1998, leading to a nomination for the Tony award in 1999. Thus, 17 years after his death, Tennessee Williams was considered better—even in his 60-year-old apprentice work—than other writers of the final days of the twentieth century.

Then in *Battle of Angels*, he tried to talk about sex and violence in the Delta. The play attracted the Theatre Guild to invest in a full-fledged professional production. This appeared to be the answer to his prayers. When the play failed in Boston, he went through a period of deep depression. Later, it was revised and produced as *Orpheus Descending*, this time with somewhat better press, but this came only after he was already famous—in 1957—17 years after the 1940 catastrophe in Boston.

This stunning failure convinced Williams that his talents lay in discovery and communication of his own inner truth. He wrote most naturally about his own family, the tensions he had known growing up in St. Louis, and the tragedy of his sister. With this recognition, he focused on his sister's decline and fall. In 1945, this story became his first Broadway success—*The Glass Menagerie*.

PLOT DEVELOPMENT

It is not a typical Tennessee Williams play. He usually built too complex a plot to fit on the stage, with too many interesting stories for each of the characters, spiced with too much violence and sexuality. In *The Glass Menagerie*, he kept it simple. This depression-era tale of a small Southern family in financial trouble is set in St. Louis. The father has abandoned his wife and two children, both of whom are now young adults. The son, Tom Wingfield, is reluctantly working in a warehouse to support his mother and sister. The daughter, Laura, is clearly unable to take care of herself, too frightened to work in an office and too shy to find a good husband. She is crippled both physically and psychologically. Although Amanda, the mother, tries to sell magazine subscriptions, she knows that she cannot support her daughter and herself without Tom's help. Having been raised to be a "lady" she has no marketable skills. Amanda seeks desperately to make Laura independent by enrolling her in business school, but that proves a failure. She then nags her son to bring home a suitor to court and marry Laura. Tom finally obliges his mother, reeling in Jim O'Connor, whose forthright and clumsy manners underscore the family's peculiar Southern habits. Jim enjoys the dinner, the conversation, and the time alone with Laura. He dances with her, kisses her, admires her glass menagerie, and clumsily breaks her favorite figure—a unicorn. Embarrassed at the hopes he knows he has raised in this shy girl, he beats a hasty retreat, mumbling that he must keep a date with his fiancée. The family bids him farewell with gracious words, knowing that this is the end of their hope—Jim will not return, Laura will not marry, Tom will escape, and Amanda will be forced to cope with an impossible future.

The story of the plans for the dinner, the event itself, and the painful conclusion are encased in a narrator's memory, frozen like figures in amber. Tom, the poet/narrator, introduces the story, underlining the social/historical background, the images, and the meaning, This device provides for a unity and a distance—giving the play a remarkably poignant tone. The open ending allows the reader to construct his or her own projection of the characters' future. Although it is clear that Tom deserts these women, just as his father had done, the fates of the other characters are left to our imagination.

CHARACTER DEVELOPMENT

The image of the absent father dominates the stage, allowing us to tie him to Tom, who is also in love with "long distances" (*Theatre, Vol. 1*, 145). We know from her conversation that Amanda loved this man, often pictured in productions in a World War I uniform, but drove him away by her constant verbal assaults. (Sometimes, a blown-up picture of Tom in a soldier's cap is used for this centerpiece, to emphasize the identification of the men in the Wingfield family.) For Amanda Wingfield, her absent husband represents a blessed memory of a time when she was secure in her roles as wife and mother.

Amanda, a traditional Southern woman, is now forced to assume the nontraditional role of breadwinner. She proves to be a practical dreamer. On the one hand, she knows she must do what it takes to keep the bills paid. If this includes selling magazine subscriptions to women in the DAR, and pressuring Tom to be more aggressive in moving up the corporate ladder, she courageously swallows her pride and stifles her sympathy with his unhappiness and marches forth. On the other hand, she cherishes the remembrances of the days back in Blue Mountain, with 17 gentlemen callers and hoards of jonquils surrounding her. She regrets her choice of the wrong suitor, one who did not become a bank president and a millionaire. She also regrets her currently diminished status: the fading of her beauty and the increasing harshness of her tone of voice. She knows she is turning into a witch, strident and unfeminine. The Delta charm, which she can turn on and off like a faucet, is more suitable to a young belle being courted on her front porch in the moonlight. In this context of St. Louis, middle age, and hard times, it has a grotesqueness to it. Williams summarizes her as, "A little woman of great but confused vitality clinging frantically to another time and place" (129). He admires her endurance, tenderness, and heroism, while acknowledging her occasional foolishness and cruelty .

Laura is the gentle portrayal of a girl fixed forever in childhood. She plays with her glass animals and enjoys her victrola but is unable to cope with typewriters, offices, flirtations, and strangers. She is too shy for this world, too withdrawn and sweet. Although the other characters rush around trying to make "plans" for her, she seems to have no instinct for self-preservation. Williams describes her as "a piece of her own glass collection, too exquisitely fragile to move from the shelf" (129). She shrinks from strangers, from confrontations. We see her as a pale shadow of her dominating mother, lacking her vivacity, courage, and grit.

Tom, an autobiographical picture of Williams in his mid-twenties, is "a poet with a job in a warehouse" (129). He mirrors Williams' appetite for literature, movies, and travel. He is having trouble at the warehouse because of his penchant for writing poems on shoe boxes when he should be working. At the end of the play, Tom Wingfield finds his own escape hatch, becoming a sailor. After investing the money for the electric bill in dues for the Union of Merchant Seamen, Tom abandons his family to save himself. Like Tom Williams himself, he becomes a wanderer and a loner.

Williams portrays Tom as a man trapped by economic pressures, forced to work at tasks that will emasculate him over time. Unlike his friend Jim, Tom is not interested in success and is not willing to spend a lifetime trapped in mechanical and meaningless chores. He must escape in order to find his own truth. In the narrator's voice, we hear the poetic, ironic tone of the outsider who has managed to transform this individual situation into a universal commentary on being true to one's self. In his double role as central character and objective commentator, he portrays his frustrations, his anger, and his sorrow. In his final sad meditations he reveals his own conflicted love for these people. Independence must be purchased at a significant price.

Only Jim is the true outsider, the "Gentleman Caller" who actually has his very conventional plans already mapped out. The antithesis of Tom, Jim is a conformist who will be content in middle management, marry Betty, his girl, and raise a family, thinking he is the happiest man alive. A kind of all-American go-getter, Jim is Williams' version of the materialistic modern dream. An "emissary from the world of reality" (145), Jim is more like a character out of Odets or Arthur Miller than Williams. He is a Midwesterner who is astonished and delighted with these refugees from the antebellum South. He enjoys flirting with Laura, is flattered to find someone who remembers his heroic days in high school. But he quickly discovers her vulnerability, is ashamed of taking advantage of her, and retreats to his own middle-class world. As Williams explains him, he is a "nice, ordinary, young man" (129).

The characters themselves are static: they discover a bit of truth about themselves or others, and they act on that truth, but they do not change. At the end of the play, Laura is still arrested in early adolescence, Amanda is still confused and tormented, Jim is still ordinary and kind, and Tom is still unhappy—though now unhappy in a new way—apart from this sad little family. He cannot escape them after all.

THEMATIC ISSUES

The Glass Menagerie quickly became an American classic. Speaking to the universal theme of the young man needing to break away from his family, to discover his own individual path, this play has touched generation after generation. It balances Tom's hunger for independence with the parallel pull of the family, the basic unit of our civilization. Amanda is not just one mother, she is "Mother" writ large. Most viewers recognize in her their own experience of the smothering love of an over-protective parent, their own rebellion against the controlling mother figure.

This American family reveals the perennial conflicts between individual needs and perceived obligations. Laura's future becomes the central obligation of this family; someone will have to take care of her. Amanda expresses eloquently the humiliation of the deserted wife and the unmarried woman in the Southern culture, and she fears that Laura will become a "front porch girl"—one who sits on the porch in the evenings watching others marry and raise their children. Williams frequently spoke of this lost lady, who is not suited for the marriage game, cannot earn a living in the modern world, and has no role in modern fragmented family units. In an earlier time, she would have been the spinster aunt, shuttled from one family member to another, becoming a collective obligation. By the 1930s, families rarely lived in great, rambling houses with enough space to accommodate long-term visitors. The shrunken family, isolated from its relatives in its apartment or bungalow, crowded into big cities, had no space for the superfluous dependents. Without that community of concern, Laura becomes Amanda's problem—and Tom's.

Thus, if we see the story from Tom's point of view, this is the battle to survive. In order to achieve his own potential as a poet, he must be a free man. But in order to behave like a good son and loving brother, he must remain in bondage. The decision to escape the "tender trap" is a necessary cruelty. Williams is telling his own story here, realizing that he escaped his sister's tragedy by transferring the full responsibility onto his mother. He rarely visited her in those first days of institutionalization; he did not participate in the decision to allow doctors to perform the frontal lobotomy. He avoided St. Louis and the agonizing decisions that his mother was forced to make. Tennessee Williams never quite escaped from the guilt of that bid for freedom.

Moving from individual experiences to a larger theme, this is also the story of a changing culture. Williams was deeply impressed by the difference between the traditions of the South, with its strong sense of family ties, community relationships and roles; its manners and morality; its faith and history. By contrast, he found St. Louis to be shallow, crude, and materialistic—an image of modern urban America. The old values, undoubtedly agrarian as well as Southern, that he had known in Clarksdale, were no longer practical in a busy city. People did not know these strangers, who tried with a certain comic dignity to maintain their pride, their speech, their habits. Amanda wanted to entertain graciously; she wanted her meals to be formal experiences; her grotesquely elegant costume mirrors her anachronistic dream. Like Chekhov's lost aristocrats, these are people the world has passed by. Even Tom, the only one who escapes this claustrophobic transplanted piece of the Old South, is sentimental about its beauty.

Yet we see also the destructiveness of a culture that would fix women and Blacks in roles that they are expected to play regardless of changing circumstances. This culture, frozen in time, would limit Tom's reading to proper works by polite writers and Laura's choices. In scene after scene, Williams shows Amanda as a victim of her own assumptions about how women should behave, how they should spend their lives, whom they should marry, what domestic chores they should perform, how they should dress, entertain, and talk. She is not just a peculiar old woman: she is a symbol of a dying civilization.

On an even more universal level, this story is about the effects of the industrial revolution on the American family. Although Williams emphasizes the Depression context of the narrative, we know that the pressures on Tom Wingfield extend beyond the span of the 1930s. The growth of big industries in the nineteenth and twentieth centuries had both forced families from the farms and small towns and lured them to great cities, where the personal needs of fragile folk are easily neglected. The polluted air, boring work, and separation from a caring community proved harmful to the mental and physical health of many displaced people.

The emphasis on the "hivelike" buildings of ugly colors with their fire escapes underscores the separation from nature, beauty, and human values. This is not the proper habitat for the dreamer, the poet, or the fragile cripple. Yet, all too often, it is the setting for the young man or woman in urban America. Williams, in *The Glass Menagerie*, is providing us a microcosm in which we can visualize the larger questions of the entire era.

STYLISTIC AND LITERARY DEVICES

Williams loved symbols. Having started his writing as a lyric poet, he explained that he had a "poet's weakness for symbols." This trait was undoubtedly also a result of his early saturation with the symbolism and thought of the Episcopal Church. He came to see almost every aspect of life as symbolic of some greater truth.

He had originally designed *The Glass Menagerie* as a Christmas story (Letter to Audrey Wood, 12/43), with the opening scene one of gift giving. The change in his point of attack to a family meal, though more secular, is nonetheless introduced by a demand that Tom come to the table so that they can say "grace," which incidentally, they then omit; but it is also to make his failed, secular "communion" a commentary on the painful relationship in this community of believers. Nothing should be more ordinary and comfortable than breaking bread together, yet the Wingfield children can perform no function without scrutiny and advice from the hovering mother. An echo of this scene is a second announcement of the impending blessing, this time a summons for Laura to come to the table when Jim O'Connor is their guest for dinner. Pretending that Laura has prepared the meal for their visitor, Amanda again dominates the event, making it her solo performance rather than a shared experience of hospitality. She turns the ritual of eating into a contest of wills. She has transformed a communion into a celebration of her personal sacrifices and a reinforcement of her children's obligations to her as their appropriately grateful response.

Amanda soon reveals herself as a symbol of the "devouring mother." Though apparently nurturing, she thwarts and hobbles her children, dominating not only their eating habits, but their entire lives, keeping them safely in the nest with her. Portraying herself as a martyr to their needs, she actually requires their submission to feed her own pride, crippling Laura by her outrageous expectations. If she could, she would emasculate Tom as well. As her own beauty fades, her appetite for adulation increases, making her a harpy rather than a saint. In a fit of anger, Tom calls his mother an ugly old "witch." Williams was to continue embellishing his archetypal monster-woman as he met more complex and powerful ogres throughout his career.

The central image in this play, from which the work takes its name, is Laura's glass menagerie. Williams' biographers have traced the origins of this image to a tragic young woman in Clarksdale, Mississippi (Leverich 1995, 55). Within the play, it allows us to see the childlike fixation on a private world of make-believe animals, and delicacy of this isolated girl.

Taking it as a symbol of Laura herself, fragile and beautiful, the author plays with the more specific figure of the unicorn. Here we see the complete development of a complex idea, hinted at in the dialogue. We know from medieval iconography that this mythical figure is identified with virgins and therefore with sexuality. Although it looks like a horse the unicorn not a horse, but is a unique (if mythical) creature. Thus, when Jim accidentally breaks off its horn, he has not transformed it into a horse: it remains a unicorn, but is now a damaged unicorn that manages to look like an ordinary horse. In some ways, this is what Amanda has done to Laura, distorted her true childish nature to make her seem like all the normal young ladies being courted by nice young gentlemen. (The "gay deceivers" are delightful symbols of Laura's underdeveloped sexuality and Amanda's pressures to appear sexy.) Laura's pained responses to her mother's cruel questions about her plans for the evening expose the anguish that this teasing causes the sensitive girl.

The mock-courtship scene between Laura and Jim contains another cluster of images. Tom, having misused the money for the electric bill, has plunged them into darkness. Amanda, always eager to adopt romantic attitudes, furnishes them with a candelabra, a relic from a church fire, and thereby returns them to the nineteenth century—the family's native habitat. Jim briefly enters into their game of playing at pre-electric life, settles on the floor, and enjoys a childlike moment of shared memories with Laura. But we soon learn that he lives fully in the "Century of Progress," which Laura is blocked from entering. Jim tries, in an act of egocentric kindness, to move her into the adult world of dancing and kissing, but Laura remains a lonely little girl who had a playmate over to visit for the evening. That scene foreshadows the final words, "For nowadays the world is lit by lightning! Blow out your candles, Laura—and so goodbye" (237).

Other images also populate the play. Williams loved the ocean and frequently used the sea as an escape symbol. His sailors, pirates, and buccaneers are the gallant figures who sail away from the dreary land to have adventures denied to most of mankind. Certainly Americans have known this imagery from their earliest days, America itself being the grand adventure for most of our ancestors. For at least three of Williams' literary heroes—Melville, O'Neill, and Crane—the sea voyage was also the escape into the life of literature.

Tennessee Williams' delight in earlier poets, novelists, and dramatists gives additional richness to the texture of the phrasing in *The Glass Menagerie*. For example, Tom's final portrayal of cities as leaves blown by the wind, "brightly colored, but torn away from the branches" echoes Shelley's "Ode to the West Wind." Fortunately, such similes work effectively even if the listener fails to pick up the source of the allusion. We need not picture the famous medieval unicorn tapestry in order to delight in the unicorn reference. Nor do we need to know about D. H. Lawrence's rainbow of sexuality in order to understand the rainbow colors at the Paradise Dance Hall. Blue Mountain is the right name for a romantic past, and Moon Lake is the ideal name for adventures in love. The words carry the message, regardless of our specific knowledge of Clarksdale's geography. Williams lets his words tell their own stories. The viewer can delight in the surface brilliance or dig deep into allusions, allowing several levels of possible resonance.

Like Clifford Odets, Eugene O'Neill, Arthur Miller, Lillian Hellman, and Lorraine Hansberry, Williams was trying to capture the dynamics of the twentieth-century American family, endowing the everyday speech and activities and concerns of these people with a kind of tragic grandeur. Unlike most of his contemporaries, he sought to broaden the range of American theatrical dialogue. For this, he blended the colloquialism of Southern dialect, Midwestern popular speech , and poetic diction. He juxtaposed Amanda's rhetorical flourishes, her monologues, and her lyrical recollections of an idyllic past with Tom's flat, often comic responses. Even more mundane are the words and gestures of Jim O'Connor, who talks of cattle, chewing gum, the Century of Progress, and self-improvement in a sharp parody of American popular culture. His comic strip quality of speech contrasts neatly with the romanticized language of the Wingfield family.

In addition to the wide range of styles and multiple levels of meaning, Williams also uses varied pace and quantity of speech for effect. Amanda is a compulsive talker, Tom a reluctant one, angry and frustrated, silent at times, bursting into overwrought expression under pressure. Laura speaks gently and at her own pace, using her simple vocabulary, refusing to respond to the usual signals, marked primarily by her quiet withdrawal. When she does speak, we attend to her words. More often, she substitutes music or gesture for language. By contrast, Jim has the skills of the social talker who is delighted with his own ability to make conversation, no matter how awkward the situation or how banal the message. His preference for the sports section of the paper (though Tom expects him to choose the comics) is a perfect summation of the strategy that American men use to avoid embarrassing silences or personal, intrusive conversation. The shared commentary on Dizzy Dean can fill the air with chatter without revealing much about the individual speaker.

The narrative voice that frames this group of players moves the range of language even further, giving a broader dimension to the domestic drama, universalizing the specifics, and lending a poignancy to the actions. Sometimes the narrator is ironic about himself and his family, sometimes he pontificates about the nature of the world, and sometimes he is sentimental. At the end, we hear Tom's voice breaking through, merging with the narrator's. It is now poetic and delicate, void of its earlier ironic sharpness. In telling the tale, he has become more sympathetic. If the play succeeds, we have also found ourselves increasingly reflective and gentle, finally moved to tears.

ALTERNATE CRITICAL PERSPECTIVE: IMPRESSIONISM

Tennessee Williams knew the possibilities of realism and naturalism and chose to reject them for this middle-class domestic tragedy. He turned instead to an interesting blend of expressionistic and impressionistic stagecraft.

Impressionism is a personal style of writing in which the author acknowledges that he is selecting his characters, scenes, and moods from his own individual perspective at a precise moment in time. The images are not photographic representations but are more akin to paintings in which certain details are in sharp focus in the foreground, others blurred and placed in the background. Thus, glimpses give the viewer the fleeting impression of a moment through selective use of significant details, just as the individual eye chooses images for the mind to consider. For the poet, such a painterly approach makes sense. As Williams tells us in his Production Notes (*Theatre, Vol. 1*, 131), "Everyone should know nowadays the unimportance of the photographic in art: that truth, life, or reality is an organic thing which the poetic imagination can represent or suggest, in essence, only through transformation, through changing into other forms than those which were merely present in appearance." This explains why he chooses to omit the real refrigerator, actual dishes, and the whole fourth-wall convention.

One of Williams' chief influences was Chekhov, whose impressionistic plays pictured a dying culture of Russian gentry, being replaced by the peasants and the entrepreneurs. He mentioned early in his career that he loved certain of Chekhov's plays and at one point developed his own version of *The Sea Gull*, which he called *The Notebook of Trigorin*. (This play has been produced recently to good reviews. In 1997, Allean Hale edited Williams' version for New Directions.) The characters in plays like *The Sea Gull* and *The Cherry Orchard* do not seem to hear one another. Each follows his own pattern of thought, picking up his individual concerns while others follow their own worries on and on. Problems do not get settled by argument but by being overtaken by events. Rather than forcing these figures into a single narrative line with a beginning, middle, and end, Chekhov hovers on the surface, letting us see, hear, and judge the characters in a carefully selected, particularly painful and poignant series of moments in time.

Williams mused that his own family was right out of Chekhov. His parents despised one another, his grandparents were unwelcome guests, his sister was in a madhouse, and he himself was rendered more miserable with each return to the family hearth. He loved these people and could not stand to be around them for long. From them he had learned the unimportance of the photographic: no photograph of Rose's pretty face and vacant eyes could capture her tragedy. No posed family portrait could portray Edwina's complexity or his own tormented love/hate relationship with her.

In trying to write their story and his own, he needed to establish distance from his subject. Over a number of years, he undertook a series of short stories in which his sister was the central character. He wrote of her as a "girl in glass," a piano student who froze at her recital, unable to function with an audience watching. (See his short stories "The Resemblance between a Violin Case and a Coffin" and "Portrait of a Girl in Glass" in *Tennessee Williams: Collected Stories*.) Gradually, he found a means to capture her shyness, her compulsions, and her isolation. But he had more difficulty in picturing himself and the other members of his family. He finally excluded the father, leaving him for later plays. The mother became an increasingly important figure in the story, a type of antiquated belle he had begun to develop in his New Orleans narratives. He was convinced that, while the tale must remain a first-person narrative, he was too close to the story to tell it effectively. He needed to give it shape and distance.

Williams settled on the device of a narrator to give both form and perspective to the story. Like Thornton Wilder, who had used this effectively in *Our Town*, Williams found it a useful theatrical technique for framing his tale. He was to return to the narrator frame in another of his episodic plays, *Camino Real*. He always had problems with tying his fragmented narratives together and found that the open admission that events were occurring inside the artistic imagination was an excellent solution to this organizing puzzle. Thus, the play opens with the narrator providing the background, the meaning, and the context for the story. It also foreshadows the end, which closes on the same setting, with the narrator again separated from this pair of beloved women who bring him such enduring pain. This bookending effect signifies clearly the continuation of the status quo. It also mirrors his creative process.

This use of the memory play format allowed him to explore the psychological possibilities of his kind of expressionistic form. Expressionism, a movement that was important in painting during his youth, had grown out of psychology. It was an effort to objectify inner experience, to use the stage as a representation of impressions or moods of the writer. It had been popular in the 1920s, especially with authors like Strindberg and Pirandello. In America, Eugene O'Neill had become the master of the form. In *The Glass Menagerie*, Williams informs us that all of the action is taking place in his memory and is therefore a projection of his emotions and distorted by his biased view.

The first scene, at the table, uses pantomimes of eating. Like some of Thornton Wilder's plays, this deliberate theatrical device emphasizes the foolishness of realistic scenery and action, pointing to the deeper reality of emotions and attitudes. The scrim, which he suggests for the opening and closing scenes, is a drop which lighting can render either transparent or opaque. Thus, when the play begins, the area behind the scrim is lighted for the narrator's words; it then rises as the dialogue commences and drops as it concludes, leaving the final words of the narrator to be accompanied by a dumb show on the part of Amanda and Laura. This forces on the audience an awareness of the unreality of the presentation, emphasizing that we have—for a few moments—entered into the mind of the narrator. The voice-over at the end, when we return to the pantomimed action and again cannot hear the words of the actors, allows our transition back into the present reality. We listen to the son and watch the women. It is a powerful theatrical effect.

Williams called his methodology the "new, plastic theatre," in which all elements of human activity and play production are important. Basing this on the belief that theatre is more than drama, he worked with a concept of total experience. A staged play is far more than the script; the sets, the lighting, the costumes, the gestures, the tone of voice, the cadence of the action, the uncomfortable silences, the haunting background music—everything happening onstage combines in a total theatre experience. For him, rushes of speech, sideways glances, nervous fidgeting, and a host of other tiny details could signal feelings and responses. He knew whether the fabric in the dress should flow with the figure or stand stiffly, how a shirt should be torn, of what fabric it was made, how much it would glimmer in the lights.

He was deliberately theatrical in his use of special lighting. Sensitive to color himself, he used the device of colored spotlights to emphasize not only the person he was remembering (he would designate a color as belonging to an individual character) but also the attitude he had toward his memory of the scene. In his "Production Notes," he describes his plans for the color and quality of light—often from medieval art—that should mark the characters in certain scenes. Williams loved art, especially painting, from the ancient Greeks to the modern Expressonists, and often keyed his plays to particular periods of art history or to specific artists. Here, he speaks of El Greco, a mannerist painter who adapted medieval religious tradition in his portrayal of suffering saints as curiously lighted, elongated figures. Williams relates this visual signal to verbal clues, portraying his women as modern American madonnas and martyrs.

He also used music in creative ways. For this play, he required a circus tune to be played in the background. As he described it, it was a tune heard "not when you are on the grounds or in the immediate vicinity of the parade, but when you are at some distance and very likely thinking of something else." This music, tied to the old victrola that reminds Laura of her father, is delicate and sad, "It expresses the surface vivacity of life with the underlying strain of immutable and inexpressible sorrow." It is Laura's music (*Theatre, Vol. 1*, 133). Often he will use musical interludes to emphasize states of mind. Paul Bowles became one of his favorite composers of music for his plays. Tennessee Williams had the ear of the musician—playing with gesture, nuance, tone, and juxtaposition. This quality of his genius has been long under-appreciated.

The dialogue is also rich with hints on action and revelations of character, a delight for actors to develop. We know immediately that Amanda is a domineering mother by her commands that her grown son "Chew!" She is treating him like a oversized child. We know that Tom is too angry to eat the meal she has prepared. We also understand her unhappiness with life in the present by her narration of an old story. And we know that this is a scene often repeated by the ritual quality of her monologue and Laura's gentle admonition, "Let her tell it . . . " Furthermore, the contrast between Laura's acceptance of her mother's memories—and the damages they do to Laura's own self-image—and the rejection of those memories by Tom is important. It tells us that Tom has the strength to resist Amanda and Laura does not.

One of the funniest scenes in the play reveals Amanda engaged in a sales pitch for a woman's magazine. The scene is introduced by Tom's caustic satire on the lascivious nature of romances in these stories. Then we see Amanda, who turns the whole force of her considerable Southern charm on the fellow DAR member who is on the receiving end of the one-sided telephone call. In her effort to overcome the obvious resistance of her sales target, Amanda displays her courage, drive, and ineptitude. She is far too proud, too aggressive for this line of work. She must stoop to selling these magazines to survive but is clearly ill-suited for the role of salesperson. When the prospect fakes an excuse and hangs up, her humiliation is palpable.

Other good scenes demonstrate Williams' skill at creating mood and revealing background through dialogue. When Amanda and Tom go out on the fire escape to look at the moon together, they show their genuine affection for one another. Amanda also touches on her love for her lost husband—a love that Tom gently acknowledges. Such a lyrical moment contrasts with Amanda's cruel teasing of Laura, suggesting that she envies this pitiful girl her youth and beauty. The pressure she employs is justified but ruthless. Here, as in most of her life, she knows full well that she is fighting a battle she is doomed to lose.

Each scene pairs different characters in different circumstances, revealing different qualities in their natures. The resultant dynamics are subtle and genuine in their complexity. Williams is trying to capture, in a net of words and in the silent language of psychological behavior, the relationships within a family triangle. This was to become his labor for much of his life.

One device he planned, which has rarely been adopted in the productions of this play, was the use of the "legend." He had planned that certain phrases be projected across the stage during corresponding scenes. It was an idea current in the 1930s, particularly among some of the theatrical people he knew at the time. Thus, to point out the poetic quality of a scene or the importance of a phrase, he would have the words, "Winter scene in a park," or "The Crust of Humility" projected on the stage by a "magic lantern." Generally, critics have commented that this overemphasis on the phrases used by his characters or the larger meaning of the scene itself is unnecessary.

The simple story tells itself. Even the narrator sometimes overstates the obvious. But no one has been willing to cut out this character's more purple lines—especially those final poetic flourishes. They move the audience to accept his valuation of the heroism and beauty of these women behind the scrim of memory.

4

A Streetcar Named Desire (1947)

BACKGROUND

At the same time that Tennessee Williams was basking in the glory of the Chicago success of *The Glass Menagerie* and looking forward to its grand Broadway opening, he was also corresponding with his agent about a new play he had in mind. This one was about New Orleans and a woman he had met there (Letter to Audrey Wood, 3/23/45, from Chicago). Earlier, in 1939, he thought of Irene, an artist he knew in New Orleans, whom he designated an "Aristocrat of the Spirit." In 1940, he had written a short story about this wild bohemian artist, who lived by her own lights, as free in her sexuality as in her art ("In Memory of an Aristocrat" in *Tennessee Williams: Collected Stories* 1985, 79–92). In the letter to Audrey Wood he expanded his original image, turned her into a schoolteacher, and burnished the new creation of Blanche DuBois. Several images had become fixed in his mind: one was of a group of men playing poker, as he remembered his father's poker nights; another was of a young woman sitting in a chair in the moonlight, waiting for a lover who never came. He tried out several endings to the story—all of which were more colorful and less effective than the one he eventually selected. Over time, he also tried out several names: *The Poker Game, Blanche's Chair in the Moon*. He finally settled on a New Orleans title, *A Streetcar Named Desire*. Audrey Wood recognized the play's power immediately. In 1947, it became his next Broadway hit, the winner of the Pulitzer and Critics Circle prizes.

STUDENT COMPANION TO TENNESSEE WILLIAMS

PLOT DEVELOPMENT

Like *The Glass Menagerie*, *A Streetcar Named Desire* describes a family and a visitor. This time, however, the visitor is not invited. The play opens with Blanche's descent on the small New Orleans apartment of her sister Stella and her husband Stanley Kowalski. Like Amanda Wingfield, Blanche DuBois has fallen from earlier affluence and status: she is again a Southern belle, no longer young and beautiful, who has lost her husband; she has also lost her family, her ancestral home, her job as a schoolteacher, and her reputation. Like Amanda Wingfield, Blanche DuBois is a small-town woman, accustomed to a position of status in her native region. Her family had, for generations, lived on the Belle Reve plantation in Laurel, Mississippi. Blanche also finds herself a stranger in the big city, this time New Orleans.

This is where the play begins, taking off in a new, more daring direction: New Orleans is far more raffish than St. Louis; it is itself the very image of decadence. The names, the architecture, the history all suggest an earlier, more elegant world. The crumbling walls and moldy stones, and the pervasive blues music take on an air of easy morality, in which anything goes. Live for the day! Her challenges are quite different from Amanda's.

The major problem for Blanche is her epic antagonist, Stanley Kowalski, her reluctant host. In *Streetcar*, unlike *The Glass Menagerie*, the masculine power-figure is present on stage. Stanley exudes a sense of ownership to the flat where he and Stella live in a state of ecstatic sexuality. Both he and his wife are far more explicitly sexual than the women in *The Glass Menagerie*. Blanche, whose background is more colorful than Amanda's, is far more isolated than she. Unlike Amanda, she was only briefly a wife and has never been a mother. Her sister is her only surviving family.

Stella, at first delighted that her big sister has come for a visit, is blissfully ignorant of the events that precipitated Blanche's departure from Laurel and her teaching job. From the beginning, Stanley is far more suspicious, picking up hints in her contradictory explanations and her evasiveness that she is a "phony." He also recognizes an antagonism and condescension in her tone toward him; this signals a challenge to his authority. The plot centers around this triangle and their reactions to one another. Both Blanche and Stanley are contenders for Stella's affection. Stella loves them both but is committed to her marriage, delighted that she is pregnant. Stanley would appear to be the clear victor, but Blanche wages a subtle guerrilla war for Stella's loyalty. Blanche's constant criticism of Stanley's crude behavior begins to weaken Stella's respect for her husband. Stella begins to see her husband through Blanche's eyes. Stanley understands this threat. When he overhears Blanche begging Stella to admit his primitive nature and run away from him, his original distrust turns into outright hostility. He must rid himself and his home of this peril; in the process, he must destroy her. If he is to maintain his dominance of the marriage, he cannot allow Stella to accept Blanche's evaluation of him.

In the meantime, Blanche searches for a way to escape from the threat she reads in his words and actions. A traditional Southern lady, she dreams of a romantic solution. At this age, she must settle for whatever she can find—a middle-aged bachelor, a mama's boy, who is one of Stanley's best friends. He proves to be a gentle person, clumsy, limited, but responsive. Mitch, like the Gentleman Caller, is much impressed by the overwhelming onslaught of Southern charm. He falls in love with Blanche and contemplates marrying her,

Stanley cannot allow his best friend to be lured into this snare. In his code, women are divided into two categories, sluts and virgins. Only virgins are allowed to marry his buddies; sluts must be exploited and exposed. Furthermore, Blanche is the snake in his garden. In his drive to undermine her growing influence with Stella, he undertakes an investigation of her background. He discovers through a salesman who travels regularly in her region of the Delta that Blanche is notorious in Laurel for her scandalous behavior. Most recently, she has been fired from her job for her involvement with a high-school student. He quickly informs his friend.

The turning point in the play is a birthday party for Blanche. As the family waits in nervous anticipation, Stanley presents Blanche with a birthday present—a bus ticket back to Laurel. Then, in a vicious follow-up attack, Stanley reveals that he has told Mitch the truth. Her suitor will not be coming back. The dinner itself is a travesty of holiday celebrations. Blanche's well-rehearsed jokes, Stanley's crude responses, breaking out into physical violence when he offers to "clear the table," remind us that these people come from different worlds. Even when humiliated, Blanche endeavors to be polite and charming; even when victorious, he drives on for the kill. The subsequent quarrel ends with the advent of Stella's birth pangs and her departure for the hospital.

Later in the evening, Blanche sits alone mourning her lost hopes and drinking in the dark apartment. Mitch bursts in, a transformed man, angry and drunken. He no longer wants to marry her, but does demand sex. She drives him out of the house and out of her life.

Meanwhile, Stella has her baby. Stanley returns to the apartment to find a delusional Blanche, wildly overdressed in all her finery to greet her fictitious lover. They argue, tussle; Stanley finally overcomes her and carries her offstage, clearly planning to rape her.

The final scene, the dénouement, takes place some days later. The family has the external appearance of having returned to harmony. Stella has returned home with her baby boy. Stanley has returned to his poker-playing cronies, including an embarrassed Mitch. Blanche, once again dominating the bathroom, seems confused and frightened. Stella and a neighbor prepare her for departure to a sanitarium; she on the other hand believes she is going to see an old lover. When an officious nurse tries to order her out, Blanche suspects the truth and resists hysterically. After a scuffle, the wise and gentle doctor leads Blanche away, offering his arm in a courtly gesture, allowing her a gracious exit scene as she murmurs, "I have always relied on the kindness of strangers." Her dignity in this exit gives her the subtle effect that marks classical tragedy—a moral victory in the face of a physical defeat.

The plot has more complications than does *The Glass Menagerie*, and more violence. It presents far more complex relationships and delves deeper into the dark side of human nature. It requires more explication of background, more nuanced acting, and more difficult stage business. The story grows naturally out of the characters, who have a kind of inevitability in their essence. We know that Blanche and Stanley are foreordained for an epic confrontation as soon as we see them on stage. In this path toward the climax, they display moments of humor, teasing, understanding, flirting, and veiled argument. At the end, Stanley has to display a kind of unrelenting face-saving in spite of his suppressed embarrassment. This is not the stuff of simple stagecraft. It requires experienced and talented actors.

Williams toyed with numerous variations on the ending, indicating that Blanche might go mad, have an affair and a baby with Stanley, or commit suicide. When we see the finished play, we are convinced that the author made the right choice. We agree with Stanley, who, when preparing to rape Blanche, announces, "We have had this date from the beginning."

To tell his story, Williams uses a series of scenes that have the cumulative effect of a single action. As in *The Glass Menagerie*, he abandons the neat structure of the well-made play. Rather, he employs the "cuts" of film production, with quick shifts in mood. Thus, he will have a violent scene moving to its climax—with Stanley hitting Stella, throwing the radio out the window, bellowing as his fellow poker players hose him down. This will cut to a scene where the sobered and penitent Stanley stands plaintively at the foot of the stairs, crying like a child for Stella, who descends to him slowly but inevitably. They come together in an image of human hunger—and the scene cuts. The next scene reveals Stella, the morning after, satiated, forgiving, ready to justify Stanley's behavior and to begin the cycle over. It is not necessary to tell the audience that we have witnessed simply a sample of the dynamics of this marriage. From Stella's contented smile, we realize that Blanche is fighting a losing battle.

This pattern of violence also foreshadows the structure of the play's climax and conclusion. Blanche once again rouses Stanley's anger. But this time, Stella is not available to shift his anger into acceptable expressions of lust and thus to tame him. He turns instead on Blanche, prepares to rape her—and the scene cuts. By contrast, this intensified brutality does not have a happy ending. The final scene reveals the aftermath of the rape and the fallout of the confrontation of these arch antagonists. Stella is disturbed but again likely to forgive and justify Stanley. She now has a baby and is a hostage to fortune. She will remain with the cycle of violence and sexuality, never quite happy again. Blanche's future is equally bleak, hinted at without promise of change. Williams was not inclined to believe that people would alter their behavior, even after facing the ugly truth about themselves. His characters may remain married at the end of his plays, but they don't remain happily married. He was not given to happy endings.

From beginning to end, *A Streetcar Named Desire* is flowing downward toward this final moment. When the gentle belle enters the picturesque slum, shrinks at the roar of the train and the shriek of the cat, we know she is doomed. As Williams says in his poem "Lament for the Moths," "Enemies of the delicate everywhere/have breathed a pestilent mist into the air" (*In the Winter of Cities* 1956, 31). The play is full of rapid action and violent shifts; it is also full of gentle scenes played out slowly. It is exciting theatre, beautifully constructed, with the inevitability of tragedy.

CHARACTER DEVELOPMENT

Blanche DuBois is Williams' most famous creation. He made her a woman with a checkered history. She had been a romantic and lovely young girl who lived with her wealthy family in Laurel, at Belle Reve—a version of Scarlett O'Hara's Tara. She fell in love when "too young" with Allan Grey, a gentle, poetic young man who wrote her beautiful letters. On their honeymoon, she discovered him in a compromising situation with another man. Later, when they were dancing at Moon Lake Casino, Blanche confronted Allan with her recognition, saying, "You disgust me. . . ." He ran from the dance floor, and she then heard the shot as he committed suicide. Her pain and guilt made this the central traumatic moment in her life. As she said, "And then the searchlight which had been turned on the world was turned off again and never for one moment has there been any light that's stronger than this—kitchen—candle" (Scene 6).

This horror trailed her home, where she was to watch Belle Reve disintegrate, lost bit by bit to debts and "epic fornications" of the males in the family. She was destined to attend to one after another of her dying relatives. By then, she had become an English teacher in Laurel and had also begun a series of sexual encounters with the young soldiers at the local military base. Her reputation was already clouded, but her double life of proper school mistress and town tramp ended with her seduction of one of her young students. The family lands were now gone, she was fired from her job and forced to leave town. This is the point at which she appears at the Kowalski household. It is no wonder she is overwrought and verging on hysteria.

She is a frantic, trapped woman, still proud, still determined to survive. Because she assumes that she must pretend to be the innocent romantic in order to attract men, she hides her past, her age, and her sexual appetites. (Part of the Southern mystique of the lady is her purity of mind and body.) The action gradually reveals that she is addicted to long baths, strong drink, cigarettes, and young men. She commands center stage by her outrageous behavior, but she also commands it by her eloquent speech and her occasionally insightful vision of reality. She is not only the best educated, the most poetic, and the most passionate of the characters; she is also the most courageous. The ending, when she displays grace in her fall, is a classical tragic triumph of the essentially noble hero.

By contrast, Stella is a thoroughly average woman, a stereotypical wife and mother, who is content to live with life-lies. She reflects little of their shared Belle Reve background, is quite content to settle into Stanley's strong arms until Blanche comes along to serve as an uncomfortable reminder of her past. Although she listens sympathetically to Blanche's hysterical discourses, she loves Stanley and their lusty life together. A little vulgarity and violence do not disturb her placid acceptance.

Some of this difference between the sisters may be attributed to the different paths their lives have taken. Stella left Belle Reve much earlier than Blanche. She did not stay to witness the family decline, but went off independently to the city. She fell in love with Stanley when he was in the service, in a uniform that disguised his different class. Thrilled by his sexual violence, she seems content to have climbed down off her pedestal. Her decision at the end of the story to stay with her brutal husband disturbed censors, who required that Stanley be punished. They demanded that she indicate that she and the baby would never return to him, but we know that Williams' uncensored ending was more likely. As Blanche is led away, Stanley reaches inside Stella's blouse and both comforts and arouses her. Of course she would remain with him; she is his woman.

This time, Cornelius Coffin Williams, Williams' father, takes his place on stage—as a model for Stanley Kowalski. He is a strutting, sexual, loud, physical man's man. A salesman, he is a natural leader who enjoys his life—the poker nights, the drinking, the wild sexuality, the fights, the bowling. Stella thinks he is destined for success. Blanche thinks he is a Neanderthal. They are both right.

Stanley is smart enough to understand when Blanche is insulting him, when she is belittling or challenging him. He also senses her attraction to him and confronts her flirtatiousness. He knows a temptress when he sees one. In his own crude way, he is sensitive to the morality of the situation and is determined to protect his home from this threat. Marlon Brando, who played the role on Broadway and later in the film, was right to discover in this character a rough charm, broad comedy, delight in battle, primitive protectiveness of his home—the qualities most frequently admired in the all-American male. He also gave the character a viciousness and a relentless drive that make him frightening.

The gentleman caller this time is Mitch, a buddy of Stanley's, at the beck and call of his domineering mother, a character never appearing on stage but always present in his thoughts. Mitch, like the long-lost Allan, is more gentle than Stanley, more dazzled by Blanche's Southern charm. He becomes an easy target for Blanche, whom he envisions as a reincarnation of his dying mother. He cannot deal with Blanche's final disclosures; she read him right. He, like most men, would require that his wife be pure and unsullied. Blanche would, at this point, be fit only as a mistress. Yet we see him as a sympathetic commentator in the final scene, now judging Stanley's brutality and ashamed at his own participation in Blanche's tragedy.

The characters are more dynamic in this play than in *Menagerie*. They seek and respond to new information about one another, deepening their understanding and moving toward action. Their power lies in their mixed natures, combining sympathetic with repellent features. Even Stanley, usually considered the villain of the piece, has his charms, his funny moments, and his justification for actions. Blanche, supposedly the heroine, does expose bawdy and mean-spirited sides to her nature. We suspect that she is secretly jealous of her sister's happiness, attracted by Stanley's animalism.

The characters in *A Streetcar Named Desire* are also representative of larger forces than in *Menagerie*. There, the struggle seemed to be a statement about the individual and the family. Here, it is expanded to comment on the "progress" of humanity. We think of Blanche's plea that Stella not "hang back with the brutes" as we watch Stella turning back toward her husband. Yet, although we agree with Blanche's plea for romance rather than "truth," we know that this is a selfish plea. She is quite willing to elect truth-telling when describing Stella's situation.

Through the interplay of these fascinating characters, Tennessee Williams explores a wide array of themes that were dear to his heart.

THEMATIC ISSUES

One theme was the very human hunger for a secure home, a place where one belonged and felt safe. Tennessee Williams knew how Blanche felt: he understood only too well the anguish of being an unwelcome guest. During his penniless days before his first Broadway success, he returned to St. Louis again and again to find himself uncomfortable in his father's house. At first, he braced himself against the barrage of criticism his frustrated parent directed at him. Later, he began to shorten his visits. Sometimes he arranged them when he knew his father would be out of town. He wanted to see his grandparents but hated to confront his father's wrath. On one occasion, he described his father's determination to keep him busy by moving a large woodpile, piece by piece, to another part of the yard. Cornelius, who was a good provider even in the depths of the depression, clearly believed that a young man should be self-supporting, with his own family, his own home.

Realizing also how awkward his grandparents felt in this unhappy house, where they were not wanted, Tennessee was touched by the pain felt and inflicted by the intruder in the home. Letters from home describing his father's insulting behavior toward these gentle old people depressed him deeply. He often expressed the hope that he might eventually take them out of there, giving them the love they deserved. Sadly, this happened only after his beloved grandmother had died.

One of his short plays, "The Unsatisfactory Supper, or the Long Stay Cut Short," elaborates this theme of the anguish of the unwelcome guest picturing the maiden aunt trying to please the crude husband of her niece. This scene was used in the film *Baby Doll*, with Aunt Rose Comfort as the pitiful victim of the brutal Archie Lee. Rose was the name of Williams' grandmother as well as his sister—his two Roses, he liked to say.

In *The Glass Menagerie*, Amanda had referred to the problem of the homeless woman as she fretted about Laura's future. She knew from experience that a woman is particularly uneasy when she has no home. For the traditional Southern woman, the home determines the person. Belle Reve is the background for both Blanche and Stella, defining them through their social class. Thus, when Stanley sneers at the place with the white columns and prides himself in pulling Stella down off "them pillars," he is speaking of a change in status and values. Blanche's admission that she and her family have lost the family home is a confession that Blanche has lost her center of stability, her identity. Now she is defined in Stanley's materialistic, pragmatic terms. She is one more person crowding his home, one more mouth to feed, one more unproductive nuisance relying on his bounty. She dominates his bathroom, his dinner table conversation, his wife. Nor does she offer in return the sexual or household services he requires. From his point of view, she is extra and intrusive.

As a gay artist in the family-oriented culture of middle-class America, Tennessee Williams could sympathize with Blanche's dilemma. Especially in the South, men are expected to marry, make a decent living, raise a family. They are not considered normal if they insist on becoming playwrights rather than shoe clerks. Williams often spoke of the loneliness of the evening hours, when most men left their offices and went home to their wives and children. By then, he was exhausted by his creative labors, ready to cruise for a partner for the evening. His long evenings in bars were the social equivalent of the home. As he indicated in his plays, the hotel was the lonely wanderer's "home" for the night; the bar habitués his "family" for the moment. The deep human need for community must be met in some manner—if not in traditional ways, then nontraditional ones must suffice.

Such nonconformity is more easily tolerated in the large, anonymous urban center. Blanche, like Tom Williams, found a freedom in moving from the small town, with its clear relationships and strong moral judgments, to the city, with its laissez-faire mode. For Blanche, who has started a spiral into madness, losing all who cared about her and who might give her comfort, this new context marks the descent into chaos. Blanche has no one here, other than her sister (and perhaps Mitch), to shelter her. Even with them, she tells lies as often as she tells the truth. She has to prove she is a lady of breeding and elegance, forcing herself to perform rituals out of keeping with her new context. When her commitment to class distinction requires that she demand respect due a lady rather than accepting tacit recognition by those she meets, she quickly becomes a grotesque parody of a forgotten age. Blanche's efforts to make the near-slum dwelling more delicate and romantic, with the Japanese lanterns over the bare lightbulbs is parallel to Amanda's jonquils and silly dress. These are empty gestures of an anachronistic cultural context. Blanche's heritage of landed aristocracy is dying of its own vices. In the urban setting of the New South, class is determined by power and wealth. Stanley will triumph because he has the will to succeed, as Stella understands. He is a type of crude new immigrant, who has no taste for the heritage of the Old South.

Even this new materialistic American culture retains much of the old Puritanism, forcing the sexual misfit to disguise his appetites and activities. The theme of family secrets was as familiar to Williams as it is to Blanche. As he ranged farther from home, he became more daring in his sexual practices and relationships. Keeping this from his parents became an obsession over the years. When he returned home, he asked that friends disguise their relationships, warning them that his mother read his letters. He knew what Blanche was feeling about harboring guilty secrets.

Although Blanche reveals the misdeeds of other members of her family early in the play, her own sexual history is slow in emerging. After all, a lady is expected to be virginal in mind as well as in practice. We catch glimpses of this bawdy nature in her foray into French with Mitch, when she asks him to go to bed with her, while pretending to be pure in her English protestations. Again with the courier of the *Evening Star*, she clearly feels tempted to "keep" him, but forces herself to let the young man go. Stanley does indeed have her number: she is flirting with him when she sprays him with perfume and teases him. In the final sexual gesture, when she breaks the bottle and begins the fight with Stanley, we recognize that she has been involved in barroom brawls before. Her sexual history, already recounted by Stanley to Stella, is here reinforced. Yet even after this full recognition and humiliation, Blanche acts the role of the lady. She takes her ritual cleansing bath, fixes her corsage of artificial violets on her lapel, and walks off on the arm of her gentleman caller/doctor. The facade is too important to her survival to abandon.

Blanche bears some resemblance to Rose Williams as well as Tennessee. The playwright suspected that his sister also had locked in her poor, mutilated memory untold secrets. Prior to her lobotomy, she frequently lapsed into nasty speech during violent spells at the mental hospital. At one point, she accused their father of molesting her, a charge that the family at various times both doubted and credited. Her own sexual needs, which were apparently never met, made her an unreliable witness. Because of Williams' frequent hints of incest in his plays, the additional suspicion of some inappropriate relationship between the brother and sister was also rampant. Later, he took space in his *Memoirs* to deny this explicitly.

All of this history of sexual confusion and frustration was, in Tennessee Williams' view, a product of repressive Puritanism. In numerous plays and public statements, Williams explored the problems of faith-based asceticism. The dualism that forces the human to deny his body's claims in order to save his soul warps him—or her. In *Summer and Smoke*, the young doctor shows Alma (whose name is Spanish for "soul") an anatomy chart. He points to the different parts of the body, asserting that each must be fed. Alma rejects this view that sexuality is just another appetite, requiring that it be spiritualized. Her self-imposed limitations result in her fragmented self, forcing her into exaggerated actions and finally into rebellion. Williams believed that the two conflicting strains in his own nature, the Puritan and the Cavalier, were also present in American thought. Neither Blanche nor Stanley, the spirit nor the flesh, is a proper expression of the fully developed human being. Her rejection of her sexuality splits her and warps her sexual expressions; his rejection of spirituality stunts him, leaving him little more than an animal.

This internal battle played out within and between these two remarkable characters is expanded to encompass the modern world. The larger theme of the story is the struggle to preserve the rich cultural traditions of the Southern heritage in the crude, but vital, modern setting, One of the finest scenes in the play presents Blanche's argument for culture, characterizing Stanley as a caveman. Yet Williams undercuts this grand oration by showing Stanley in the wings, listening, understanding that she is attacking his marriage as well as his values. The physical contrast between this over-the-hill belle and virile male animal makes the outcome inevitable. When Stella chooses him over Blanche, we understand she is choosing survival of the species rather than the dream of a dead past. Stanley has a vigor and a dynamism that are essentially American. He has no interest in traditions or subtlety, only in the preservation of his family.

Blanche draws the audience to her side by the complexity of the scene: she is arguing her points without facing Stanley honestly; she has herself failed to live the ideal life she cherishes; and she has been flirting with Stanley when her sister is out of the house. Like the South itself, which built this idyllic life on the sordid foundations of slavery, miscegenation (interracial mating), and exploitation, Blanche's idealism is blighted. Thus, Williams refuses to allow the audience to settle comfortably into either Stanley's arms or Blanche's. He instead presents balanced alternatives.

This reveals Williams' complex sense of the ambiguities of "Truth." He was one of our first postmodern playwrights, always challenging the clear and discoverable nature of ultimate Truth We want something we can hold up to the light and examine and understand. We want to measure morality as "straight" and fixed. Yet, as Blanche complains, the human being cannot be measured this way. Terms like "straight" cannot apply to the human heart.

Although we are determined to understand the "real" world, to look clearly at life, we also have a perennial hunger for romance, which relies on exaggeration and imagination. We want human relations to be more than sexual need, we want human life to be something more than animal existence. We want beauty as well as truth. This is part of what Blanche means when she pleads with her sister not to "hold back with the brutes." It is Tennessee Williams' overarching plea to his audience—to hold on to the "flag" of art, poetry, music—"In this dark march toward whatever it is we're approaching" (*Theatre, Vol. 1*, 323).

STYLISTIC AND LITERARY DEVICES

Setting *A Streetcar Named Desire* in New Orleans was a stroke of genius. At the very end of December 1938, the first moment he descended into this bohemian center, Tennessee Williams discovered a city totally unlike the rest of the American South. He was delighted with its ambiance. Here, if anywhere in this funny old world, he asserted in his journal, he had found "home." He especially loved the French Quarter, or the Vieux Carré, a few blocks of narrow streets and decaying buildings that combine Spanish architecture and French nomenclature. The wrought-iron balconies, the blues music, and the intermingled population of street artists, tourists, beggars, and vendors struck Williams as natural theatre. The bells of the cathedral rang out over the moan of the saxophone, the clanging of the streetcars, and the warning blasts of the barges on the river. The symbolic nuances were obvious.

He overlaid this with his own memories of small-town upbringing in the rural Delta to project Blanche DuBois's amazement as she stepped into this scene. For her, Belle Reve (Beautiful Dream), and Laurel (glories of a golden youth) form natural symbols of the aristocratic Old South—with the gracious neoclassical homes set in the midst of vast acreage. This lost, lamented heritage mirrors the end of the antebellum South. Her flight to the city and to the grim apartment of the Kowalskis reflects the coming of the New South—urban, cramped, entrepreneurial, materialistic, and crude.

Blanche is both a victim of history and a participant in it. Her decision to step onto the streetcar ironically named "Desire"—an actual trolley in New Orleans at the time—is a conscious and disastrous choice. Driven by events in her own past, her family's decline, and her insatiable needs, she tries to skirt the realization that the streetcar is headed for "cemeteries." She gets off at "Elysian Fields," but this debased dream is no classical resting place for the happy and illustrious dead. Instead it is the temporary home of the lusty couple who have settled for a sexual paradise that has no space for a third adult. For Blanche, the scene is replete with threats: she is frightened by the train noises, the animal cries, the street vendors. In this evocation of mood, Williams is able to select actual sounds and symbols of the city. Tamale vendors cry out, "Red hot!" Flower sellers call, "Flores por los muertos!" ("Flowers for the dead!") While Blanche cringes, Stanley laughs and mimics the sounds around him, joining with his own boisterous shouts and rages. This is manifestly his native habitat.

The stifling heat also reflects the passions building on stage, intensified by the steam from Blanche's ritual bathing. Tennessee Williams, ever a student of theological iconography, reminds us constantly of Blanche's sense of sin and her need for cleansing. She frets over stains and insists on cleanliness, preferring to wear white to signal her lost innocence. The gentle rain from heaven brings momentary relief from the intense heat, reminding us of God's grace, allowing for a few quiet moments in this violent play.

New Orleans is a colorful place, with dramatic contrasts between the vivid scenes of the evening and the fresh light of the morning. Williams made powerful use of this light/dark imagery, reinforcing it with stage directions for colored spots. He first envisioned the play in primary colors, with Cezanne's painting of the poker game in his mind. The poker players, who have center stage in two scenes, provide strong masculine imagery and energy. They contrast with the delicate music and shaded lighting of the feminine back room. The glare of the lamp over the poker table illuminates the scene, contrasting with the rose-colored Japanese lantern Blanche uses to cover the bedroom bulb. It is obvious why Williams first considered naming this play *The Poker Game.*

In the recognition scene, when Mitch snatches the rose covering off the "naked light bulb," Blanche shrieks that she doesn't want realism—harsh truth—but romance. Her insistence that she meet him only in dim light allows her to pretend to be young and pretty. She wants to retain the image of the innocent virgin. The shading of light bulbs obviously follows Blanche's shading of facts. When Stanley peels off her tissue of lies, she stands in the glare of his cynical gaze as nothing more than a pretentious tramp with a taste for liquor.

New Orleans' love of music is another strong element in *A Streetcar Named Desire.* Blanche's taste is for the old songs—the "Varsouviana"—which was the polka tune to which she and Allan were dancing when she uttered the words that destroyed him. Dim traces of this tune are used to signal her tragic memory and to introduce reminiscences. She also has a taste for saccharine popular music on the radio, and likes to sing ironically appropriate songs like "Paper Moon": "It wouldn't be make believe if you believed in me. . . ." In the background of the play are the haunting echoes of the blues, the indigenous music of New Orleans, combining sensuality with violence, exactly right for these folks. It is no wonder that some productions were to emphasize the music, even including silhouetted dancers, or that the composer André Previn would be tempted to turn the play into an opera.

While Blanche loves music, Stanley loves machines. He speaks of motors and appears smeared with grease, enjoys demonstrating his understanding of things mechanical. We know that he is the one adapted to the twentieth century. Like the imagery in *The Glass Menagerie*, we see that electricity is replacing candles, that realism is trumping romanticism. Blanche may insist that the poker party is nothing but a gathering of apes, but we realize that it is also the image of twentieth-century man—seven-card stud. Her brand of gentility has been dealt out.

The play is full of double entendres, crude observations, and explicit sexuality; it is also full of idealism, poetic allusions, and subtle insights. The censors had a terrible time with it, realizing that by scrubbing it clean, they risked destroying a masterpiece. At the time, films were not allowed to mention homosexuals or show rape. Nor could a villain escape unpunished. Williams and Elia Kazan, who directed the movie as well as the play, had to fight for these key elements. To eliminate Allan's feminine sensitivity was to miss much of his poetic nature; to avoid the rape was to miss Stanley's brutal destructiveness; and to punish Stanley by having Stella desert him was to fly in the face of reality. Kazan was able to handle each of these elements by making them implied rather than explicit: he avoids mentioning the scene between Allan and the other man, uses a broken mirror and a fire hose to substitute for the rape scene, and allows Stella to protest that she won't go back to Stanley—though we know she will.

Through the symbolism and its implied meanings, these artists were able to produce what has been called Hollywood's first "adult film." (See Schumach 1964, 71–79.)

ALTERNATE CRITICAL PERSPECTIVE: FEMINIST CRITICISM

This story lends itself quite naturally to feminist criticism. Feminism, a movement whose roots can be traced back to the middle ages, had come into its own in the twentieth century, though it was not a major force in the American South. Feminist critics, who accept the idea that gender differences are culturally determined, not inborn, interpret literature as a record of male dominance—particularly the repression by white, heterosexual, European men. The attitudes of men who impose their will on women and try to convince then of their inferiority are evident throughout this play: the way they interact with women, discuss them, look at them, talk to them, use and abuse them.

Even so, looking at *A Streetcar Named Desire* from a feminist perspective proves enormously complicated. This is a woman's story: Blanche, the key character, whose point of view dominates the story, is a woman; her problems are distinctly women's problems, her limitations and strategies are peculiar to powerless women. In addition, the character who is faced with deciding between the warring parties, Stella, is another kind of woman. Yet her choices are also peculiarly female choices, and her final decision is a concession to the constraints on a woman, not only in twentieth-century America, but in most of human history.

One important tenet of feminism is that gender is a social construct. If womanhood is a role defined by society rather than a natural condition, few societies have defined it more tightly than the American South. The mythology of Southern womanhood, developed most completely in the middle of the nineteenth century, elevated the white woman to a position of veneration. Nineteenth-century Southern gentility considered the Southern lady to be a nonsexual creature, helpless and fragile, unlike her black sisters. In *The Mind of the South*, W. J. Cash (1960) described in detail the distinction between black and white women, the black woman being perceived as lusty and compliant, the white as Puritanical and lily-pure (87–89). As a Southern lady, Blanche's narrowly defined social role has kept her from admitting her natural appetites and pursuing them forthrightly. She has felt obliged to lie to herself and to others.

Within the Western tradition, from early Hebrew times, the woman's sexual purity was essential. "Thou shalt not commit adultery," proclaimed God in His seventh commandment to the Israelites. Although intended for everyone, this commandment has usually applied primarily to the woman. Patriarchs and kings had many wives, but the unfaithful wife or the sexually active maiden was anathema. The prostitute or adulteress could be stoned to death for her behavior. Although Jesus admonished those intent on stoning such a sinner to look first to their own sins before casting the first stone, this fierce judgment against women guilty of sexual transgressions has continued. Increasingly, by medieval times, the "fall" for women meant sexual misbehavior—the loss of virginity outside of marriage. For man, Adam's fall had a far more impressive theological meaning—the refusal to serve God, Satanic pride.

The medieval veneration of the Virgin Mary brought this celebration of chastity to a climax. The elevation of Mary in medieval iconography and thought resulted in the subsequent elevation of European upper-class women. Out of a convoluted identification of the "lady" with Mary and the knights' lavish tributes to her beauty and purity came the cult of chivalry. Williams—like many educated Southerners—was well aware of this tradition. He often read Romantic reconstructions of this mythology, especially works like "The Lady of Shalott." He loved to play with the idea of the knight, often in the ironic mode of Don Quixote. This romanticized chivalry is the approach that Blanche requires of Mitch when she demands that he bow before he presents his flowers to her, acting as her "Rosenkavalier" (*Theatre, Vol. 1*, 339). ("Der Rosenkavalier" was a romantic German story set to music in an opera by Richard Strauss. The cavalier figure in the story behaves with exaggerated chivalry, setting his lady on a pedestal.) In the final confrontation with the drunken Mitch, when he knows she is not the virgin of his dreams, but the slut of his desires, she accuses him of being "uncavalier" (379). She knows that he too recognizes her as "fallen," no longer a lady.

Blanche's Southern version of Puritanism probably contributed to her husband's suicide, and her inability to comprehend her guilt led her into promiscuity. A Southern teenage girl from her background would have almost no information about sex. She would certainly have none of the understanding required to deal with the problems facing a bisexual husband. Blanche's passionate love for Allan, her elopement with him, her hideous discovery of his affair with another man, her equally passionate disgust for his deviation, and her shock at his violent response became the central plot of her life. She lived it over and over, like a movie that ran endlessly in her head. Most of her behavior derived from this cluster of events. Her exclusive focus on young lovers, even as she grew older, indicates a fixation on the young poet-husband whose letters she carries in her trunk. When Stanley handles the letters, she becomes hysterical and nauseated. She is attracted to Mitch because he too has lost someone. She seems to be a prisoner of her memories.

On the other hand, Williams has said that he considers Blanche liberated: for a woman from a small Southern town to have lived so independent a life during the middle years of this century was courageous indeed. Still, this was not a life of which she was proud. Her central hunger at this stage in her life is for a good husband, even one as dull and clumsy as Mitch. His deep concern for his mother, which makes him appear a sissy in the masculine mind, makes him sweet and appealing to Blanche—a gentle man. She discourages his aggressive masculinity whenever it rears its ugly head, forcing him into the role of the adoring suitor. She knows that it is only during the courtship that the woman has the advantage, which she reinforces by withholding sexual favors and demanding rituals of respect. Blanche understands the rules of the courtship game.

She and Stella both realize that the traditional woman has few choices: she must be the good daughter, sheltered and virginal; the good wife, protected and faithful; or the good mother, loving and wise. If she is forced by circumstances to work, she must undertake womanly tasks—teaching the young or nursing the old. It was not really appropriate for a gentlewoman to labor outside the home, but some accommodation became essential when women increasingly found themselves without male providers. Even within the home, the lady was not expected to do the heavy labor. Her ideal role was to be a pampered doll, waited on by servants, cherished by husband and children.

Both Blanche and Stella seek the security of marriage, but both find marriage has its own problems for the wife. Both sisters married for love, but both chose unsuitable husbands. Blanche's disappointment in Allan's ambiguous sexual identify may have led Stella to select an aggressively heterosexual man of the wrong social class. (Williams often portrays the "good boy" in the Southern home to be sissified, the crude "bad boy" to be the manly alternative—as in *The Seven Descents of Myrtle*.) Stella has her own problems with marriage to Stanley which are only beginning to appear in the play. She does not, at this point, acknowledge that she is in "something I want to get out of"—as she puts it in their confrontation (*Theatre, Vol. 1*, 320). If she is to hold her husband, she must adapt to his clumsy manners and insulting gestures, accept his violence, enjoy his cycles of brutality and penitence, believe his improbable denials, accept his protection and his ascendancy. In return, she will have her home and her children.

Some feminist critics have attacked Tennessee Williams for portraying these women as victims and losers. They are especially appalled at Stella's easy acceptance of spousal abuse. This is not a fair criticism: Williams was not interested in a political agenda. He wrote most of his plays long before the modern wave of feminism had defined its position on such issues. Williams was not prescribing behavior for his female characters. He was describing the behavior he had witnessed. Women all too often remain in abusive relationships, curiously attracted to their persecutor in a painfully passive response. In other cases, like his own mother's, the woman might be forced by economic circumstances to endure years of either physical or psychological abuse. When she had an alternative—that is, money—she did rid herself of Cornelius.

As a gay man, Tennessee Williams felt he was particularly sensitive to the status of women—powerless and defined as "other." He himself was on occasion the victim of sexual abuse. He knew how frightening it could be. In fact, Blanche is often seen as the spokesperson for Williams himself. (He occasionally referred to himself as Blanche and acknowledged that his sexual orientation made him sensitive to women's concerns.) She is frequently described as a homosexual in drag, therefore attracted to Stanley for somewhat more ambiguous reasons. The play does have some coded gay messages, but this language is not aimed at the general audience, who see Blanche as fully female.

Certainly, his women characters are among some of the finest ever portrayed. They are also among the most complex and anti-stereotypical. Blanche is both a villain and a victim, the cause of her husband's suicide and the suffering widow as a result of it. She seeks her forgiveness and her penance in sexual pursuits that reverse her earlier aversion to sexuality outside of a prescribed code of conduct. She pretends that she wants to save Stella from her cave-age mate, but she appears interested in taking over either Stella's husband or her life. She unconsciously invites the violence that destroys her, appearing as a masochist who seeks out her matching sadist to precipitate the final violence. She is a "truth teller" who tries to avoid her own truth, judging others in superficial ways, while trying to escape their reciprocal judgment. She refuses Mitch's sexual advances, but is willing to accept the role of mistress to "Shep," her mythical lover, and she allows herself license to service multitudes of young soldiers at the "Tarantula Arms." While pretending to be feminine and weak, she is really sharp and predatory, even a pedophile. Everything that feminists despise in the construct of the Southern Lady is somehow undercut in this ultimate example of that image. As a critique of hypocrisy demanded of women, she should be a favorite of the movement.

A particularly complex problem for feminists is the issue of rape—the ultimate outrage. In this invasion of the female body, the woman is uniquely vulnerable to masculine attack, frequently for purposes of domination, not for sexual release. The rape victim is most often portrayed as the maiden in distress, though the feminist most often admires the strong woman, who fights for her own rights, kicking the aggressor in the crotch. In the case of Blanche, she has flirted with Stanley, engaged him in verbal combat, and challenged his authority. He confronts her in his role of the alpha male facing the attacker of the herd. It is less lust than power that motivates him. In her, he sees a foe. Furthermore, she is no gentle maiden facing this beast. She smashes a bottle, threatens to twist it in his face. She is, as he realizes, a "tiger," a worthy adversary. This explains Williams' difficulties in writing the ending of the play. He knew that the censors would want Blanche destroyed, but he was tempted to let her have a triumphal departure. This is certainly not the attitude of a man who belittles women. On the other hand, it plays into the ultimate insulting defense used frequently in courts of law, that the rape victim "asked for it." In the case of Blanche and Stanley, she incited the outrage, he needed the victory. Both have their share of guilt.

Williams' sympathy, by and large, lies with the women. Furthermore, unlike traditional writers of romantic fiction, he is not fixated on nubile young virgins. His interesting women tend to be older, experienced, and subtle. From classical literature on, the older woman could be the mother figure or the shrew. It is primarily among modern women writers that the middle-aged woman can serve as the heroine. The sexual woman, in confrontations with the younger hero, was traditionally the "devouring mother," the Medusa image. In Williams, the young men are not heroes; they are rarely even central characters. Nor are the older women simply monsters. He knew too many "witches" over the years who had been hardened into that role, like Amanda, seeming vicious to the less experienced. Life turns old women into ogres.

In addition, instead of seeing marriage as the end of a woman's life, he sees it as the beginning. When Stella and Stanley marry, they do not automatically live happily ever after. He is no Prince Charming. We know that, even if Blanche and Mitch should marry, they will not live a life of bliss. Mitch cannot live up to Blanche's dream of the ideal lover any more than she can live up to his dream of the perfect little woman. Stanley and Mitch are realistic portrayals of men who try to force their women into neat categories. Williams knows that a woman like Stella would choose to stay with a brutal husband, once she has children, rather than risk the poverty and bleakness of life as a single mother. Only a blind romantic would expect her to make the grand gesture at the end of the play. Williams' recognition of this essential pragmatism in playing the cards one is dealt demonstrates his sensitivity to women's issues.

It is not surprising that a man raised by an unhappy mother, always at odds with her husband, would see marriage as less than idyllic. Having watched his sister struggle to become the kind of Southern belle that his mother expected, he knew how cruel this definition of roles could be. Although he felt no romantic attachment to women, Williams was close to various women all through his life—his grandmother, his agent, actresses, and friends. He studied them, captured their phrasing, their gestures, their ideas. He knew that they had to occupy a frightening territory, where they pretended they were younger, prettier, more innocent, and less savvy than they actually were. He saw them working through the strategies of the weak and the excluded. He loved and admired many women for their courage and their integrity.

5

Camino Real
(1953)

BACKGROUND

In 1946, Tennessee Williams wrote his agent Audrey Wood (2/18/46) that he was working on a "Mexican poetic fantasy." His travels in the southernmost parts of the United States—New Orleans and Key West—and his extended visits to Mexico had inspired him to create a kind of "plastic poem," about the romantic attitude toward life he found in these spots. As he said in a later letter to Cheryl Crawford (2/10/52), a famous director and producer on and off Broadway, he envisioned a wild theatrical event that would combine music and dance with "grotesque mummers with gargoyle masks." In this serious fun, he thought he might experiment with a new kind of drama, one that was unusually creative and free in its use of space and language. He wanted to see characters running through the audience the way clowns do in a circus, blending slapstick action with tragic experience, American huckster-talk back-to-back with delicate lyricism, like the contrasting styles of the ringmaster and the trapeze artists.

Williams knew full well that his theatrical success to this point had come from his rich blending of realism and romanticism. He had found the way to enrich the drab surface of life by giving it resonance, making the immediate and trivial seem universal and significant. Stanley Kowalski would be nothing more than a nasty brute without Blanche DuBois as his foil. She, in turn, would be a down-at-the-heels Southern belle without Stanley to shine a light on her virtues. Their story underscored the natural stresses between the practical and the ideal. Now he was tempted to gamble his popularity as he abandoned the realistic grounding and aimed the spotlight at the high-wire acts. He had occasionally tried to write verse drama and fantasy, but discovered there was no market for these plays. Such early pieces as "The Purification" and *Stairs to the Roof* never became favorites, in spite of (or perhaps, because of) their richly lyrical language. Even so, Williams felt sure he could bring his public with him into this new arena.

When he mailed his agent, Audrey Wood, a mad piece he called "Ten Blocks on the Camino Real" in 1946, she recommended that he put it away in his trunk and try again (*Memoirs* 1975, 165). She wisely advised him, for his own good, to continue mining the vein he had found to be successful. He did publish the play in 1948, along with other early pieces, in a collection he called *American Blues*, but he was dissatisfied with this retreat in the face of market values. He thought an unproduced play was like a stillborn child. To live, the play must be acted on a stage. As he said in his "Afterword" to *Camino Real*, "A play in a book is only the shadow of a play and not even a clear shadow of it. . . . The printed script of a play is hardly more than an architect's blueprint of a house not yet built or built and destroyed" (68–69). He required the "vulgarity of performance" to turn his words into living creatures. Audrey's response hurt and discouraged Williams; he loved this little fantasy. Although he reluctantly took her advice, he harbored a grudge against her, which grew stronger over time.

Over the next few years, even though he went from success to success with other, more realistic plays, he kept returning to this poetic favorite, expanding it, including fresh observations from his travels and experience. As he recalled it in *Memoirs*, Tennessee Williams dropped by the Actors' Studio one day when he was in New York to discover Elia Kazan conducting an exercise with Eli Wallach and Barbara Baxley. He was using Williams' old, but not forgotten play. Williams was delighted, discovering in this bare-bones production the magic that the play contained. Kazan prodded him to consider a Broadway production, but then went on to other activities and was unable to help his old colleague bring it to fruition. With this encouragement, Williams continued developing it until it finally became a full-length play which he called *Camino Real*. In 1953, it finally had a full-scale production on Broadway, with Cheryl Crawford as director. It was a flop. He blamed the failure on her, on the producer, and on the benighted public. Deep in his heart, he also blamed his agent.

Audrey Wood was proven right. In spite of the delightful production with outstanding actors and staging, most of the critics were puzzled. The play seemed too preachy, the rhetoric too purple, the symbolism too personal.

Stripped of his nuanced characters and subtle interactions, the play revealed all of Williams' flaws. Although the critics had applauded poetic fantasies by William Saroyan, T. S. Eliot, and Christopher Fry, they thought Williams' play was obscure where it was not obvious, pretentious where it sought to be profound. The lyricism seemed overwrought. Most of the critics (except for Brooks Atkinson, an old Williams defender) panned the play. Williams was devastated.

PLOT DEVELOPMENT

Williams went on the defensive for *Camino Real,* writing at least two of his best essays in an attempt to explain its symbolism. This was a fantasy, he insisted, and should not be judged like his earlier plays. It was a different genre. The "plot" was a construct of mental associations, with one event having little obvious logical relationship to the next. In such a play, he was justified in feeling liberated from the standard rules of probability. A surrealist poem should not be criticized for its failures in narrative construction. As he said, this is more like a comic strip read backwards, with characters who pop up out of nowhere, and then disappear, often without explanation or consequence; events that lack prior buildup or subsequent reference; there are sudden interruptions and disappearances. It is the pattern of the cartoon, or the dream.

Recent critics have begun to discuss Tennessee Williams' debt to the funny papers and to filmed cartoons, which he would have known as popular "short subjects" at the movies, introducing feature productions. He used these fragments of popular culture to make serious statements about life. Earlier, in a short story about a one-armed male prostitute facing electrocution for murder, he had also included a cartoon that he drew himself as an illustration. (He sometimes did this in letters as well. Some of the drawings show real talent.) The young hero-victim of that story responded to letters to his many fans, sometimes ending with a sketch. To illustrate this childlike need to expand expression beyond the limited scope of words, Williams drew a grotesque sketch of an electric chair with a tack in the middle and a scribbled note: "the hot seat!!@?HA-HA!!?@*!!" (*Tennessee Williams: Collected Stories* 1985, 180). He discovered, as had Shakespeare, that inserting a comic commentary or interlude in a tragic scene intensified the anguish and revealed a curious human quality of objectivity and heroism. (This particular story shares with *Camino Real* the simple-minded hero, who is an earlier version of the Kilroy character.) He was to return to this device of gothic cartoon comedy in his late works, most impressively in "The Gnädiges Fräulein."

Williams was an enthusiastic fan of modern psychology, particularly Freud and Jung, and was fully aware of its enormous impact on modern art. Like other moderns influenced by psychology, he thought it imperative to reveal inner experience by projecting that experience into external forms. Artistic evocations of the subconscious were very popular in Europe among playwrights and painters whom Tennessee Williams admired—Strindberg, Baudelaire, the symbolists, surrealists, and the German expressionist painters Kandinsky, Klee, etc. Their refreshing freedom, their playful use of color and image struck him as ideal for his articulation of human experience. He liked the idea of free association of ideas rather than logical progression, interior monologues rather than the action-oriented plotting of realistic drama. He resonated to their bizarre admixture of pain and pleasure, their illogical combinations of disparate elements that mimicked the pattern of the dream. Williams, who had a vivid imagination, delighted in the wildly creative possibilities that lay in rejecting materialistic realism with its pretense at a fourth wall and instead "constructing another world" (*Where I Live* 1978, 63).

He crafted *Camino Real* as a series of "blocks" that constituted Don Quixote's dream, giving his hero a voice at the opening and closing of the play. The old knight errant frames the play and lies dormant during the main action. The play becomes a Quixotic vision of reality at the final stage of his adventures. Shortly after it opens, when Sancho Panza, the perennial realist, goes home and abandons his old friend, we know that we have lost the practical side of the story, leaving us with unchecked romanticism. The play consequently is an unrelieved poetic vision. Since Quixote is the mad optimist, eternally victimized by his brushes with reality, the dream play becomes the story of human heroism in the face of constant and inevitable defeat. The gentle innocent, eternally seeking the impossible dream, is slapped down by the cynical brutes of the world, who consider him a fool. For those who know the career of Don Quixote, the failure of his surrogate hero—Kilroy—is inevitable. In many ways, Don Quixote is also Tennessee Williams, the perennial dreamer, who tilted regularly with windmills, and whose cry to the very end of his life was "En avant!" He was always ready to dream dreams and to sally forth on new adventures.

The play is set in a port city, with a dried-up fountain at its center. As in many of the world's port cities, the rich and poor sections are clearly separated. In this mythical place, we have a compendium of all the Central American and Gulf cities that Williams had discovered, with the same run-down buildings, dead-end situations, and opportunities for exploitation. A walled town, at the end of the "Royal Road," this "Real Road" is an echo of the early bicycle trip young Tom Williams made in 1939, down the coast of California to Mexico and back. An older, more cynical Williams had since known many such desperate places, from which he might escape only by venturing through the gate into the "Terra Incognita." This term for unknown lands appears on medieval maps, describing the vast, unexplored land outside of our closed-in little worlds. Here this unknown territory looks suspiciously like T. S. Eliot's *The Waste Land*. In the far distance, there are blue mountains, a place for dreams, if the hero has any adventure left in his soul. But most of the inhabitants of this dead-end city allow the walls to block any vision of possible escape, accepting this loveless community as the unchangeable reality of their lives.

Into this bleak setting comes a carnival crowd of classic characters, who act out their traditional roles. Gutman, a totalitarian leader, barks out his orders. The street cleaners, his lackeys, become the harbingers of death. Grinning and snickering at the suffering immigrants, they pick up the corpses and stuff them into barrels. We meet a range of characters in rapid succession—Marguerite Gautier, Jacques Casanova, Lord Byron, the Gypsy and her daughter Esmeralda, Kilroy, and numerous others. Kilroy, an archetypal American sailor, comes in wearing dungarees and an undershirt with a pair of golden boxing gloves slung about his neck. He tries to get his bearings, find a place to spend the night, a friend to tell his problems to, but he is soon robbed and humiliated, stripped of his possessions and his dignity, forced to put on a fake nose that lights up, a fright wig, and baggy pants to play the role of patsy. The Survivor, who runs on stage at the opening, wounded and seeking help, is a possible ally, but he soon ends as a pile of rubbish, ignored by those who have their own problems.

When the Survivor is carried off, we begin to understand the "plot" design. Characters run onto the stage, seek information about this place, and look for possibilities of escape. They are battered by circumstances but find little sense of brotherhood here. In this place, where the dry fountain signals the shriveled hearts of the people, sufferers will find no sympathy, the dead will find no mourners. Gutman strips the newcomers of their dignity, other locals rob and confuse them, his henchmen shoot them, and the street cleaners carry them off. Kilroy has his brief chance at "love" in return for hocking his last possessions, his golden gloves. He discovers quickly that the Gypsy's daughter, whose virginity is restored monthly, is all tease. She wants money, travel, certainly not selfless love. Kilroy sums it up: "Stewed, screwed and tattooed on the Camino Real! Baptized, finally with the contents of a slop-jar—Did anybody say the deal was rugged?!" (157).

Some random breaks in this routine treatment provide moments of false hope for him. The "Fugitivo," for example, is an unscheduled airplane that mockingly promises an escape for those with funding and papers. The flurry of activity that accompanies its arrival and departure allows a moment of hope that is then cynically destroyed.

Kilroy is not the only one who discovers that love is no escape from this cruel reality. The romance between the classic old lovers, Casanova and Camille, moves from a touching sensitivity to a cruel betrayal and then back to a painful acceptance. The crass arrangement between Kilroy and the Gypsy's daughter culminates in a frustrated effort to lift her veil, followed by disappointment and betrayal. Love proves to be nothing more than one more commodity for sale on the Camino Real.

The overall pattern of the plot is downward. All of the characters in this play—as in most of Williams' plays—are facing the end of their dreams, the loss of their dignity. The Patsy-of-the-day briefly amuses the antagonistic crowd, tasting humiliation and despair, and then unnoted and unmourned death in a ritual reminiscent of the medieval Dance of Death. The feverish conclusion.

It is only in the final scenes that Williams provides a softening effect, his tribute to the heroism and essential goodness in the human heart. La Madrecita de los Perdidos ("the little mother of the misguided") begs God for understanding and love for these lost creatures. The old lovers do come back together for a final, gentle moment. Kilroy bounces back from death. And the dreamers, Kilroy and Don Quixote, launch off into the bleak Unknown, hoping against hope for a successful journey to the Blue Mountains.

CHARACTER DEVELOPMENT

The characters in *Camino Real* are deliberately cartoon characters without shading or subtlety. While Williams had become famous for using his real people—often folks from his own family—and expanding them into universal images, here he reverses the process. He turns them into recognizable modern people, but without depth. For the most part, he leaves them simplified and static in order to serve the purposes of his "masque." To develop a deeper characterization would defeat his purposes. Rather, these are like the masked and painted figures we would see in a circus—comic, sad, and two-dimensional. Their grotesque slapstick does not provoke much sympathy because we do not believe in them. We can laugh at their pratfalls and delight in their rapid recovery from loud blows knowing that the bats are balloons, the screams faked. They are not real people experiencing real pain.

Some of the characters are standard types—the street cleaners and the pawnbroker, for instance. Some were taken from literature—Dumas' Camille from *The Lady of the Camelias* (*La Dame aux Comelias*) and Proust's Baron de Charlus from *Remembrance of Things Past* (*Recherche du Temps Predue*); some were actual people—Lord Byron and Casanova; and some were mythic—la Madrecita and Kilroy in particular.

The events of the play involve a series of fictitious and historical characters who take the spotlight briefly and then retreat to the shadows. The protagonist is Kilroy, the American Golden Glove champ with a bad heart, the archetypal stranger who wanders into this arid scene, lost and dying. While among the other outcasts, he is robbed, humiliated, tempted, and killed. But he bounces back in a comic resurrection, like Road Runner.

Kilroy was the name given to American soldiers overseas during World War II. Signs appeared on walls everywhere proclaiming, "Kilroy was here." Williams came to see him as the American version of the Wandering Jew, taking the middleAmerican culture with him all over the world. In his flat Midwestern American speech, he sounds a bit like Stanley Kowalski or Jim O'Connor, celebrating the movie queens and "good old American" values. He expects fair play from the people he meets, has a generosity of spirit that allows him to share his last dollars with a stranger, loves his wife, and brags of his athletic prowess. He is crude and sweet, a Joe Palooka character right out of the contemporary comic strips. We laugh at his innocence when he approaches the Baron as "A normal American. In a clean white suit." The Baron sardonically corrects him: "My suit is pale yellow. My nationality is French, and my normality has been often subject to question" (*Theatre, Vol. 2*, 468).

Williams expands his hero to make him the athlete from Housman's poem "To an Athlete Dying Young," whose laurels came too soon. Housman's athlete is blessed with an early death, rather than facing an anticlimactic life, painfully prolonged after his great moment in the sun. Kilroy, the "champ," the winner of the Golden Gloves is the celebrated American athlete, quickly discarded when he can no longer compete. A parallel to the prizewinning playwright, Kilroy was to linger in Williams' mind, reappearing in both *Cat on a Hot Tin Roof* and *Sweet Bird of Youth*. His name (Kil-roy) has echoes of the archetypal king-that-must-die. More literary audiences might respond further to the implied comic allusion to Shelley's lament for Keats in "Adonais" and Byron's subsequent dramatic act of mourning Shelley, another Romantic who was also lionized at an early age and died young. When Shelley's drowned body was burning on the beach, Byron is said to have reached in and ripped out his heart and then swum out to sea, carrying this flaming symbol.

Williams took some of his other figures from his reading—not only the biographies of Byron and Shelley, but also Casanova's letters and Proust's great novel, *Remembrance of Things Past*. As we have seen, from his youth Williams had been a great reader of letters and biographies, always interested in the way creative people lived their lives. In a writer like Byron—and the other Romantics—Williams saw something of his own confused path. Byron was slightly deformed, with a club foot, which Williams uses symbolically as leading him in a twisted path. Byron's infamous life style, involving brutal affairs with many women, and his brilliant poetic ability, his dissipation, and his haunting conviction of his own sins made him a fascinating study in the tormented and sinister artist. In a number of ways, Tennessee Williams identified with him. A great swimmer himself, Williams delighted in the outsized lives the Romantics lived and occasionally tried to cast his own career in their pattern.

His readings included other nineteenth-century English and French writers from which he took images that interested and delighted him. For instance, we have Camille, *La Dame aux Camelias*, Dumas' heroine Marguerite Gautier, the consumptive prostitute—delicate and beautiful, the doomed lady of the flowers. A source for Blanche DuBois, here she is far simpler.

The Gypsy's daughter, Esmeralda, comes from Victor Hugo's *The Hunchback of Notre Dame*, another nineteenth-century romantic tale. Rather than the innocent heroine of that tale, she is transformed into a carnival sideshow. Her mother, the old Gypsy whore, is the barker who hawks her daughter's perennial recovery of virginity to the suckers, paying their money to witness the comic "miracle." She contrasts with the sympathetic Madonna figure, la Madrecita, who is a Pietà image—an older Virgin Mary, mourning the dead Christ.

Other figures are simply types: the loan shark is the typical thieving merchant; the medical students and wealthy Mulligans are quickly drawn caricatures. A. Ratt is the hotel manager that Williams knew only too well from his many arguments with his ilk over bills and damages to furniture.

In some ways, many of these characters are images of Williams himself: certainly Don Quixote and Sancho Panza are a portrayal of his dual nature. These figures, taken from the renaissance-era Spanish novel, were two of Williams' favorites. Don Quixote was the classic idealist, denying the cruel reality as he fought for his dream of truth. Sancho, his squat sidekick, was the balanced contrasting realist, loving his master, but flatly denying the vision he could never share. Ironically, his very love of Don Quixote proved a kind of madness for this little peasant, who came to relish their sallies forth into one adventure after another. Cervantes' rich parody of medieval romance is a delightful meditation on madness and individual concepts of truth that Tennessee Williams found a mirror of his own cherished ideas.

In addition, Williams shared the sense of damnation that haunted George Gordon, Lord Byron, as well as his delight in travel. With Casanova, he shared the ironic combination of romantic idealism and promiscuity. Even Kilroy, the eternal innocent, had certain characteristics of the very American Tennessee Williams. The playwright, always returning to the theatre, was as vulnerable as any fighter entering the ring. He could only remain champ for the time being.

Although the play contains a summary of his favorite character types, none of them is developed as fully as in his other—more successful—plays. He sketches an outline of these people in a few stylized strokes, brushes onto the page a wash of vivid colors but avoids the final shading that would give the portrayal depth and reality.

THEMATIC ISSUES

The play is fascinating for the light it sheds on other Williams works. In it we have a neat summary not only of his favorite character types but also of his prevailing themes, symbols, and influences. Tennessee Williams returns here to the thematic premise that we all live in walled-in cities surrounded by a frightening wasteland. Earlier, in *Battle of Angels*, he used the even lonelier image of solitary confinement. This isolation was made more painful by the general lack of sympathy—even when we share a prison setting. He was convinced that few people care about another person's distress, suffering, or even death. In his journals, he acknowledged his own hardness of heart in the face of incredible pain felt by members of his family and projected that egoism to others. In later years, he faced a series of deaths with little outward display of emotion, an emotional paralysis that shocked him. He knew he required distance in order to shape experience into art, but the cruelty of his objective eye was painful to acknowledge.

This insight became a recurrent theme in his work: man's terrible isolation and his hunger for relationships. Only when we break through the walls that separate our claustrophobic little worlds—through compassion or love or brotherhood—do we have those rare moments of communication. Many of Williams' plays lead up to the scene when a character reaches out to touch another in a gesture of understanding. Then, as Blanche says of her special moment, "There's God, so quickly." Williams believed that man was both an individual and a social creature, hungry for human contact and frightened of the vulnerability involved in touching or being touched. The characters in *Camino Real* discover that this contact need not be sexual. In fact, the old married couple show little sympathy with one another. It is instead the old lovers and the young ones who show genuine affection for one another. At the end, Kilroy and Don Quixote, two old dreamers, discover that they are brothers under the skin, able to escape the walled city because they retain their vision and hope.

Over time Williams had come to believe that the Camino Real—the actual road along the California coast—was an image of human experience. Life may at first appear to be the Royal Road, but by the end, it is the Real Road. He enjoyed this play on words, the difference between the Spanish and the English translations of the name, preferring that the play itself be pronounced the English way. Even the term "Real," the name for Mexican currency, ties in nicely with his experience of reality. In his life, money was the key to social acceptance. The poor man could hope for little sympathy. Certainly, in this play, money is essential for housing, food, companionship, and even for survival itself. When Kilroy is robbed, he is immediately reduced to vagrant status. All of his accomplishments, his Golden Gloves, his memories of his "one true love," become jokes for the locals' amusement.

This "reality" also emphasizes Williams' hatred of totalitarian power. The strong man, with his henchmen, can strip a stranger of his dignity without trial or contradiction. In some productions of *Camino Real*, the presence of uniformed, jackbooted military men and the punctuation of the action with gunfire intensify the fascistic tone and mood of fear. All of his life, Tennessee Williams disliked a powerful state. He was distrustful of the forces of government mobilized by the United States in World War II, and even more wary of the country's involvement in Viet Nam. When he was living in Macon, Georgia, in the early years of World War II, he was picked up for suspicious behavior. Because he could not produce his draft card, the police assumed he was a draft-dodger or a spy. At other times, he found himself stranded and penniless in a variety of locales, always under suspicion for his down-and-out appearance. A healthy young man of draft age, wandering around the countryside during a period of all-out mobilization, was necessarily suspect. (Williams' bad eyes kept him out of service, but his brother did serve in the war.) A non-conformist like Williams was inclined to hate any uniformity or regimentation.

As we can see in *Camino Real*, Williams was half in love with communism, which he failed to identify as a totalitarian form in itself, with its own jack-booted, uniformed leaders who often looked much like Gutman. He was quite fond of Castro, a revolutionary he could romanticize as a freedom fighter. On trips to Cuba with friends, he had a hard time understanding that Castro was also a dictator who murdered his enemies and threw thousands into jail for disagreeing with him. Williams never came to a full understanding of the iniquities perpetrated by communist governments around the world. The cry of "Brotherhood," which rocks Camino Real, is an echo of Williams' leftist background. He came to intellectual maturity at a time when many intellectual leaders were left-leaning. Unlike a number of his colleagues, he never actually joined the Communist Party, but he did remain sympathetic with leftist causes all of his life. Knowing that this political commentary was not his talent nor were the ideas popular for most of his career, he usually kept his plays apolitical. *Camino Real* is his most outspoken theatrical critique of government power.

Tennessee Williams on several occasions explicitly denounced the capitalistic system on which the American economy is based, believing that capitalism rewards greed and promotes cruelty against the fragile members of the human community. (See "The Malediction" in *Tennessee Williams: Collected Stories*

1985 for an illustration of this theme.) This economic/philosophic/ethical judgement was at heart largely personal—the fruit of his own experience. Having determined that his father was the very personification of capitalism, and having nothing but unhappy memories of his own labors in the business world, Williams had a visceral hatred of big business. Although he was always eager to succeed, he despised the system that produced factories and mindless labor. He knew the value of money from having lived so long without it, counting every penny he could beg from his mother or borrow from his friends. He knew something of Kilroy's experience of hocking his prize possessions with the pawnbroker and then being robbed by the first stranger he met. Williams' letters are full of statements about pawning his clothes and occasional acts of theft.

Williams' own experience—including his pathological attention to his own health—is also reflected in thematic elements of the play. Kilroy's bad heart has separated him from his great loves—the prize ring and his wife. He can no longer fight or make love. He is doomed to witness the death of his marriage and his reputation. Williams, never married, and only for a time in a committed relationship, was convinced that the bonds of love are exceedingly fragile. Though some of his characters remain together at the end of his stories, they are rarely happy in a fixed and legalized relationship. From watching his parents' love-hate marriage, and from his own experiences of betraying and being betrayed, he had no faith that any love lasted forever.

The theme of fame's impermanence was recurrent in Williams' work. Because he wanted so desperately to be famous, and because fame came in such a rush, he cherished it and tried his hardest to preserve it. In America, most famous playwrights dazzle us for the moment and then disappear. Only a few have lasted as long as prizewinning boxers. Williams was determined to be a survivor in the game of theatre. He wrote a particularly revealing essay on "A Streetcar Named Success" (included in *Where I Live*, 15–22) in which he describes the experience of waking up one morning to find himself famous. Later, as we shall see in the chapter on *Sweet Bird of Youth*, he wrote extensively about the temptations of the "Bitch Goddess Success." Like Kilroy, he knew that he might have to hock his Golden Gloves to survive. He also knew his sometime goddess would betray him in time—as she did in the failure of *Camino Real*.

STYLISTIC AND LITERARY DEVICES

The play was not only a comic strip read backwards, as Williams had described it, but also a "masque," a medieval English form of theatre that involved spectacles of masked figures. In Elizabethan times, these masques were frequently presented at court as a display of color and light. They included a succession of rapidly changing scenes and tableaux, blending classical, contemporary, and religious imagery with music and extravagant costume. Sometimes they even included mists of perfume to involve all the senses. This total theatre would have delighted Williams, whose zeal for plastic theatre (see earlier discussion) encompassed an operatic dimension akin to the older idea of the masque.

An even more obvious term for the play would be "*commedia dell'arte*," the remarkable form that combined serous and comic features much like a puppet show and flourished in sixteenth-century Italy. Bands of strolling players developed colorful dramas of comic and romantic themes, using stock characters and a wide range of stage business, blending zany costumes and delightful music with antic behavior. Sad clowns had a long history from the middle ages, when the Christ-figure himself was sometimes the subject of laughter. Medieval paintings sometimes displayed the suffering Christ surrounded by leering gargoyle tormentors. The idea of the "fool" for Christ has Biblical roots, reinforced by medieval pageants in which the crafts made grotesque accommodations to their audiences. A famous example of this peasant literalism is the *Second Shepherd's Play*, a remarkable blend of comedy and tragedy, in which the baby Jesus, the lamb of God, is replaced with a real lamb. The weeping clown has been revived in recent years as a sacred image, grotesque and dramatic—particularly adaptable to Tennessee Williams' baroque symbolism.

He tried to recreate something of the serious fun of these older forms—and of the modern circus—in *Camino Real*. The two-dimensional characters are all stereotypes; their actions are quick and funny—even when potentially tragic. This is what he was later to call "slapstick tragedy." Kilroy becomes his modern day pathetic clown, blending irreconcilable modes. Although he was disappointed by this failure, one of many, he never abandoned the basic strategies he used in *Camino Real*, which were to form the core of many of his final works, notably *Slapstick Tragedy* and *Out Cry*.

The story is structured as a dream. The expressionistic device of the dream and the dreamer as a frame for the play gives it a unity much like that achieved in *The Glass Menagerie* with its narrator/poet. In this case, the dreamer does not participate in the "masque" (except at the end) nor does it serve as a recollection for him. The characters in this town, much like those in many of the walled towns Don Quixote visited, have no obvious ties to him. He does, however, shape our judgment of them through his suffering from brutality and his faith in man's capacity for love and generosity.

The play is rich in symbolism; it is sometimes characterized as a surrealistic poem. The symbolism is of a different sort than Williams characteristically used. In *Where I Live*, he described one image of the portmanteau being thrown, demonstrating in that action the meaning of "fragile memories"

(66–67). It is such an obviously symbolic gesture that it serves as an effective focus for understanding why this play failed. Williams noted that the first critics of the play were inclined to list the symbols and try to decipher each of them. He protested, "I can't deny that I use a lot of those things called symbols but being a self-defensive creature, I say that symbols are nothing but the natural speech of drama" (66).

We are accustomed to Tennessee Williams' developing a sensitive, realistic tale of people we know, using a recognizable set of tensions and actions. From these very natural scenes, gestures, words, we find delight in discovering larger meanings, subtler truths. By contrast, *Camino Real* tells us flatly that it is full of symbols. Some of these have no natural context, are apparently included for the sole purpose of their meaning. In this play, there is little for us to discover on our own; Williams has done our work for us, leaving us with a handful of glitter but no deep satisfaction. He apparently intended the play to prod us to cosmic contemplation, but most audiences respond to it as nothing more than dazzling entertainment.

ALTERNATE CRITICAL PERSPECTIVE: ARCHETYPAL CRITICISM

For Tennessee Williams, symbols were indeed a natural language. He had spent many of his earliest years immersed in the Episcopal Church, specifically St. George's in Clarksdale, Mississippi. With its stained-glass windows detailing biblical narratives, its American gothic architecture and careful placement of furniture, its precisely selected music, vestments, and liturgy, this tiny descendant of the ancient Christian Church became near and dear to the growing boy. Living in the rectory, he found that his days were divided by preparations for religious services, from matins to evensong; his weeks were patterned by the Church calendar. He saw the liturgy, the readings, the colors of the vestments change with Advent or Pentecost, and his mood mirrored the alterations. Having been born on Palm Sunday, Williams found that Passion Week was always important to him. Several of his plays have a background of Easter bells and songs, and many echo the Last Supper, the agony of Gethsemane, the betrayal, the Crucifixion, the last words from the Cross, or the Resurrection. He was known to begin a letter written on Easter Sunday with a mockery of his grandfather's proclamation, "Hallelujah! He is risen!" Christmas was particularly important to him as a time he should be with his family. Three of his plays were designed to have Christmas as their setting. The images of the Christian Church left a permanent imprint on his mind. No student of Tennessee Williams can understand the full meaning of his plays without reference to the Christian symbolism that permeates them.

Because his grandfather's library was his earliest source of stories and pictures, he also came to know a wide array of saints and the martyrs. He discovered detailed stories of their backgrounds, their faith, their trials, and their deaths. It is no surprise that his plays are populated by the saints—Catherine, Sebastian, Mary, etc. Although he rarely expands on the relevance of the name to the character, scholars have found boundless treasures to discuss in his variations on old images.

In these same books of hagiography (study of saints), the growing boy also discovered lavish illustrations, often by European masters, who had portrayed saints' contortions in the throes of death. Williams loved the medieval paintings of religious materials, and frequently described his scenes and his lighting by reference to specific art works. In *The Glass Menagerie*, for example, he describes the lighting for Laura as having "a peculiar pristine clarity such as light used in early religious portraits of female saints or madonnas. A certain correspondence to light in religious paintings, such as El Greco's, where the figures are radiant in atmosphere that is relatively dusky could be effectively used throughout the play" (*Theatre, Vol. 1*, 133–134). Not only in his first travels to Europe, when he visited numerous cathedrals and galleries, but throughout his life, he demonstrated a genuine interest in Christian art. In his plays, the language, the characterization, the lighting, and many of the ideas reflect his study of Christian art and iconography (symbols used in paintings).

The same library that introduced him to the saints became also the beginning of his acquaintance with the legends of the Greek heroes. For an imaginative child, with the encouragement of a doting grandfather, it must have been a natural transition. The parallels between the classical and the Christian led him to see that Christ's harrowing of hell bore a strong relationship to Orpheus' rescue of Euridice. It is no wonder that he would be tempted to use the Christlike character as his hero in *Battle of Angels* and later transform him into Orpheus for his revision of the play as *Orpheus Descending*. For Williams, the myths were interconnected, rooted in the same need to rescue life from the forces of darkness and death.

Later, he read the plays of classical Greece, which were based on these myths that had delighted him as a child. Seeing what liberties the Hellenic authors took with their religious tales, he must have been tempted to follow their lead. If Euripides could develop an alternative myth of Helen of Troy, for example, why couldn't Tennessee Williams create some variations of Christ? He was to discover that audiences in Athens and Boston saw their orthodoxy in very different ways. In fifth-century B.C., Greek audiences were still struggling with the meaning of their religious ideas. In twentieth-century A.D., American audiences were inclined to believe in a creed and centuries of battle over every jot and tittle of its meaning. Scripture was not acceptable as a springboard for lively imaginations to use as a point of departure. If he was to make his theological statements, Williams was forced to translate his ideas into Greek mythology. He did find, however, he could make free use of the saints without creating a furor.

By the time he finished college, he had also become acquainted with the famous psychologists' use of myth. He knew about Freud's study of Oedipus and found in his imagery considerable material he could use. Sigmund Freud (1856–1939) was an Austrian neurologist, the founder of psychoanalysis. He used mythic characters to explain psychological problems. For example, Oedipus, a classical Greek tragic hero, who killed his father and married his mother, was interpreted as a symbol of a common drive in young men, which Freud called the "Oedipus Complex." (See Hoffman, 1945, for an explanation of the impact on several modern authors, though without reference to Williams. Williams did know the plays Hoffman discusses, and probably saw a number of them.) Much of his sexual symbolism in the plays is based on Freudian phallic and female imagery—canes for old men, guns for impotent middle-aged ones, women trying on shoes, holding purses rather than babies, playing with strings of beads that look like eggs. His early plays are full of fairly obvious Freudian imagery, which delighted him as a way of titillating his audience without specific reference to pornography or obscenities.

Far more important was his interest in Jung's idea of archetypes. He even says in "Foreword to *Camino Real*" that the people in the play are "mostly archetypes of certain basic attitudes and qualities" (*Where I Live*, 63). Carl Jung (1875–1961), a Swiss psychologist and psychiatrist who founded analytic psychology, developed the theory of archetypes and the collective unconscious that proved influential for the next century in the study of literature and religion. He believed that varieties of human experience are genetically coded and transferred to successive generations as primordial image patterns that evoke startlingly similar feelings in both authors and readers. Our ancestors expressed this shared memory of the entire human race in their religions, dreams, myths and fantasies. The literary use of these primordial, pre-logical images can be enormously powerful. The archetype may be expressed through plot pattern, character type, or images that endow the story with certain symbolic meanings. T. S. Eliot was particularly interested in the concept, noting that the poet was the modern civilized man most capable of tapping the rich resources of the primordial images. (Numerous Eliot musings on tradition, poetry, the classics, and drama were published during Williams' formative years; the young man even named one of his first dramatic efforts *April Is the Cruelest*

Month [*later titled Spring Storm*], in reference to the opening of *The Waste Land* [1922], a long poem replete with archetypal patterns.)

He also was fully aware of the use that contemporary intellectuals made of comparative mythology. He was intrigued by the idea that the heroes and the gods from a wide range of cultures shared characteristics and adventures. (See Campbell 1956.) He knew about Frazier's idea of the corn god, described in *The Golden Bough*, which was widely discussed in the twenties and thirties. Any college student of the time would have been acquainted with these famous works, especially a young man who studied in Eliot's hometown, St. Louis, at Washington University, which was founded by Eliot's grandfather.

In *Camino Real*, we see archetypal patterns everywhere. For example, the setting is a walled town with a dried-up fountain. The town, or community of people, is cut off from the outside world, totalitarian and cruel. In much of literature, we see contrasts between such communities: Jerusalem and Athens, the City of God and the "eternal" city of Rome, the shining city on a hill and Sodom. For much of biblical history, the incarnation of evil was Babylon. In Eliot's *The Waste Land*, the city is modern London, which has only sordid echoes of its earlier splendor. In Bunyan's *Pilgrim's Progress*, the pilgrim leaves the city of Destruction, goes up the narrow path by way of Vanity Fair, arriving finally at Zion, in Beulah Land, where God is the Ruler of the Celestial City.

At the center of older towns was the public square, the gathering place for the townspeople. It was in such a place that the well or the fountain furnished the life-giving water for the community. Water, of course, is the archetypal image for life, for purity. Christ's meeting with the woman at the well is a classic treatment of this imagery. The water was also a source of spiritual renewal through baptism to the new life of the spirit, a cleansing of sins. Thus, the dried-up fountain at the heart of Camino Real is indicative of the cruelty, the sinfulness, the soullessness of the town and its people.

Williams' bleak town is surrounded by wasteland—a desert. The barrenness of this imagery reminds us again of the lack of water, of vegetation, of life. The sterility of this land, like Eliot's landscape, can be relieved only by the coming of rain—a God-given act of mercy. In Frazier's work, and in Eliot's, the land demands a sacrifice of the corn god, the King that must die. This Christ-figure, who willingly goes into the wilderness for enlightenment, sheds his blood to bring fertility back to the people—a new life. In Christian thought, the imagery is of Christ's sacrificial death; in Greek, it is Dionysus, the god of wine, who dies annually, only to be reborn in the springtime.

The wall around the town protects it from intruders and imprisons its citizens. It mirrors the isolation of the individuals in the town, who themselves are like walled citadels. The medieval city was also an image for the Metaphysical poet John Donne, who begged God to batter his heart and capture the city, imprisoning him and thus freeing him from sin.

The means of departure from the walled city to the "Terra Incognita" of the wasteland is up a great flight of stairs that "mount the ancient wall to a sort of archway" (431). This would seem a natural enough bit of scenery, except that we also know that stairs have traditionally symbolized a change in levels of reality. When the Pilgrim starts toward the Celestial City, he has to climb; so does Dante, when he reaches Mount Purgatory. The place of worship is usually high above the townspeople. It is also the traditional place of sacrifice, whether for Hebrew or Inca altars.

We know that this town of Camino Real is the place of last resort, the final stop before death. Concerned with the approach of death from his middle years, Williams frequently described people faced with their last chance—in God's waiting room, as he once called the situation. The manner in which the human confronts defeat and the sure knowledge of approaching death fascinated him. He was convinced that the true heroism of the human spirit emerged in this ultimate confrontation.

Occasionally, some lucky citizen manages to escape on the unscheduled Fugitivo, an airplane that has the aspect of a miracle. Tickets and plans for its random comings and goings prove puzzling and unavailable. The only reliable escape is to make a journey over the desert to the mountains—a journey requiring courage and stamina. The archetypal journey echoes Bunyan's book, an old favorite. But these moderns, like Eliot's modern Londoners, are too enervated to try the pilgrimage to the holy mountains. It is typical of Williams that he would have his poetic dreamer, Don Quixote, serve as the pilgrim, willing to attempt voyages. Of the folk that the old warrior for the faith meets in this barren town, only the innocent Kilroy can escape. This symbol of the New World's citizen, innocent and decent, has the corn god's capacity for resurrection from the dead. He bounces back to life, escaping from the street sweepers in a parody of Christ's resurrection.

The Gypsy's daughter, by contrast, is a parody of the Virgin Mary, with a capacity for renewed virginity. She is the figure often described as the Lady of the Rocks or the Lady of Situations—the Temptress figure. Her clear linkage to the moon and its cycles of renewal is taken out of mythology, the Great Goddess figure. She lures Kilroy (Everyman) to sell his soul for a night of pleasure with her, and then denies him satisfaction. Like the Sirens, hers is a powerful voice, drawing men to their destruction. Odysseus can resist her only by asking his sailors to lash him to the mast of his ship. The romantic hero is more susceptible to her call than is the stolid realist.

Most of the characters and the actions in the play are open to this sort of expansive interpretation. From the first words, Williams notifies us that even the colors in the play have symbolic meaning. We are expected to indulge in reflection and fanciful interpretation as we see his whirling masque. From this series of recognitions the play's themes quickly emerge: The mass of mankind are victims; they drop dead on the public square and are swept up by the grinning street sweepers, the grotesque images of Death. Modern communities are walled off, protective and sterile. Only at the end of the play, in response to a gesture of generosity, does the fountain begin to flow, as Don Quixote proclaims, "The violets in the mountains have broken the rocks!" The world thirsts after sympathy, compassion, love.

One of the clearest marks of archetypal presentations is the dramatic use of symbolic opposites—dark and light, good and evil, water and desert, flowers and rocks. The play is full of such contrasts, beginning with Sancho and Don Quixote, the realist and the romantic, traveling together. Characters are presented as either good or evil, usually measured by their response to Kilroy or to one another. Women are either virgins or whores; men are brutes or wimps. The town itself is starkly divided into rich and poor, the haves and the have-nots. They are either voyagers or survivors, victims or victimizers. Such a design does not provide much opportunity for subtle distinctions; the colors are primary and vibrant.

This abundance of symbols, especially the symbols of transcendence, is typical of Williams. He loved to universalize, to generalize the particular. In every action, he tended to see the larger pattern; in each person, the type. Usually this creative pattern works effectively for him, but this play is the exception. Here, stripped of the need to develop realistic characters in a believable situation, he allowed his fantasy free rein. This is a temptation we also see in his short stories, when characters suddenly fly off into space, in a kind of magic realism. Some readers love these flights of imagination. Most find them irritating displays of his lack of discipline. Whatever the judgment, they are signature Williams.

6

Cat on a Hot Tin Roof
(1955)

In his Broadway production *Cat on a Hot Tin Roof,* Tennessee Williams returned to his tried and true path to success. This powerful play once again employed his popular realistic/romantic structure. He used a linear plot line, recognizable characters, and colorful themes drawn from the American South. He played this time to the prevailing myth of the plantation South, though with his very own twist.

The major shift in this play, foreshadowing the emphasis in his subsequent works, was the increasingly open presentation of homosexuality. In his public persona and in his major works, up until this point, he had been extremely cautious to cloak his own sexual orientation, but the world was becoming a bit more accepting by 1955. He had watched with interest the reception of another gay drama, *Tea and Sympathy.* In that play, a student worries about his sexual identity, finally "proving" his heterosexuality. Williams was encouraged by its success, and even worried that critics might think he was copying Robert Anderson's ideas in his own work. But *Cat on a Hot Tin Roof* was too different a play to arouse such suspicions. Most critics realized that this treatment of gay characters and ideas in *Cat* was a natural progression for Tennessee Williams, who had been hinting at homosexual themes from the beginning of his career.

PLOT DEVELOPMENT

Cat on a Hot Tin Roof at first appears to be the most traditionally Southern of Tennessee Williams' full-length plays. It is set in Glorious Hill, a fictitious location near enough to Clarksdale to have its characters' activities covered in the *Clarksdale Register*. This detail places it in the Mississippi Delta, the region where cotton is king, the land is rich, men are men, women are women, and no deviant patterns are allowed. The home, with its long second-floor verandah, wicker furniture, and ceiling fans, is an old-fashioned plantation-style setting. Williams had made a point of visiting such a place early in his career and had clipped a piece from the local paper about the family who lived there.

Yet underneath this latter-day *Gone with the Wind* exterior, we discover a more realistic and contemporary truth: this rich land was previously farmed by two old bachelors, Jack Straw and Peter Ochello. Big Daddy Pollitt had happened by their place when he was riding the rails of the Yellow Dog train. He stopped off at this junction to pick up a few dollars doing yard work. He stayed to become overseer of the plantation and finally inherited it from the gay couple. In his introductory notes to the play, Williams describes the setting as "Victorian with a touch of the Far East. . . . gently and poetically haunted by a relationship that must have involved a tenderness which was uncommon" (*Theatre, Vol. 3*, 15).

Thus, Big Daddy, an ex-hobo, is a redneck without family or formal education, a shrewd, hardworking, hard-driving man who shares the dream of William Faulkner's Thomas Sutpen: he seeks to establish a dynasty on these "twenty-eight thousand acres of the richest land this side of the valley Nile" (80). He marries slightly above himself. Big Mama is a woman who shares some of his crudeness and comic sense but possesses a great deal more generosity of spirit. Their two sons both married gentry. Gooper, the attorney, married Mae Flynn, new wealth from Memphis; Brick, the sports announcer, married Maggie, from an old Clarksdale family, who had her debut in Nashville. It is Gooper and Mae who have subsequently produced a pack of potential heirs, while Brick and Maggie remain childless. The play is set in the bedroom of this latter, barren couple, with their double bed center stage—ironically the same bed shared in earlier years by the old gay lovers who built the fortune the Pollitts now enjoy.

Although we see only one bedroom out of many in this rambling old mansion, Williams as usual points to the larger implied context. Voices echo from a distance reminding us of the host of children and black servants whose destinies are tied to the action on stage. We can hear the fireworks on the lawn and see the flash of the explosions; a thunderstorm dramatically underscores the passionate exchanges at the climax of the play. The cool, refreshing breezes after the storm echo the cleansing power of the truth-telling we have witnessed.

The plot of *Cat on a Hot Tin Roof* derives from an earlier short story—"Three Players of a Summer Game" (in *Tennessee Williams: Collected Stories* 1985, 303–25). In that story, Brick Pollitt falls in love with a young widow, spends his summer evenings playing croquet with her and her fat little daughter, has an affair with the widow, and is eventually discovered and repossessed by his strong and capable wife, Maggie. The story's final scene reveals the drunken Brick lolling in the back seat of their Pierce Arrow touring car, with Maggie in the driver's seat. Williams describes Maggie's strong brown arms and her "wonderful male assurance" as she blows the car's "silver trumpet at every intersection." He compares the handsome Brick to a prized captive being paraded through the streets of Rome in a victory celebration honoring some ancient conqueror" (*Tennessee Williams: Collected Stories*, 324–5).

This beautiful—and painful—little story derived from some childhood memories, including a young man in Clarksdale named Brick and a friend in St. Louis who loved croquet. The play is full of references to the Delta of Williams' youth—Moon Lake, Old Miss, the Yellow Dog train, the church with its stained-glass windows, etc. He harvested many such memories to give this play the its richly realistic texture.

Big Daddy Pollitt, the head of the family and the central force in it, is celebrating his birthday. He is also dying of cancer. The old man, filled with pain and premonitions, has just returned from the Ochsner Clinic but has not been told the truth about his condition. Big Mama has also been kept in the dark, encouraging her to make loud, ironic proclamations of her husband's robust health.

His elder son, Gooper, does know the truth about Big Daddy's health and plans to tell him and the rest of the family at the end of birthday festivities. For Gooper, the unloved and unlovable obedient son, the main concern is an orderly transition of the estate into his capable hands as trustee. His fecund wife, Mae, is his eager partner in this self-serving endeavor. He is practically salivating in his hunger for this power.

For Brick, the younger, beloved prodigal son, neither Big Daddy's estate nor his death holds much interest. He is a disillusioned idealist, an alcoholic, who can't understand why anyone would care about either possessions or life. Through alcohol, he is trying to escape his own demons that seem more frightening than death: his best friend, Skipper, who had played football with him all through school, college, and afterwards, developed an unnatural attraction to Brick. In an effort to prove his masculinity, he had an adulterous night with Maggie. His deep remorse led to a slow death through drugs and drink. Brick, while denying Skipper's homosexuality or his own attraction to his friend, has firmly shut Maggie out of his life and bed. He is now following Skip's torturous path toward suicide in his own alcoholic way. Maggie, who lusts after her handsome husband and the family estate, wants to bring him back to life. She believes that she can accomplish this only by forcing him to face his friend's homosexuality and her own benign motives in seducing Skipper.

Big Daddy also wants Brick to face his own homophobia and take charge of his life. He must produce children so that he can take charge of the estate; so he should either return to Maggie or abandon her for someone else. Once Big Daddy realizes his own impending death, this gentle wish becomes a compelling need. It is clearly important that the land stay in the family. For both Big Mama and Big Daddy, only Brick's line should inherit; he is the heir most like his father.

The design of the play is a set of conversations, using different mixes of the characters, to unravel the motives, relationships, and ultimately the truth for each. It moves relentlessly from the news of Big Daddy's doom and the hint of Brick's homosexual tendencies toward a confrontation in which each tells the other the "truth"—out of a combination of anger and love. Ironically, the solution is based on a lie that Maggie hopes to transform into truth: she tells Big Daddy that she is pregnant. In the final scene, she pressures Brick to return to their bed, to produce the heir for the Pollitt dynasty.

In the original design of the play, Big Daddy disappears after the shocking revelation of his cancer, only surfacing as an offstage bellow of pain in the third act. The final scene has Maggie locking up Brick's liquor until he sleeps with her. This loving victory of the strong woman over the beautiful, weak man is much like the conclusion of the short story.

Elia Kazan, Williams' favorite director, thought this plot pattern had three basic problems:

1. The absence of Big Daddy from act 3,
2. The need for Brick to "undergo some apparent mutation as a result of the virtual vivisection" in act 2,
3. The need to present Maggie as a more sympathetic character (*Theatre, Vol. 3,* 167–168).

Williams obliged, and the Broadway version had a transformed third act. Big Daddy reappears after the family conference. He is more mellow, ready to hand over his estate and show some grudging sympathy for his obviously distressed wife. Maggie is therefore able to tell her lie/prophesy of the coming heir to Big Daddy, while she kneels before him. She repeats this act of obeisance in the final scene: after pitching out Brick's liquor bottles, she kneels before him in a final proclamation of love and hope.

The big change is in Brick, who shows some fight, taking Maggie's side in the argument, admiring her vigorous defense, accepting her victory graciously—without the ambiguity of the original script. This final change in the character of Brick was to prey on Tennessee Williams' conscience. Although the transformation of the character made the audience happy, it worried Williams. He thought it was dishonest to pretend that Brick would reverse himself because of a single conversation. He insisted that the "moral paralysis" was a "root thing" of Brick's tragedy (*Theatre, Vol. 3*, 168). Although Elia Kazan believed that people could change, Williams did not. At best, he thought they might discover and accept the truth about their fixed nature.

Williams was very proud of this play because, for the first time, he was able to observe the Aristotelian unities. Aristotle, a Greek, philosopher who lived at the close of the great period of drama, had described Greek classical tragedy as being unified in place, time, and action. A group of characters, gathered in a single place, during a single day, and moved through a single action. In the case of *Cat on a Hot Tin Roof*, the Pollitt family has gathered at the homestead to celebrate the birthday of Big Daddy, a day on which he ironically discovers that he is doomed to die of cancer. In the course of this tempestuous day, the characters come to understand one another better, to face their own truth, and to deal with the shock of Big Daddy's fate.

The unity lies in the relentless focus on the major concerns of life: death and continuity. The pressure on Brick to accept his sexual nature is a pressure to continue the family line—to procreate. Like Abraham, Big Daddy wants his seed to survive him. In Brick, rather than in his firstborn, he sees his true lineage—spiritual as well as physical. With little faith in a supernatural afterlife, Big Daddy wants a memorial more impressive than stained glass windows. The fortune and the land are not enough; the estate must be in the hands of the one both parents consider the "true" Pollitt heir—the son of Brick and Maggie. From the opening scene, in which both Maggie and Brick are undressed, facing one another across the double bed, until the closing scene, when Maggie leads Brick to the bed in a ritual of conception, this is the point of the arguments. The play is very simple and unified in this powerful line of action.

CHARACTER DEVELOPMENT

This is a family story. We are witnesses to the dynamics within segments of this family and the interactions of the entire social and emotional construct. We see three generations of Pollitts, a wealthy, egocentric, dysfunctional family, not very different from many upper-middle-class Americans in the mid-twentieth century. The struggle for survival is over; the squabbles are now at the edge. Who has the most love? the most power? Who will inherit the land? None are threatened with poverty; all will eventually face decline and death. It is only Big Daddy who must face the Grim Reaper right now.

At first we are aware of the three pairs of players: Big Daddy and Big Mama, Brick and Maggie, Gooper and Mae. We come to know a great deal about each individual and each marriage. Big Daddy is the driving force in the family, proud of his wealth, his sexual prowess, his life. Sadly, it is his marriage that sets the nasty tone for the others. He makes no apologies for his crude behavior, including the comic-rude treatment of his wife. He has no background in genteel courtesies and no interest in cultivating them. It is typical of Big Daddy that he would tell the off-color joke about the elephants. (This story was censored from most performances and from the film.) His language is as salty as the audiences would allow—shocking for the period. Though a redneck who dropped out of school at the fourth grade, he is shrewd and sensitive in many ways. Having lived and worked in a variety of places, he is more worldly wise than the more sheltered members of the family. He recognized, when he first arrived at this plantation, that his employers were gay, but made no moral judgments. If Brick is a bisexual, Big Daddy will love him nonetheless. He seems to understand the people around him—except for Big Mama. He asserts that, though he has slept with her all these years, he can't stand the sight of her. He seems startled to hear that she loves him. He needs to be in charge, to dominate the family circle. The news of his impending death is a powerful blow for him. The question that split Williams and Kazan was whether he would face his suffering alone like a dying animal, or come to terms with his destiny in the midst of his family. In the Broadway version of the play, when we see him again after his confrontation with truth, he has become a more gentle old lion. The epigraph from Dylan Thomas, "Rage, rage against the dying of the light" is clearly addressed to Williams' fierce conception of this cornpone Lear—who would not go "gentle" into that "good night."

Big Mama is an ideal partner for Big Daddy, larger than life, crude and emotional. The one character most shocked by her husband's news, and the one to whom he is cruelest, she clearly loves him. There is a subtle tone of pain that underlies her conversations with Big Daddy, as he insults her with lacerating humor and she swallows her pride, forcing herself to laugh at his ugly jibes. For a lifetime, she has loved him openly and enthusiastically while he has mocked that affection, never believing that he could be loved. A painful moment in the play comes with the exchange, when Big Mama cries out that, for all of these years, he has never believed that she loved him, "And I did, did so much. . . . I even loved your hate and hardness, Big Daddy!" His response is under his breath, to himself, "Wouldn't it be funny if that was true" (78). This moment does not signal a change in their relationship: in the remaining moments of act 23, he tells Brick that he wants to indulge his appetite with women, young and beautiful ones, whom he will strip naked, choke with diamonds, smother in minks and "hump to hell" (96). In act 3, he continues to insult Big Mama, even insisting that he can't remember what she looks like when she leaves the room. Yet, in their final appearance together, he says he is going to the roof to survey his kingdom a final time, and she begs to come with him (209). Accepting his silence for acceptance, she trails along, still loving and still unloved.

Unreciprocated love is repeated in Big Mama's relationship with Brick, her favorite son. She wants him and his wife, Maggie (the Cat), to inherit the plantation and to manage the estate. But Brick is a drinker, an ex-athlete, and a reluctant husband. He is matched with Maggie, a fiercely loyal wife, who is ambitious and angry. Maggie, in turn, mirrors both Big Mama (in her devotion to an unyielding husband) and Mae (in her hunger for position and wealth). Maggie is the most aggressive of the wives, not content to follow Big Mama's path to a life of martyrdom. She says that, in the early days of their marriage, Brick had been a "cool" lover, impassive and confident. When she suspected that his overly close friendship with Skipper was interfering with their marriage, she seduced Brick's friend, thereby forcing him to recognize his unnatural love. This led to his self-destruction. Although she is sorry that this struggle with Skipper turned out so disastrously, she is not likely to give up in her battle for Brick now. She is aware of the weapons she has to work with: she keeps herself in shape, she dresses carefully, and she nags interminably. She wants more than the property, though that is important to her. She wants love, sex, and children. From the moment the play opens, we know she will win. She dominates the stage, her voice, her gestures, her humor, her appetites, her beauty make her the clear power in the family. She wants to become what Big Daddy has been, master of all she surveys. Her will to power makes it probable that she, like her predecessor in the short story version of this tale, will be the triumphant conqueror.

The other son, Gooper, is the absolute opposite of Brick. Hard working, lawyerly, married, henpecked, the father of numerous "no-neck monsters," poor Gooper is the classic loser. The more he tries, the worse he looks. We see in him the faithful son in the Prodigal Son parable—with the same grudging sense of duty and hunger for reward.

Mae, his wife, is an ideal match for him: she follows the dictates of society, becomes the proper kind of mother and wife, joins him in seeking to advance the fortunes of their growing family. She is catty with Maggie, whom she views as a threat. She is saccharine with Big Daddy and Big Mama, whom she hopes to replace. She is conspiratorial with Gooper, whom she schemes to promote. Williams' disgust at her fertility parallels his disdain for Gooper's industriousness. Theirs are the virtues applauded by most of the modern American South, but not by Tennessee Williams.

Each of these characters is at once individual, regional, and mythic. Each has roots in Williams' own memories; each is deeply embedded in Southern culture; and each has a transcendent human meaning. For instance, Big Daddy is Williams' tribute to his own father, a man with whom he could never communicate. In numerous remembrances, including a beautiful short story, "The Man in the Overstuffed Chair," written after the tormented old salesman's death in 1957, Tennessee Williams describes this blustering character. He was a man's man, a drinker, a womanizer, a poker-player, a man with a booming voice and a colorful vocabulary. The title image of a "cat on a hot tin roof" came from Cornelius. Over the years, the son had resented the father; their letters suggest a careful politeness rather than love. The young writer hated to go home, where he would have to face the wrath of this man who could not understand his son's devoting all those years to poetry and theatre. After Williams had some successes, his father grew proud of him, though he was never able to express this to his son. It was clearly a painful relationship, but one rooted in a strange kind of love.

Big Daddy is also a Southern type—the aggressive, hard-driving poor white. Uneducated and uncouth, this redneck is a target of ridicule in much of Southern literature. Authors who wrote of the Old South sneered at such hill folk for their vulgarity. Authors of the modern South were more inclined to write of their remarkable ability to endure. The Snopes family in Faulkner's fiction is a wonderful, many-faceted portrayal of a stratum of Southern life. Erskine Caldwell's (another 20th century Southern writer's) people are less varied, more sociological types. In the New South, where money and industry mattered more than family and culture, such men as Big Daddy could become giants. Williams knew of specific examples of such personal triumphs in the region around Clarksdale. He also admired those qualities that they shared with the original frontiersmen and pioneers who first built the fortunes and the plantation homes. They were not true "aristocrats," according to historians, but hardworking folk who were smart enough and ruthless enough to fight the wilderness and the native Americans for a legacy to hand down to their families. (See the extended discussion in W. J. Cash 1960, especially Book I.)

This is the kind of man who becomes the "king of the mountain" in any culture—the man who takes risks, dominates others, wins the day. Big Daddy's enormous size, his booming voice, his gargantuan appetites would make him the "hero" of barbaric epics—except he was no aristocrat. Only in a democracy could this figure achieve his true potential. It was in an aftereffect of the traumatic Civil War and Reconstruction that this type of man was transformed into a mythic "aristocrat" with elegant manners and understanding of classical culture. Most plantations—as Williams realized—were nothing more than big farms, with strong farmers in charge. Money provided them with a veneer of class, but it was only a generation deep. They were not descended from European aristocracy, had little formal education. The courtly manners of the Southern gentry, much celebrated in antebellum literature, were not the result of generations of breeding. The residue of this courtliness, still retained among the upper class in the modern South, has shallow roots. Even so it is important in a region where tiny distinctions are very important.

Anyone who knows behavior patterns among Southern gentility would immediately recognize that Big Mama is no blue blood. She comes from circumstances only slightly better than Big Daddy's. Her family had some property but no breeding. She matches her husband in strength of character, zest for life. She is overdressed, loud, and loving—the ideal mate for this man. No lady, she gleefully pulls a protesting and embarrassed preacher into her lap in a bit of horseplay. She tells Maggie that her marriage is on the rocks in all likelihood because of trouble in bed. She minces no words in asking blunt and intrusive questions: Why does Brick drink? Why is Maggie childless and catty? Not diplomatic enough to pretend she loves both of her children equally, she makes it clear she prefers Brick, her "only" son—who has never wanted to be kissed. She is outspoken about her plans to protect Big Daddy against Gooper's plans for a takeover. She even resorts to his rhetoric—"CRAP!"—in putting the over-eager heirs in their place.

Though blunt, she is far more loving and selfless than her husband, paraphrasing scripture in her plea that they must love one another. In this generosity of spirit, Williams is pointing to the universal figure of the Great Mother, the earth goddess from whom all life derives, and who serves as the source of comfort in the face of death. Her name, Big Mama, places her in the line of the classic mammies of Southern literature, those black women who nurtured the children and to whom the grown men and women could return for comfort. The "lady" of Southern literature rarely has this earthy quality, but the white "cracker" suckled and raised her own children. Big Mama is Tennessee Williams' tribute to such good, plain folk.

Maggie, on the other hand, is a Southern lady. She has grown up in an old family, now down-at-the-heels, who apparently lived in the Delta, sent her to Old Miss, arranged her "coming out" as a debutante in Nashville, and taught her all of the rituals of proper Southern behavior. She knows the advantages of wealth, the problems of poverty, resents those—like Mae—who have wealth but not class. She hates hand-me-downs and is still bitter that her dress for the debutante ball was secondhand. Hers is a sharp tongue, the clever speech of an educated and well-bred lady who sees the perils of a loveless and penniless future. (Williams had used facets of this character before in Blanche, in *A Streetcar Named Desire*, and Cassandra, in *Battle of Angels*.) The language she uses demonstrates a range in education and understanding. She is funny, tells wonderful anecdotes, provides sharp insights, displays a range of intellect and emotion beyond anyone else in the play. She sees herself as both a saint and a cat. She doesn't mind self-referential animal imagery. Her announcement of the coming of the child, for instance, is drawn from horse-breeding. The child, by

Brick, will be "out of Maggie," connoting the good bloodline of the anticipated thoroughbred.

In part the character of Maggie is a portrait of Williams' friend the Lady
Maria St. Just. Claiming to come from White Russian aristocracy, she also had
a sharp tongue, with a delight in the bawdy, a satiric manner, and (according to
some reports) a voracious appetite for money and sex. An artist like Williams
inevitably draws from the entire wealth of his experience and his reading, yet
the influence of Maria (which she claimed in her collection of letters called *Five
O'Clock Angel*) is unmistakable in this remarkable characterization.

The ever-pregnant Mae is less fully developed. Williams sees her, like
Gooper, as a by-product of the New South. Her family, the Flynns, have none
of Maggie's breeding and wit, but they had plenty of money. Her debut in
Memphis (eight years before Maggie's in Nashville) was a thing of splendor; she
was in addition the Cotton Carnival queen, a moment of triumph that she
never allows Maggie to forget. Maggie sneers at the Flynns, who "never had a
thing in this world but money and they lost that, they were nothing at all but
fairly successful climbers" (*Theatre, Vol. 3*, 25). She insists that "old Papa
Flynn" barely escaped going to jail for "shady manipulations" of the stock market when his chain stores crashed. This neatly sketched detail signals that their
wealth was commercially based and they are without ethics. To the true Southerner, wealth should come from land, family, or a profession, not from commercial enterprises, and certainly not from chain stores. (Notice how
completely Williams envisions his characters: they have family heritage and individual traits as well as universal appeal.)

These nouveaux riches Flynns represent the type of new Southerner who
has no roots in the culture, cares nothing for the land, the history, the moral
and religious traditions of the region. They want money, position, power. Mae
even uses her flock of children as pawns to lord it over Maggie, to ingratiate
herself with Big Mama, to flatter Big Daddy. Maggie is right in seeing these little "no-neck monsters" with their cute, animal names, as show dogs, who do
tricks for the public. Williams portrays Mae as basically greedy and nasty, a totally unlovable character.

Mae is a type of middle-class matron Williams knew and disdained in his
own mother—a woman who bragged about her children, sought always to
move to a better neighborhood, eagerly sought office in the DAR. These bour-
geois values metamorphosed in Williams' imagination as he saw them as his
audiences. These were the kind of middle-aged, middle-class matinee patrons
he was expected to satisfy with his plays. He couldn't resist taunting and shocking them.

Mae is the perfect mate for Gooper, the Southern Babbitt figure. He is a type
still living in any Southern town—the middle-class business man with the ex-

pensively dressed wife and the proper associates, memberships, and activities. Gooper vacations in the Smokies, watches football on television in the evenings, the very image of proletarian self-satisfaction that the bohemian Tennessee Williams despised.

Gooper is a cruel satire on Dakin, the lawyer brother that Tennessee resented and loved much of his life, the son ironically that their own father both loved and celebrated at the expense of Tom/Tennessee. This cruel parody was Williams' revenge for years of sibling rivalry. After law school, Dakin served in World War II, married, adopted two girls, and had a respectable law practice while Tennessee remained single and often penniless—a true prodigal. It is interesting that Brick is more handsome than Gooper, more appealing to women, since Dakin Williams was usually considered the more attractive of the Williams brothers. Poor Gooper is not even provided with a proper name, but survives in our memory as a comic strip character, the eternal straight man for everyone's jokes.

In any just universe, this good son would inherit the fortune: he is prepared by legal training to manage it and has led an orderly life so as to deserve it. But the whole play is designed to reward the prodigal, who cares nothing for love, reputation, or property. Brick is "cool" and reserved; Gooper is sweaty, talkative, agitated. It is Brick around whom everyone revolves. They beg him to love them; they kneel before him—as Maggie says, as if he were "a Greek god."

In such an unjust universe, the weak and beautiful triumph over the hardworking and humdrum. The strong, masculine force is defeated by time and decay, and love remains unreciprocated. As Kilroy exclaimed at the end of *Camino Real*, "Did anybody say the deal was rugged?!" (*Theatre, Vol. 3*, 587) Williams clearly thought it was. The best we can do is to play the cards we are dealt, with dignity and good humor.

THEMATIC ISSUES

The Pollitts' long day's journey into night forced them to recognize a handful of home truths about rugged deals. One major theme of the play is articulated by Big Daddy, who learns that, regardless of owning "twenty-eight thousand acres of the richest land this side of the river Nile. . . ." he can't buy his life (*Theatre, Vol. 3*, 86). "Yes, sir," he tells Brick, "that's how it is, the human animal is a beast that dies" (*Theatre, Vol. 3*, 88). This grand pontification, pronounced when he thinks he has a new lease on life, takes on ironic intensity when he discovers Death is knocking on his door.

His real hunger is for immortality. In this family immortality is not a promise of an afterlife in heaven or hell. It is holding on to the property, continuing the family line—the seed of Big Daddy Pollitt. Even their pastor, who has apparently been invited to help the family deal with the devastating news, is more interested in a memorial window than in comforting the dying or encouraging this old man to prepare his heart and soul for the Last Judgment. Everyone but Brick is concerned with who will inherit the estate. With all the emphasis on producing heirs, we know that these folk are only one step above the animals. Unless Brick produces a son, Big Daddy will be dead indeed, for he will die without a "true" heir. Poor Gooper, the son denied the blessing, can never become the favorite, the true inheritor of the tradition. (This has a biblical flavor of dynastic continuity from Abraham, with the brothers fighting over the birthright from old Isaac, and battling over favoritism like Joseph and his brothers.)

Another theme is apparent in Brick's response to life's challenges. At the same time that Big Daddy is contemplating his own impending demise, we discover an ever sadder death is possible, a death-in-life that Brick has chosen. He is throwing away his life, like something dirty. His refuses to engage in the battle, withdrawing to spend his waking hours seeking obliteration. Maggie, Big Mama, and Big Daddy all plead with him to come back into the game of life, rather than remaining a spectator, sidelined by injuries. The sports imagery reinforces this, explaining that he is unhappy with any but the ideal game, wherein the players are young and handsome, the grand aerial passes signal perfect coordination, and the victory celebration but one more joy of the comradeship with teammates. If he cannot play, if he does not have teammates, if he is now sidelined and forced to describe other people's activities, then he wants to quit entirely. The night before the opening scene, he thought briefly to recover that youthful vitality, leaping over hurdles, and breaking his ankle. Brick faces a different kind of reality from Big Daddy's: how to live life after heroism.

It becomes clear that Brick has chosen death-in-life because of his own guilty participation in his buddy's destruction. His real error lies in choosing to avoid the truth. The climax is the epic confrontation of Brick and Big Daddy (act 2). When Brick insists he is disgusted with "mendacity," with "lies and liars," Big Daddy responds that he will have to learn to live with mendacity—there is nothing else to live with. Refusing to accept the real, material, disgusting, corrupt world, pretending to an idealism too pure to touch the earth, is itself a lie. As Williams demonstrated in *Camino Real*, the royal road inevitably becomes the real road.

Big Daddy then challenges Brick to face his own truth: his homophobia is so deep that he could not forgive or reach out to his best friend to save him. Brick is such a puritan that he cannot acknowledge this form of "love" in Skipper (and perhaps in himself). At this point, Brick lashes out with his secret knowledge of the other unspoken truth, using this as a weapon of last resort against

Big Daddy. The old man has cancer and will soon die a painful death. This shocking news floors Big Daddy, who swears, in an echo of Brick: "CHRIST—DAMN—ALL—LYING SONS OF—LYING BITCHES!" (*Theatre, Vol. 3*, 128).

In the course of this play, Williams considers a number of explanations of this mendacity. We may love one another too much to reveal the truth. We may have our own profits to consider, making the other person's ignorance a part of our calculations. We may want to use the secret understanding of the other person against him, to make ourselves feel good or look better. We may be self-deluding, too prim and proper to acknowledge a disgusting reality. We may be too polite to use the ugly words "queer" or "cancer." Or we may be malicious, delighting in our superiority, gaining pleasure from the other man's illusions.

Williams was obsessed with the need for truth, making this a central theme of the play. Whatever the motivation, lying is like a deadly disease that eats at the individual and the family. Only when it is laid bare, cut out, can healing take place. This is what happens as a result of the cleansing confrontation in act 2. If we see act 3 as played on Broadway, this is the aftermath of that moment of truth. Big Daddy has changed into a gentler, more understanding man. As a truthteller himself, he has the courage to face his own truth, making him even more courageous.

Big Mama's response to the truth is more nurturing, in keeping with her different role in the family. She suggests we must support one another when this "black" thing comes among us. "Time goes by so fast. . . . Death commences too early. . . . Oh, you know, we just have got to love each other, an' stay together all of us just as close as we can" (202). Ironically, even as she says this, she turns to her "only" son Brick and encourages him to grow up, to take charge.

Brick is forced to face a series of truths: he must recognize that fame is fleeting, that we have to learn to live with aging and with disappointment and with guilt. People must finds ways to cope with life in the real world, to live past youth into maturity, to accept marriage without romance, to accept the passing of that wonderful moment when they were handsome and young and the center of the universe. In one of his poems, Williams states this recognition in another way, saying that everyone must learn that there is a passion for "declivity" in the world. There is an impluse to fall that follows the rise, just as in a fountain's flow.

Once Brick has come to this understanding, he can also forgive himself, Skipper, Maggie, and the god that let him live beyond his golden youth.

In his relationship with Maggie—as in his relationship with Big Daddy—Brick is discovering that real communication is impossible. They talk, but they do not really listen to or believe one another, or make genuine contact. Once again, Williams works from the premise of man's radical isolation and the rarity of those moments when we can break out of this isolation. We see a few such moments in the Broadway version of the third act of *Cat*—when Big Daddy acknowledges the "life" inside Maggie, when Brick tentatively admits the possibility that Maggie really loves him. Notice, however, that these moments are included in the version Kazan insisted on and Williams repudiated. This author does not really believe that these people will alter their solitary ways. Williams believed that language breaks down just as we need it most, blocking our hope of explaining our truth to those we love.

Behind all of this is another Williams motif: no matter how much people may desire to do so, they almost never change. This fatalistic worldview is clearly delineated in Williams' introductory remarks to the "Broadway Version" of act 3. He had spent years discovering that he was what he was, an artist and a homosexual. No conversation or event in his life would alter that. The trick was to find a way to live with this truth.

Williams uses the Delta region, with its rich soil, pride in family and land ownership to build an Old Testament tragedy and also blast the antebellum aristocratic Southern myth. The Pollitts are not aristocrats, the life they live is no more genteel than are most of our lives, their conflicts are as common as dirt, and the land they think they "own" will outlast them all. In the long run, for all of their passionate pretenses, they are children at play in the fields of the Lord. The final theme is this, that their games will stop at the end of the day, and it won't matter much who won and who lost.

STYLISTIC AND LITERARY DEVICES

As usual, Tennessee Williams dug into his bag of tricks and came up with a fistful of them to develop and press home his ideas. By making certain characters attractive, articulate, funny, sensitive, or sad, he involved the audience in a sympathetic response to them. Others, who are sharp-tongued, rude, intrusive, cruel, pregnant, sweaty, or fat become the objects of our wrath or ridicule. His talent appears in his ability to make the ironic speech of Maggie comic and winsome, the crudeness of the older couple touching. He knew how to make Mae's hovering solicitude for Big Daddy's cancer nasty. She is too delighted at cataloging the most gruesome details. In these bits of dialogue we hear the echoes of gossip about disease in the guise of concern. In another bit of quick and subtle revelation, we see flashes of the love that Brick and Maggie still share. Brick's terse defense of Maggie, when he inquires laconically about being at her "level," has a neat, understated gallantry. We see in those few words that these two are still engaged in a battle of wills. They admire one another as strong contenders and resent outsiders' taking sides.

Williams uses patterns of imagery to reinforce the impression created by his characters' physical appearance: Mae is heavier and older than Maggie, and she is at an advanced stage of pregnancy. The slim, agile Maggie has the clever lines and the classical imagery. She is the huntress Diana, the one with idealistic speeches about love and lovemaking. By contrast Mae's animal imagery, pregnancy, and "no-neck" children with dogs' names identify her with as the more matronly Hera. Maggie and Brick are natural aristocrats, athletic and stylish. Brick is dressed in white satin pajamas; Maggie fastidiously changes her dress dirtied by Mae's piglets. She admires her own body in the mirror and elicits a lecherous glance from Big Daddy. Full of vital energy, she appears to be the virgin with the bow and arrow in the wild woods. (See Rose 1959, 134 ff.)

Williams' baroque mind often elaborated on such imagery, expanding it, though subtly, throughout the play. Maggie, for example, mentions that when she and Brick met, they were at Old Miss (the University of Mississippi), where she was an accomplished archer. She loved to run through the woods with her dogs chasing deer, and therefore won the Diana trophy. Unlike the huntress goddess, jealous of her chastity, Maggie is eager to reject her chaste life, to lure Brick to the bed. Like Diana, Maggie punishes those who get in her way. Skipper is no Actaeon, but, as in the myth, he did look on her naked beauty and found himself pursued by his own "hounds" of fear and self-deception until he too was torn apart. (In the original myth, Actaeon watched Diana, the huntress queen, as she undressed. In her wrath, she transformed him into a stag, who was pursued by his own hunting dogs until he was finally killed by them and by his friends, who could not recognize him in this new shape.) Perhaps Williams is saying that Brick is one of these erstwhile friends, who joins the pack in destroying his friend who, once he has become the unspeakable homosexual, is no longer quite human. Shelley's "Adonais," which used this myth, was a poem he knew and loved. It was not beyond Tennessee Williams to reference it as a subtext—or hidden message—about the treatment of gays in a heterosexual community.

Brick is the image of Artemis's twin brother, Apollo, celebrated in Greek statuary. (Perhaps the close ties but failed love between Maggie and Brick is rooted in their implied sibling relationship: they are more nearly brother and sister than husband and wife.) Brick has plenty of parallels with Apollo: Renowned for his physical beauty, this sun god was the ideal male figure, whose sacred plant was the laurel. (Brick's mother talks of his red curls when he was a child, pointing to his own "golden" nature.) His preference for white clothing testifies to his idealism, his dream of purity. His "deep friendship" with Skipper implies that he shares with Apollo a preference for boys. In fact, even the death of Skipper seems to be parallel to the myth of Hyakinthos, a beloved youth who was accidentally killed by Apollo when he was hurling the diskos—the ancient version of the football.

We know that Williams was steeped in Greek mythology, especially the myriad tales of the beautiful and athletic Apollo. His use of the Orpheus legend in *Orpheus Descending* clearly testifies to this. In his short story "One Arm," he pictured the broken kouros (young male) statue, the oft-repeated image of Apollo. Brick's broken ankle shows us that, if we follow all the leads and hints in a Williams' play, we find ourselves deep in classical lore.

Brick has a cluster of linguistic and dramatic tricks that keep him at the center of the stage: his constant return to "Echo Springs," (a fancy way of announcing his alcoholism and alluding to the Greek myth of Echo) gives a rhythm to the play. The constant refrain of the characters that he should stop drinking gives it a refrain. We wait with him for the moment he will hear the "click" and be relieved of all ties with this caterwauling. When Maggie breaks the rhythm by smashing the bottles, she provides the dénouement. Brick's detachment and coolness in this supercharged family quarrel are a neat physical contrast, ironically making him the object of "gaze." The nonparticipant becomes the center of attention. The beautiful and distant Brick, apparently crumbling before our eyes, is forced to play the hero who takes over the fortune and fathers the heir.

At its deepest level, the whole story is about the cycle of life. The marriage bed, the "altar" on which Brick's idealism must be sacrificed, is center stage. This historic old bed, once the site of homosexual lovers, must be transformed to a heterosexual marriage bed. The thunderstorm, with its cleansing effects, not only reinforces the onstage catharsis, but also ties the fertility of the humans to the fertility of the land and the reliance of both on superhuman powers for sustenance. The ironic birthday/deathday celebration brings us face-to-face with the cycle of dust-to-dust.

As always, Tennessee Williams imagined his play visually. He filled it with colorful words, stage business, a range of moods, and delightful contrasts. We move quickly from laughter to tears, despair to hope in the course of the three acts. It is a wonderful play to produce or watch.

ALTERNATE CRITICAL PERSPECTIVE: GAY CRITICISM

Gay criticism uses the devices of feminist criticism, with a particular focus on sexuality, specifically same-sex desire—homosexual, homosocial, and homophobic themes inside cultural and literary artifacts. Like the feminists, the gay critics are concerned with sexual identity, the problem of perceiving self as "other," the object iof the "gaze" that reduces the person to an object of desire.

A key concern, especially during Tennessee Williams' life, was the portrayal of homosexuality as a perversion, an abnormality, a pathology. Freud had seen homosexuality as a form of narcissism, really desiring the self in another, but some gay critics have argued against this, insisting that men want other men, not self, that Narcissus rejected both boys and girls in his love of self.

Gay critics have been split in their view of this play, partially because Williams himself appeared ambiguous about the nature of homosexuality. We suspect he identifies with both Brick and Big Daddy in his statements. He certainly understands homosexuality; he also seems to despise it. Big Daddy speaks of the previous occupants of the bedroom and of his sympathy with their love. Unlike the prissy Brick, who uses loaded words like "queers" and "fairies," this worldly wise man is not judgmental about human love, no matter where it occurs. This is ironic, considering that the character is modeled on Cornelius Williams, whose implied judgment on his effeminate ways dogged much of Tom's life. (See "The Man in the Overstuffed Chair" in *Tennessee Williams: Collected Stories*, vii–xvii.) Tennessee himself grew more sympathetic as he aged, coming to understand how thoroughly unhappy his father was.

Critics insisted that the play was "evasive," refusing to confront the central issue of Brick's sexual orientation. Walter Kerr asks, "Is he a homosexual? At one moment he is denouncing 'queers,' at another describing the way he clasped his friend's hand going to bed at night" (*New York Herald Tribune*, April 3, 1955, sec. 4:1 reprinted in Crandell 1996, 119). This ambiguity about homosexuality has been a major source of concern by critics who looked at this and later plays, trying to establish exactly what Williams was saying. Sometimes, he seems to believe that homosexuality can coexist with heterosexuality in a single character. (Brick is described by Maggie as a good lover, though his "disinterested" manner seems to be a curious source of delight for her.) In this case, the bisexual male decides on the sex of the partners he selects. Williams describes his own early sexual attraction to women, though he was to become far more enamored of men and boys as he matured. He did not agree that sexuality was as clear-cut a choice as many of his critics have insisted.

The play is embedded in its period: because of the homophobic response of American society to gay men, at least in the 1950s when the play was written, an athlete such as Brick Pollitt would be shocked at the very idea that his friend was gay—or that he was suspected of homosexual proclivities. Even if he felt this in himself, he would not be able to face this "truth." That is the point that Big Daddy is making in their confrontation: Brick would rather destroy Skipper and himself than admit his feeling for other men. This sense of self-loathing that leads Brick to drink is repeated in other Williams plays. In *A Streetcar Named Desire*, Blanche's recognition of Allan's homosexuality drives her young husband to suicide. In *Small Craft Warnings*, the gay writer Quentin makes a long speech about the horrible life of the homosexual. Williams' own efforts to hide his sexual orientation from his family and his public for so many years must have increased this sense of disgust at his own life.

On the other hand, he was compelled to speak of his drives and his experiences, writing of them in story after story. Many of the early short stories were quite explicit about the sexual activities of gay characters, but Williams could publish these in limited editions for a special audience. Plays are intended for a larger, more general public, that perforce includes the matinee matrons who buy blocks of tickets. Thus, he made Allan Grey's sexuality a minor part of the play, a segment of memory, and the character himself was conveniently dead. Some believe that the narrator in *The Glass Menagerie* is gay, but Williams disguised this well enough that critics have only recently unearthed the evidence. Only just prior to the production of *Cat* was a homosexual theme accepted in a main-stream play—in Anderson's *Tea and Sympathy*. Williams knew that he was risking public wrath by presenting homosexuality in a sympathetic manner. If the play seems ambiguous, it is in part because Williams was himself ambiguous.

Williams was convinced that this problem of sexual orientation was not a trivial concern. He called it the "root" of the tragedy in *Cat*.

John Simon, a prominent critic, thought that both Maggie and Brick were disguised gays. Brick he characterizes as a "fairly typical figure from the homosexual world: the beautiful but mediocre young man who coasts along on his looks, and drinks because he is beginning to lose them" (Simon 1974.) This golden boy is the center of adoration among his lovers, who are often brighter, more artistic, or more accomplished men. They, however, cannot overcome their "fatal obsession with mere looks, mere youth, and the indolent passivity" of this perfect partner. He is a love object, which later critics would identify as the "object of gaze." Certainly Brick does fulfill this role, standing partially nude at the beginning of act 1, then lounging about in his clinging white satin pajamas. (Stanley Kowalski had also undressed on stage, strutting around in his seminude fashion, flexing his muscles.) For the gay playwright, the erotic on-stage scene is the striptease of the well-built male.

If Brick is the homosexual ideal, Simon insists, then Maggie becomes the "disguised, sentimentalized portrait of the gifted, worldly, passionate homosexual lover" who finds herself frustrated by the passionless beloved. Although Maggie is a good-looking woman, she does not elicit many adoring comments from others that Brick does. Although other men look at her with lust, we see no evidence of sexual desire for her on Brick's part. She speaks of him as a "disinterested lover"—hardly a flattering portrayal of one's mate. What seems admirable in her is her boyish vigor, not her womanly curves. By contrast, Mae's pregnancy is pictured as repulsive and animalistic.

We have already seen that Maggie is modeled after the virgin goddess, who is a man-hater. Apollo, her brother, is her beloved—and a forbidden sexual partner. This imagery reinforces the sense that there are barriers here to a satisfying heterosexual marriage. This theme of incest recurs in Williams' work and in his thoughts. Perhaps he is relying on his own life and his deep love of his sister—the only long-lasting love of his life—and perhaps he is drawing from literary classics. Not only the Greeks, who saw the brother-sister, mother-son ties as sexually complex, but also such modern masters as Strindberg had explored the ideas. In *The Father*, for instance, August Strindberg described an embattled marriage, in which the strong woman tormented her husband, while also serving as a substitute mother to him. This love-hate relationship makes the marriage a battleground and the struggle for superiority a lifetime of hell on earth.

Simon suggests that Williams is vindictive in his treatment of women because of his own orientation. This seems an unfair comment, given the host of sympathetic female characters in Williams' plays. This strong woman, coupled with a weak man, is not a peculiar character in Southern fiction, and probably in Southern life. The woman need not be seen as a castrator nor her portrayal as "vindictive." In order to survive, to have a family and a life, Maggie must assume control. She does it with love, in order to save Brick as well as herself. Perhaps this transforms her into a mother figure, but for Williams, she is not hateful or nasty as a result. Unlike Strindberg, he creates in Maggie a sympathetic motherly wife.

Other critics have picked up on this first critique of the play's hidden agenda. Richard Vowles insists that "the play is really about that shadowy no-man's land between hetero-and homosexuality" (Crandell 1996, 128). Williams would probably agree. He has said that he prefers to retain some mystery in his representation of the complexities of human relationships.

A more forceful critique was rendered by Eric Bentley, who wanted to know whether Brick could be cured, "and, if not, whether homosexuality is something this individual can accept as irrevocable truth about himself" (128). He insists that the story is "fatally incomplete." But Williams could not have heeded this advice without becoming a didactic and obvious spokesman for the diagnosis and treatment of homosexuality. He was writing at a time when the psychological community, like the rest of the world, was struggling over whether homosexuality was an inborn condition or a lifestyle choice, and whether therapy could alter the orientation. He felt it necessary to respond to the critics at some length, insisting that this is not "evasion" on his part. (See "Critic Says 'Evasion,' Writer Says 'Mystery'" in *Where I Live* 1978, 70–74.)

From his youth, Tennessee Williams' effeminacy had alienated him from his father and from others in a culture that despises homosexuality. He read biographies and correspondence of the artists, trying to understand how the artist can live in the antagonistic world. His poetry is full of celebrations of moments of sexual delight, followed by the pains of guilt and alienation, followed by embarrassed boredom with sexual partners. His constant efforts to hide his truth from his mother led him into disguises that probably enhanced his storytelling ability. He insisted that his sexual ambiguity made him sympathetic with both men and women and contributed to his ability to draw sympathetic female characters. Some critics have insisted that his women are often men in drag. He frequently referred to himself as "Blanche," yet he despised homosexual "camp" and had a number of good friends among women—often older women.

Perhaps he could not describe a happy marriage because he had not been close to one. Certainly the relationship between his parents was a constant battle, finally ending in divorce. His grandparents had a long, companionate marriage, that involved a great deal of sacrifice on Grandmother's part and a great deal of self-indulgence on Grandfather's. The grandfather, who became the model for Nonno in *Night of the Iguana*, lived with Williams and his partner, Frank Merlo, off and on for some years. At least one biographer suggests that the grandfather had some tendencies toward homosexuality himself—and perhaps even some hidden history of it. (See Leverich 1995, 151–152.) This may not be the actual explanation of the grandfather's sympathy with the gay partners; he may have been so pleased to see Tennessee happy and settled that he was willing to overlook the fact that his mate was a male.

Gay critics in recent years, especially such distinguished authors as David Savran (1992) and John Clum (1992) have explored Williams' sexuality in considerable detail. They are frequently unhappy with his critique of the gay experience, especially his occasional outbursts of self-loathing. Williams was never an unambiguous advocate of homosexuality. He did have a large network of homosexual friends; he did advocate civil rights for gays; but he never said that this was a happy condition. His nervous laughter at his own life, his compulsion to confess every nasty detail of drunken orgies he had attended (not only in *Memoirs*, but also in *Moise and the World of Reason*) testify to his anguish.

Out of this pain came the complex message that makes plays like *A Streetcar Named Desire* and *Cat on a Hot Tin Roof* powerful and realistic. His anguish was a source of his creativity; his failure to make his own family understand his problems forced him to spend his life seeking to communicate with audiences in darkened auditoriums.

7

Sweet Bird of Youth
(1959)

BACKGROUND

America is no country for old people. The cult of youth is central to our national life: our films, clothing, education, music, health, and our entire system of values. The burgeoning cosmetic industry in this country, now aimed at men as well as women of a certain age, attests to this obsession with appearing perennially youthful.

Tennessee Williams was painfully aware of his age. From the time in his twenties when he started lying about the year of his birth so that he could qualify as a "young" playwright, through his prolonged apprenticeship in the theatre, living like an adolescent with no home or family of his own, Williams counted each advancing year with apprehension. His companions, many of whom changed daily, seemed younger and younger as he advanced in age. Increasingly suspicious of the motives of those handsome young men around him, he recognized that they were attracted to his fame and fortune. These golden boys only accentuated his loss of innocence and physique. He hated the monster of cynicism that he was becoming.

There were obvious compensations that came with fame and fortune, including the freedom of movement, which he enjoyed to the fullest. As soon as he became successful, Williams indulged his love of travel, spending every possible vacation in Europe, where he relished his international celebrity and enjoyed meeting famous members of the art world. His all-time favorite city was

Rome. This splendid ancient city, ironically, celebrates glorious youth every bit as much as does the New World. Responding to this sad discovery, he wrote *The Roman Spring of Mrs. Stone* (published in 1950), a novel about the aging artist in this city so full of stone carvings of beautiful young bodies.

The actress at the center of the novel, Karen Stone, had been a Broadway star for years. When she hit menopause, however, she also came to the end of her career. To escape those who continually reminded her of her early beauty and talent, she decided to fly with her timid little rabbit of a husband to Rome. On the plane trip across the Atlantic, her husband suffered a heart attack and died, leaving her to face the rapid approach of old age alone. She determined to fight her fate. She thought she still might discover romance—love among the ruins.

The Roman Spring of Mrs. Stone, which was made into a beautiful film with Vivien Leigh and Warren Beatty in 1961, echoes elements of *A Streetcar Named Desire.* Once again, the heroine laments that the sweet bird of youth has flown the coop, never to return. She restricts her public appearances to evenings, to places with dim lighting. She lavishes attention on every detail of dress and make-up to pursue with art and determination that which had come easily and naturally a few years earlier. In the case of Karen Stone, her wealth and talent protect her in a way denied to the penniless Blanche. They also expose her to new indignities and temptations. She is a powerful woman who can use wit and charm for her own purposes. Over the years, Mrs. Stone discovered that she could easily dominate young actors who played opposite her; she could seduce them and upstage them. Now, stripped of much of that power, she cannot escape the awareness of her own mortality. Will power alone is not sufficient to allow her to continue playing Juliet when she looks more like the old nurse. The Romeo she discovers has no interest in her person, only in her gifts.

The story chronicles her flirtation with a handsome young gigolo, who proves more beautiful and vain than she, ending with her humiliation by him. The shocking conclusion of the story has her dropping a key from her balcony to a vagrant who has been stalking her, repeatedly exposing himself without a word. She no longer pretends that the anticipated relationship will be romance. Lust will suffice for the time being. Sex will take her mind off her fate.

Williams was, of course, talking about himself. He often referred to himself as an "old bitch." He was also describing the many actresses he had come to know over the years. Early in his apprenticeship years, he met Tallulah Bankhead, a southerner and an outrageous character, whom he came to love as a good friend. Later, he watched with admiration and anguish the heroic final days of Laurette Taylor, who died in the role of Amanda in *The Glass Menagerie.* A great parade of such wonderful old actresses, powerful, fierce, and heroic, took roles in his many plays and films.

As early as 1948, Williams had drafted a one-act play called "The Enemy: Time" (Kolin 1998, 137). By 1956, he had developed the theme into an early draft of *Sweet Bird of Youth,* which opened in Coral Gables, Florida. After its good reception, he developed a more polished script for Broadway, opening finally in 1959. It had a fair run—383 performances—largely because of the brilliant acting of Geraldine Page as the Princess Kosmonopolis. Although critics pointed to problems in the plot structure, the unloveliness of the characters, and the trite pronouncement at the end, audiences found it exciting and entertaining.

The success of *Sweet Bird of Youth* (and his own compulsion to write masked autobiographies) encouraged Williams to continue pursuing this theme of the aging artist, but with less and less public acclaim. In 1963, Williams elaborated his views of the theatre's aged ogres in a less successful play, *The Milk Train Doesn't Stop Here Anymore.* This painful story of the dying actress would seem to be almost a sequel to *Sweet Bird of Youth.* "The Gnädiges Fräulein" (1966) is one of his last and best variations on the character. This time, she is stripped of wealth and dignity, left with failure and a drive to continue performing. His obsession with aging never did diminish. Like his heroine in *Slapstick Tragedy,* he was driven to continue writing these painful self-revelations.

PLOT DEVEOPMENT

Sweet Bird of Youth is set in St. Cloud, a coastal town, where a grand old hotel overlooks the blue waters of the Gulf of Mexico. The townspeople and customs are modern-day Southern. The town itself is controlled by Boss Finley, a redneck who has come down out of the clay hills of Mississippi. He dominates this region's politics and plans to expand his realm.

His daughter, Heavenly, whom he uses quite cynically as a symbol of white supremacy, has frustrated his ambitions for her disposition because she has long been in love with a poor, handsome youth, Chance Wayne. Blocked from marriage to her by Finley's grand plans, Chance goes off to seek his fortune on the stage. At first, he has some modest success in small roles on Broadway and in Hollywood. Then the war puts an end to this promising career. He reluctantly joined the Navy, which he quickly seeks to escape. A dishonorable discharge severely damages any chance at an heroic status at home. With thinning hair and diminished physical appeal, he also finds his chances at stardom have waned. He soon degenerates into a beach bum and a gigolo, contracts a venereal disease, and infects Heavenly on one of his sentimental visits home. When the play begins, he has returned to St. Cloud, after a prolonged absence, not realizing that Heavenly has had to have a hysterectomy because of her disease and that the whole community now despises him for her sake.

Along with him is Alexandra Del Lago, traveling under an assumed name, the Princess Kosmonopolis, Chance's current source of income and hope. Some time prior to the opening scene, this grand old dame of the theatre had tried a comeback in films and was horrified at the transformation in her image which the screen magnified at the premiere of the movie. She ran from the theatre, tripped and tumbled down the stairs, picked herself up, and then continued running and hiding for the next few months. Alexandra, confused and dissipated in her flight from truth, has employed a number of young companions along the way to be her caretakers and lovers. She barely recalls their names. To her, they are like the pills she takes and the drugs she ingests—nothing more than a means of escape.

These two ogres—the Princess and Chance—are alone together at the beginning of the play. Alexandra, calling herself "the Princess" to avoid recognition, is trying to establish where she is and why, and who this stranger is in her hotel room. This process, of course, provides the audience with essential exposition as well. Chance uses her befuddlement to set up a clumsy blackmail trap, taping her inadvertent confession of drug use. When he springs the trap on her, she sneers at his petty trickery, quickly dominates and subdues him, forcing him back to bed, and then rewards him with traveler's checks. She never seriously considers endorsing his elaborate and hopeless plot, which is to stage a fake beauty/talent pageant which he and Heavenly will win. He fantasizes that Alexandra will be his ticket to Hollywood. She knows that he will be her companion only so long as he amuses her.

Through their conversation, Williams provides background exposition: we learn of Chance's background, his love for Heavenly, and his grandiose dreams. By means of the Princess's cynical comments on this type of young actor, who has nothing but transient beauty, we recognize Chance to be a common figure in the theatre world. When his looks disappear, he is through.

Chance leaves the room, hoping to find Heavenly, to drive the Princess's fancy car with its silver horns around town, to brag and strut and play his old role of returning hero. As the play opens up and introduces more local citizens, different characters reveal that Chance has neglected not only Heavenly, but also his mother. She died while he was away and was buried by charitable members of the community. His stony heart is obvious in the calm manner in which he responds to this news; he is more concerned with defending his negligent behavior than in mourning his mother. We also discover that Heavenly is now engaged to marry the doctor who performed the surgery on her. Because the locals blame Chance for ruining Heavenly's good name, the men of the town are poised to castrate Chance unless he leaves quickly. His only hope is to escape under the protection of the Princess.

As the day progresses, we see Chance vainly disregarding the mounting threats, seeking a rendezvous with Heavenly. She, now reduced to a zombie-like shell of the young woman he remembers, has been ordered to avoid him. She meekly seeks to obey her father's commands.

The scene then shifts to the bar in the hotel, where the sounds of a political rally can be heard in the background. Boss's mistress discusses her disgust with her crude lover, her sympathy with Chance, and her support of a redneck heckler who has been following Boss wherever he goes to ask embarrassing questions about Heavenly's operation. (Boss Finley likes to parade Heavenly on stage, dressed in dazzling white, as a living symbol of the purity of white Southern womanhood.) Miss Lucy, the mistress, warns Chance that he is in great danger in this town.

In this climactic scene, when Chance is aware of the threatening noises of the local lynch mob being whipped to a fervor by Boss Finley, he realizes that the wrath which earlier ended with the lynching of a black man might next turn on him. The Princess suddenly appears—as if from another life. She has discovered a real sympathy for him, a return of human feeling to her dried-up old heart. In this mood of goodwill, she offers to help him escape. Chance, focused entirely on his own immediate objectives, rejects her offer, unceremoniously ordering a wheelchair for her ignominious return to their room.

The dénouement comes when both Chance and the Princess are back in their room. Chance once again tries to force Alexandra to stage a fake contest that will make him and Heavenly stars. She reverses their roles, using the phone call that he places to a Hollywood gossip columnist to discover the truth about her own success. As it turns out, her comeback film was not a failure after all, but a fresh victory. She immediately forgets all about poor Chance and begins to map out her own future, planning a revival like an old phoenix. Chance, accepting this final failure, refuses to accompany her as part of her luggage, like a pet dog on a leash. In a rare moment of dignity for him, he stays and faces the lynch mob that is clearly intent on castrating him. His final speech directed to the audience asks for understanding and recognition of Time as the enemy of us all.

The plot pattern we see here has certain unities: it takes place in a single day—as does *Cat on a Hot Tin Roof*. It also stays in a single town, though not in a single setting; but the action of the play is not unified. The characters are a bit scattered, some of them appearing only briefly. The central stories never quite merge. Williams' plan was apparently to trace the Princess's final ascent to a new fame, while tracking Chance's final descent to a new ignominy. This chiasmatic structure (like an X) works neatly for such carefully balanced paths of these two characters. They are united by their isolation from others, their brief union on the road and in bed, and their moment of sympathy with one another. The three-act structure, with a truncated final act, allows the standard use of act 1 for rising action and complications, act 2 for the climax and recognition scene, and act 3 for the dénouement and the statement of the theme.

CHARACTER DEVELOPMENT

In *Sweet Bird of Youth,* Williams portrays a common type of show biz failure: a young man who has only modest talent, no training in his craft, and little taste for hard work. The would-be actor lacks everything but good looks and ambition. The motive for his adventure is an inflated sense of his own talent, a need to be famous. He quickly loses his innocence, even as he fails to grab the brass ring on the carousel of success. Poor Chance doesn't even have luck. He doesn't run into a generous old tycoon eager to give him a lift, recognizing his sterling qualities. Instead, he finds himself surrounded by conniving egoists like himself. The Princess invites him into her bed, but not as a prelude to real love or generous sponsorship of his talent. She is just as selfish as he. Even true love turns out to be sordid and destructive over time, ending in the corruption of both people involved. Both chance and Heavenly lose their fertility, having only the dream of romance, but neither the public joy of the wedding, the companionship of married love, nor the hope of children. The old folks who thwart their romance do not repent of their evil ways, but continue to hoard all the prizes for themselves.

The whole thrust of the play is deeply, cruelly cynical. It is the characters who are the source for this cynical reversal of the plot line. In the opening scene, instead of focusing, as is typically the case, on a lovely young woman we can all admire, Williams spotlights an aging hawk rising out of a rumpled bed. The young character in the scene is not a hero, but a weak and foolish man, not master of the game, but merely a pawn. For all of his twisting and turning, Chance is designated to serve as the sacrificial victim in the play.

Usually stories deal either with pairs of young lovers or with an older man who finds himself attracted to a younger woman in a December-May love affair. Here we see a role-reversal, typical of Williams, who prefers the older, wiser, and more powerful woman as the transcendent character. The man is usually the more passive (effeminate/heroine) figure, who needs to be saved. It is he who is celebrated as a beauty. It is she who has the power of the purse. We soon realize that they are in some curious way yoked together, providing us with the two faces of the theatre, of art and of age. They are both consummate egoists, both capable of incredible highs and lows—some of which are alcohol or drug induced. The plot is primarily, as we have seen, a battle between these two antiheroes for supremacy.

Alexandra Del Lago explains to Chance Wayne that they are both monsters, both living in Beanstalk Country. Reminded by this indirect reference to the fairy tale of Jack and the Beanstalk, we soon discover that Chance is the greedy and curious little boy who climbs out of his own very ordinary world, only to find himself faced with monsters who will devour him. The Princess is the chief ogre in this oversized world, but Boss Finley proves the more vicious one.

Chance/Jack is the silly innocent who thinks he can outsmart professional tricksters; when he trades those things he has for a dream (in the myth, the family's cow for a bag of magic beans), he has gone too far. He has climbed beyond the familiar world he can control. After a mad struggle with flesh-eating giants, he falls back to the little world he had hoped to escape. In spite of his gigantic ego, he proves unsuccessful even as a monster. Williams draws this would-be hero as the classic victim, subject to a variety of forces. Like most modern playwrights, he has created an anti-hero as the protagonist of his tale.

Originally gentle and innocent, Chance has become selfish and ambitious. He was at first a beautiful young lover, deeply in love with his ideal mate. But the interference of her father forced him to find a means to win her love. He wanted to be the romantic hero in the fairy tale. Without education or prestige in a socially conscious town, he had to rely on his average abilities to win him spectacular results. Having displayed some modest theatrical talents, he succumbed to unjustified faith in his own genius, largely because his sympathetic society applauded too enthusiastically. There were warnings when he tried to move beyond his small-town triumphs, failing at the state level of competition; yet he could not settle for mediocrity. Poor and hungry for attention, he remained staunchly loyal to the American dream of success. He thought that his handsome face would take him to the top of the entertainment business, without training in his art. He believed that his quick access to roles in major productions signified the beginning of a grand career, but he found he never moved beyond bit parts. Chance Wayne, finally, is nothing more than one of the many disposable bits of handsome flesh that stage and film producers buy and use. A fresh crop is always available.

The Princess is a contrasting figure. She too is egocentric and amoral; but she has paid her dues, learned the lessons of the theatre, moved into real stardom based on talent and art. Unlike Chance, she has moved beyond shame. Looking back on the world with some perspective, she is cruel, but also comic and wise in her commentary on his situation and her own. Alexandra Del Lago is one of Williams' finest creations.

She is an image drawn out of modern American culture, particularly the movies. At about the time of this production, some wonderful old actresses had found roles in Hollywood films, making comebacks as horror queens, modern day witches. A series of these films used the talents of the actresses that were no longer appropriate in ingenue roles—*Arsenic and Old Lace* and *Sunset Boulevard* are prime examples. The gothic delight in seeing the celebrated beauty become a spooky old lunatic sent chills through audiences. Williams, an avid movie fan, must have been fascinated by the aging process in the various appearances of actresses through the years in different of his plays: Vivien Leigh, who had been Scarlett in *Gone with the Wind* became Blanche in the film version of *Streetcar* and then Mrs. Stone in *The Roman Spring of Mrs. Stone.* Each role showed her older and more skilled.

In an essay published in 1961 (included in the collection *Where I Live*), called "Five Fiery Ladies," Williams wrote about some of these women he had admired in his plays: Vivien Leigh, Elizabeth Taylor, Geraldine Page, Anna Magnani, and Katharine Hepburn. The colorful anecdotes and insights in the essay reveal clearly why great actresses loved to work with Williams. He understood them, and the roles he wrote for them allowed a full display of their brilliance. Williams had always had enormous admiration for such powerful actresses; he loved to watch them perform in his plays and occasionally dedicated his plays to one of them, in hopes of tempting her to take a part he designed especially for her.

A second pair in the play, Heavenly and Boss Finley, are also counterintuitive characters: they are stereotypes representing pure good and evil, and (in a just universe) should be rewarded and punished in accordance with their merits. Instead, they remain in their incestuous bonds to the very end, with Heavenly neutered and pressured into a loveless marriage, Boss unloving and dominant. They, like Chance and the Princess, derive from a curious combination of Greek classics and modern American movies. He is the thundering Jove figure, the heartless god of the thunderbolt. She, tied to love and water, is Venus, the creature of beauty and desire. In classical myth, she can usually persuade Jove to listen to her requests—but not in this tale. He is deaf to her deeply felt pleas. Or perhaps Williams was still mulling over the Orpheus myth, making Boss the lord of the underworld, Hades, and Heavenly his lovely prisoner, Persephone. With Williams, everything is possible; he loves to jumble his allusions together, allowing his critics to pick out one bit of the jumble after another, each time thinking that this is the solution.

Boss Finley was drawn from the myth of Huey Long, the archetypal Southern politician. The Southern political tradition was a rich one, beginning in the eighteenth century with the Virginia gentlemen who gathered to debate political theories and practice, moving through a more folksy image of the Tennessee frontiersman, Andrew Jackson, and settling into the folksy swamps of Louisiana with the populist Huey Long. His blustery manner, colorful speech, rhetorical power, largess with the masses, and early death at the hands of an assassin made him a cult hero among poor whites in the deep South. Boss Finley believes that God has called him down from the hills to lead the people of this region. His brutal use of his own son and daughter as tools for his aggrandizement, his cruel treatment of his mistress and Chance are indicators of his lust for power and ruthlesslessness. His rhetorical skills are on display in the set speech we hear broadcast in the bar.

Boss Finley's public persona depends on the public's faith in his log-cabin origins, his authentic calling from God, and his crusade to keep the South safe for the flower of white womanhood. In forcing Heavenly to be part of his myth, he makes her live a lie. The public proclamation of this deceit comes from the Heckler, a type of religious fanatic common in the South, who follows Boss Finley and cries out his truth in the face of oppressive guards. Boss's own public lies and private sexual license make his crusade a joke. He must prop up his crumbling story with violence, even if it involves his mistress, his daughter, and her lover.

Heavenly complains to her father that he married for love, yet will not let her marry the man she loves. He tries instead to marry her off to political allies or proper young men whom he chooses for their position or wealth, using her as a pawn in his game of power broker. He has warped her life and destroyed Chance's, corrupting them through his drive for power. He thereby undercuts his image of himself as God's servant, bringing hospitals and schools to the needy citizens of his region, revealing himself as a megalomaniac.

Williams' audience would have readily recognized this figure. The American politician had been much analyzed in recent times, largely because of the increasing power of such men as Franklin Roosevelt and Huey Long. For good or evil, they were so popular that they could change the rules freely. With the rise of foreign despots like Hitler and Mussolini, the potential for fascist thuggery had frightened writers from Sinclair Lewis (*It Can't Happen Here*) to Robert Penn Warren. *All the King's Men,* dealing with the rise of Huey Long, translated into an American myth, was an enormously successful novel, and later a popular film. A series of movies and plays followed, dealing with the complexities of American politics, the challenges to idealism, and the temptations of power. Williams himself had briefly considered writing a play about such a figure, finally abandoning it because of Penn Warren's success. Williams' Boss Finley would have been interpreted by the audience, as by the Heckler, as the proto-fascist voice of the racist South, the poor white who rises only through stepping on the blacks in his path.

The faintly incestuous father-daughter relationship in *Sweet Bird of Youth* is unusual for Williams. Generally he hints at incestuous feelings between mother and son or brother and sister. Finley would never acknowledge this to be a part of his own story; he would see his relationship with his daughter as entirely appropriate and protective. Heavenly is aware of his destructive possessiveness of her, turning her into a trophy virgin. Her long affair with Chance, now at an end, appears to be her only act of defiance.

The possessive Boss's portrayal of Heavenly as the lily-white virgin is a caricature of the anachronistic tradition of the Southern lady, set on a pedestal, protected and revered. (See Cash 1960.) She is an image of the Virgin Mary, curiously defended against the ravages of African American men, who are presumed to be lusting mightily after her. As a pseudo-aristocratic type, she must be asexual and innocent, idolized as virgin, wife, and mother. Suitors are expected to lavish her with praise and flowers—as in the warped memories of Amanda—but should harbor no expectations of sexual favors in return. This is part of the reason that Boss cannot acknowledge the physical relationship that Heavenly gladly shared with Chance in their younger days. Again, audiences would recognize Finley's plans for Heavenly, having seen *Gone with the Wind* and being thoroughly familiar with the expectations for the Southern belle.

This conflicts with Chance's vision of her. For him, she is the image of Aphrodite, rising from the waters, beautiful and pure. She is the ideal of first love. Her simple response to his love echoes the character of Rosa in *The Rose Tattoo*. Williams loves this natural woman who worships Venus rather than the Virgin.

When Boss Finley's sterile image triumphs over Chance's fertile one, the love is frustrated, the characters destroyed. Instead of ending as in a fairy tale, living happily ever after, the ending is more like *Romeo and Juliet* in modern American dress. Both are castrated by an evil world. The disease that Chance brings back to infect Heavenly is a symbol of the society's corruption. Heavenly's hysterectomy and her very public humiliation end the dream of walking hand-in-hand into the sunset. We have instead the nightmare of Heavenly's loveless marriage and Chance's mutilation—and perhaps death.

The remarkable accomplishment we see in this wild reversal of established norms of art is that Williams moves us to empathy. We are drawn along to climb on an emotional rollercoaster with these unappealing characters. We know they are monsters of selfishness, but we keep looking for redeeming qualities. When the Princess thinks she has found a real tear on her cheek—when she sympathizes with another human being—we are delighted with her compassion. At least the grubby little Jack-and-the-Beanstalk character has some vestiges of his former vulnerability and looks, but she is the flesh-eating giant of Beanstalk Country. It is testimony to Williams' power that he forces us to feel for these creations. In *Sweet Bird of Youth,* we are face-to-face with some of Tennessee Williams' favorite monsters.

THEMATIC ISSUES

Southern political and social patterns are crucial in understanding the characters and the ideas of this play. The South's caste system, which has prevailed since the nineteenth century, had become increasingly malevolent in the twentieth. The old aristocratic ideal has been replaced by a money-based status system. (See Dollard 1949.) The young doctors and businessmen who attack Chance at the end of the play are part of the new middle class, the nouveaux riches of the New South. Their wives are the country club set, well dressed and empty headed. Ironically, Chance and Boss Finley have come from the same poverty class. Finley's objection to Heavenly's marriage to this lad lies in her family's effort to move up to the next social level. Without ancestors of note, culture, or remarkable ability, they will need wealth to obtain status. They can arrive at this through political power and arranging the right marriages for their children. Their neat little world of upward mobility is threatened by the anarchy of the non-conformists who have invaded St. Cloud preaching the gospel of love and art. Alexandra is wealthy and famous, making her immune to their bullying tactics. Chance, who flouts their whole system of values, has no such protection. He refuses to respect middle-class values, calling them into question in his own proclamation that he is free to love whom he chooses, to do what he likes. This kind of rebellion is intolerable. These folks know he is vulnerable if they can separate him from his powerful protector.

From his earliest plays in St. Louis, Williams had preached against the status quo, especially the conservative Southern cultural system. That traumatic uprooting from Mississippi to St. Louis had impressed him with the snobbery of the middle class, the alienation of the misfit. His later deepening interest in poetry and awareness of his sexual differences encouraged him to believe he was the archetypal rebel—even in his own family. In *Stairs to the Roof,* an early play, he described his separation from the other workers in the shoe factory, escaping to the roof to see the sky. In *Battle of Angels,* Valentine Xavier, like Chance Wayne, is a free-living, free-loving spirit, who comes into a small town (very like Clarksdale, Mississippi) where he upsets all the women and antagonizes all the men. He is a prophet of sexual liberation, a writer like Williams. He too ends up as the victim of the angry lynch mob.

Like most Southern gentlefolk, the Williams family had little contact with the poor whites, an indigenous group who were an embarrassment to their fellow whites. Many Southern authors believe the poor whites are the most lethal elements in Southern culture, the real source of violence in the region. Aware of the powerful class/caste system that excludes them from moving ahead, they can maintain their pride only by turning on black people, who are the only ones ranking lower than they. Thus, they are frequently the most vicious racists, the ones most likely to be involved in lynchings.

In *Sweet Bird of Youth,* Boss Finley is just such a type. He is what Southerners would call "poor white trash." Big Daddy was from this same crude and uneducated class, but he worked hard and long to build his empire. In the process, he expanded his sympathies so that he eventually became a man who displayed considerable generosity of spirit. Boss Finley, also in pursuit of power and dynasty for his heirs, used his gift for rhetoric to become a political power broker. By appealing to the grossest elements in the South, the racism, the violence, the "protection" of Southern womanhood, he is able to enlarge his realm. Less concerned with his children's development than Big Daddy, Boss Finley willingly sacrifices them to his ambition.

Chance is a preordained victim of such a system and of such a man. He challenges the whole system that Finley has spent his life manipulating. Chance is also ambitious to rise and is willing to use other people as his stepping stones in this process. Challenging the older man in the love of Heavenly, ruining her as a symbol of purity, interfering with his plans for her use in his career, he becomes a target for destruction. This spark of anarchy cannot be tolerated by a totalitarian like Boss Finley. In this dynamic, Williams points to the peril that any challenge to the status quo might posit. The struggle for power in this jungle is deadly.

Chance Wayne, eager to succeed in the theatre, also introduces the theme of success. By following the path of popular theatre and films, Chance becomes the typical American phenomenon of the transient celebrity, the star of the moment. Andy Warhohl said that everyone gets fifteen minutes of fame; we sense that Chance has had his. Lacking true self-knowledge, which Alexandra has in abundance, he overestimates his talent and the market for it. The entertainment industry is highly competitive, requiring a fresh supply of young faces and bodies to provide background for top stars. New York and Hollywood are mobbed by attractive young people who expect to "make it big." Many have won acclaim in high school musicals and exaggerate their flair for acting and singing. Once separated from the friendly audiences of friends and neighbors, they discover that their modest talents will not serve in the rough-and-tumble competition of the theatre or film industry. They will need serious talent and staying power. Tennessee Williams had seen plenty of these young actors. When he first visited his agent in New York, he found himself in a room full of aspiring actresses, hoping for a part on Broadway. Every one of his plays had its tryouts for casting the handful of roles; he had watched as one after another of these near-successes was turned away in disappointment.

In this mad scramble for success, some find sex their best weapon; they sleep their way to the top. Williams shows that cynical exploitation of others results in exploitation in return. Among those who try this strategy, most find themselves discarded with the morning light. Lusty producers and directors can have their pick of the pretty faces and handsome physiques that surround them. This use of sexuality as a disposable commodity is clear in the opening scene of *Sweet Bird of Youth*. It sets the tone of cynicism that saturates the play.

The contrasting age of the couple on stage, the violation of private moments of confidence by threats of blackmail, the battle for supremacy as the Princess acts the sexual aggressor, Chance's humiliating response to the command performance in the bed—these are all far crueler statements of sexual warfare than we saw in *Cat on a Hot Tin Roof.* At the end of that play, Maggie led a reluctant Brick to the bed in order to beget his child, using his thirst for Echo Springs. In this new play, no one pretends that love is involved. There is no marriage, no child, no future. There is nothing gentle about the imperious command of the Princess Kosmonopolis. She states quite clearly that sex is a distraction, like alcohol or hashish.

Yet for all of her nastiness and self-indulgence, she is the character who prevails, the one who finally defines *success.* This would seem to suggest the theme that the persistent, powerful artist is the dominant force in this sick world. She compares herself to Cleopatra, as ancient as "Egypt." Recalling Shakespeare's characterization of that great woman, hers was a beauty that did not fade with time. She found a means to use her brain, her charm, and her skills to win her wars. The Princess is ruthless but also self-critical. Unblinkingly honest, she analyzes her own perceived failures. She also quite accurately estimates Chance's third-rate career opportunities. In a stark portrayal, she does him the favor of laying out his future for him. Sadly, it is a future he cannot acknowledge and continue to live.

The split ending of the play points to the two characters' separate modes of confronting the tyranny of Time. Over the years, Williams has played with the theme of Time's relentless pace. In an essay called "The Timeless World of a Play" (*Where I Live,* 49), which he wrote in 1951 as an introduction to *The Rose Tattoo,* he quoted Carson McCullers: "Time, the endless idiot, runs screaming 'round the world." He insisted that it was this "rush of time that deprives our actual lives of so much dignity and meaning." An ancillary theme is that Art is the antidote to this experience, because art arrests time, giving dignity and meaning back again. The great artist, therefore, is in a war against Time. It should come as no surprise to discover that the working title of the first draft of the play was *The Enemy: Time.*

At the end of *Sweet Bird of Youth,* Alexandra prepares to reenter the world of art—though only briefly. She will prepare her face and her figure to be seen in public once again—foreshadowed by the sleep mask she wears at the beginning of the play. Chance, by contrast, refuses to go along as another piece of her luggage. He stays to face castration, an experience which Time has already performed on him. This small-town Prufrock has already "seen it all," that his hair is thinning and his appeal is evaporating. He is no Prince Hamlet, nor was he meant to be. He returns to the world where Time is the monarch and he is nothing but a captive slave, doomed to extinction.

Out of this decision comes the final implied act of violence. The threatening chorus of local men moves ominously toward him. His sexuality has been the center of his pride. Castration is tantamount to murder. Where a man's treasure is, there will his heart be also. Williams insisted that all of his life he had been haunted by the obsession that "to desire a thing or to love a thing intensely is to place yourself in a vulnerable position." This produced a fear, "which was sometimes terror," which in turn gave him "a certain tendency toward an atmosphere of hysteria and violence" in his writing—"an atmosphere that has existed in it since the beginning" ("Foreword to *Sweet Bird of Youth*," in *Where I Live*, 107). His characters love life, take chances, sally forth on adventures to become the targets of the dark, dreary, ordinary people who resent them as if they were brightly plumaged birds that must be caught and put in cages.

Sweet Bird of Youth finally reminds us of one of Tennessee Williams' favorite poets, John Keats. In "Ode on Melancholy," this poet said that the most intense pain comes to the one who cares most about Beauty, Joy, and Pleasure, the one who

> Can burst Joy's grape against his palate fine;
> His soul shall taste the sadness of her might,
> And be among her cloudy trophies hung. (*Poetical Works*, 209)

STYLISTIC AND LITERARY DEVICES

The play reads as a cluster of familiar mythic characters: the ideal woman, Heavenly, is pursued by the beautiful youth. In his struggle to win her hand, Chance confronts first the possessive father, Boss, and is aided by the friendly Aunt Nonnie. He vows to win her by winning fame and returning on his white horse, finds his adventures take him to the Big City, then to war, and finally to the bed of the Wicked Princess. To achieve victory, he must shake off this obsession with big chariots and satin sheets, return to his ideal, and accept the challenge posed for suitors to the daughter of the king. Unfortunately, the test for suitors involves wealth and status, and the lady is now sullied and sterile. Chance fails to become the hero, win the lady, or live happily ever after. This fairy tale has an all-too-realistic ending.

The play employs many of his traditional devices and symbols. For example, the setting is a grand old hotel, a perfect context for the Princess Kosmonopolis, who also is an American copy of Old World grandeur. Her name may echo the splendor of Alexander the Great, her pseudonym may recall the cosmopolitan quality of her success, but she is an ersatz princess nonetheless. She has no palace, only a temporary bit of splendor that she rents by the day and is expelled from by nightfall. The hotel, the scene for many Williams plays, is a temporary harbor for the night, not a real home. At the center is the bed, this time with rumpled satin sheets, with one of the actors still asleep and masked. The separation of the bed partners from the beginning foreshadows their separation at the end. The double bed, a traditional image of union, particularly of marital union, is here the temporary locus for sexual escape, not union or communion. Rather than a joyous scene of the ritual mating, the bed soon proves an altar for the sacrifice/payment at the command of the Princess.

This use of images of transience continues into another locale, the cocktail lounge at the Royal Palms. This is no festive scene for family dining—a ritual of bonding that Williams had mocked from the opening scene of *The Glass Menagerie.* Instead, it is the place where strangers gather in an artificial communion over a drink. The bar imagery is to become more prominent in the subsequent plays *Small Craft Warnings* and *In The Bar of a Tokyo Hotel,* both based partly on O'Neill's setting for *The Iceman Cometh.* Williams, who spent much of his life in bars to escape through alcohol and to find a partner for the night, saw these encounters as a painfully inadequate substitute for a real family. A temporary gathering of strangers fortified by alcohol and forced conviviality provides a fake sense of community that is no substitute for the real thing. In this world of "lonely crowds," such meeting places serve many people.

In the bar scene, when Chance callously orders a wheelchair for Alexandra, we see a cluster of interactive images: she has come to offer him real friendship, but he is so intent on his illusions, puffed up with pills and ego, that he cannot consider her moment of tenderness. The command for a wheelchair is his insulting signal that he will not serve as her crutch, instead sending her off in the care of others, a broken old woman. (Alexandra's dignified acceptance of an "anonymous" arm for her exit from the bar reminds us of the final scene of *Streetcar,* with Blanche leaving on the arm of the doctor.) In this action, Chance invites his own catastrophe. The Princess, by contrast, signals her resurgent power, an old phoenix rising from her lethargy, as she rises from the bed in the first scene, to execute a triumphal exit. Their paths cross, with her now in the ascendancy.

Williams uses a number of ingenious—and not entirely successful—devices to make his points in the play. For example, his employment of the microphones and television in act 2, scene 2, to give an unreal sound to the scene, broadcasting the fake images of Boss Finley to the region, reminds us that this is not the actual quality of his voice or his personality. Like the Wizard of Oz, he uses the electronic enhancements to provide him grandeur. All of the flashbulbs, the noise, the music, the heckling, and general confusion are mirrors of both Chance's mind at this point and the chaos of the moment of fame. The outside activity, as in expressionist drama, echoes the interior life.

Williams is particularly imaginative in his use of movies. The flickering images of a past performance become permanent transcripts of genius. Like the written word, the film image has a longer life than the stage performance that lives only in the memory of the actors and the audience. He always thought it a tragedy that Laurette Taylor's performance as Amanda was not recorded on film. The theatre has its own kind of magic because it is live and subject to disasters at each performance. When the words of the playwright, the arrangements of the director, producer, set-designer, lighting experts, and others all come together in a sensitive performance with talented actors before a responsive audience, we see a moment of wonder. By contrast, the film is a more carefully edited and slickly produced construct, creating a single perfect performance, fixed firmly in celluloid. Williams loved the theatre, but he respected the film industry that preserved the artifacts.

The comeback scene, recounted as memory in the first act, and then repeated in the telephone conversation in the final act, demonstrates the ease with which Williams built his complex imagery: frightened by the magnified film image of herself as an old woman, Alexandra shrinks in horror at the stranger on the giant screen. She races from the theatre (thereby abandoning her career), trips over her regal train (her vain attempt to restore dignity to her persona), tumbles down the stairs (a ceremony of descent from her fake splendor), "like a sailor's drunk whore" to the bottom (*Theatre, Vol. 4*, 35). In a recapitulation of the scene in act 3, she uses the eyes of another as her mirror, allowing this flattering image to justify her return to the stage. Once again she picks herself up, brushes off stragglers, fixes her face, straightens her clothes, and prepares for the curtain.

The play is full of such rich symbols and rituals, as is suitable given its deep roots in myth. From the moment we step into the Royal Palms Hotel in Glorious Hill, Mississippi, and watch the Princess Kosmonopolis (aka, Alexandra Del Lago) rising from her drugged sleep, we know we are in the presence of greatness, a phoenix rising out of its own ashes.

ALTERNATE CRITICAL PERSPECTIVE: INTERTEXTUAL CRITICISM

As moderns have approached stories from feminist and gay perspectives, they have become more convinced that the concept of the "story" or "truth" depends on the point of view, the influences on the author, his or her sources for understanding reality, the traditions which the author has internalized. This awareness that the old controlling myths of our culture no longer apply to many writers and readers has led to a sense of "decenteredness"—an abandonment of old explanations based on a logical, orderly explanation of meaning.

Modern critics see writing as the construction of "texts" that build themselves as a mosaic of quotations, allusions, sources, influences. The study of this complex interrelationship between the text and other texts becomes the basis for intertextual criticism.

Tennessee Williams allows each of his characters to build an individual story, to see his or her own life through a particular prism created by "intratexts"—the books, magazines, and newspapers they have read, the movies they have seen, the popular songs they have learned. Over and above each of these individual clusters of influences is the author's own shaping of the tale, which relies on his vast collection of influences and experiences and is termed the "metatext." Thus, Williams' play may be analyzed in the immediate influences—such recent films he has seen—or in the merging of a complex of individual stories, or in the deeper pattern of his own favorite mythology. The intertextual critic investigates the complicated relationship of these outside "texts" to the published text of the work itself.

At least one critic believes that Williams had a particular movie in mind when he sat down to write *Sweet Bird of Youth*. He had just seen Billy Wilder's film *Sunset Boulevard* at a preview showing in 1950, telling a friend afterwards that he found it shattering and "wonderfully awful" (Spoto 1985, 257). This is the story of Norma Desmond, a once-great film star, who now lives a gothic life in a gorgeous mansion on Hollywood's Sunset Boulevard. Her younger lover, a mediocre writer, enjoys this lavish life style. He relishes the closet full of shirts and suits, the costly jewelry, the illuminated swimming pool and private screening room for movies. When he falls in love with a nice young girl, he sees himself as a powerless gigolo, abandons the girl, and seeks to escape from the old actress. She chases him down the stairs, calls to him to come back, and shoots him. He falls face down into the swimming pool he loved. The final scene, when the police arrive to arrest her, provides her comeback as a mad scene. She marches majestically down the grand staircase as the cameras roll, believing she is finally back in films.

Williams himself seems to be playing against this movie, making subtle changes to press the message into more powerful statements about art, success, modern culture, small-town tyranny, and numerous other topics. One biographer, Donald Spoto, suggests that the background of this film may explain the narrative voice that breaks out at the end, when Chance comes forward to announce his role. In the film, the dead lover continues speaking even after death, the narrator in spite of his character's demise.

In spite of this authorial voice, the drama itself demands that all of the characters speak in their own voices, drawing from the texts they may know to draft the story of their individual lives. Drama demands presentation rather than narration, requires individual voices rather than an overarching voice of the author. Each of the characters in this story is a unique modern American type; each is keyed to popular culture; each constructs his or her own story using texts from films, newspapers, songs, or magazines of the era. In addition, Williams provides each with a grounding in myth or fairy tales, thereby making them resonate with a larger community of viewers who are not interested in John Wayne or Marilyn Monroe.

Each of the characters, while a good critic of other people's stories and silly beliefs, is so egocentric as to believe his or her version of the story is the only truth. In constructing this maze of contradictory tales, Williams draws on a vast array of literary and cultural allusions, from ancient Greek classics to modern American pop art. Anything can serve as his "text," from corn gods to comic strips. Unraveling some of these stories allows the critic to understand the various "truths" that Williams sees at the core of his world.

The myth of the Hollywood star, reinforced by films, movie magazines, gossip columnists, and fan clubs, is central to the thinking of both Alexandra and Chance. Tennessee Williams has made Alexandra shrewder than the star in *Sunset Boulevard* and Chance cruder than the gigolo. By this time, Hollywood had an abundance of superannuated film stars, still dragging their fame behind them. People tended to merge the actors with their roles, reading movie magazines for tidbits about the rich and the beautiful. Williams himself had been the writer for Lana Turner when he briefly served an apprenticeship in Hollywood at MGM. (At the time, he referred to the film to which he was contributing as *The Celluloid Brassiere*.) He knew the fakery behind the glitzy facade. It takes a strong character to handle this fame: Alexandra is a bona fide citizen of this fantastic country; Chance is only a visitor.

Chance Wayne, as his name indicates, is a transitory figure tied to popular culture who dreams of becoming a movie hero—like John Wayne. Those who grew up in the heyday of the American film industry were thrilled at the Cinderella story of the small-town boy or girl discovered by a film mogul, transported to Hollywood, and transformed into a star. According to prevailing myth, looks and luck were enough to explain the success stories of Lana Turner or Marilyn Monroe. Talent shows or beauty contests might well prove the springboard for the miraculous discovery. The silly little plot that Chance lays out for the skeptical Princess draws on this cultural context. Thousands of young people in America dream that becoming the winner of a state drama contest or being chosen Miss Georgia Peach Princess will set them on the road to stardom. Williams had a genius for capturing the icons of pop culture, the songs, dances, television shows, sports, and movies. Here he pictures an era of big Broadway musicals—like *Oklahoma!*—full of happy songs, lively dances, young lovers, happy endings, and middle-class values. A familiarity with the pop culture helps the reader understand Chance's dreams of popping out of the pack, making it big.

Chance sees this as his final opportunity to become something special, not just an average kid from a decent family in a small Gulf coastal town. Unfortunately, a series of wars in the middle years of our century interrupted the sentimental dreams for a host of young men. For Chance, the call to service also broke his fragile string of successes at a crucial moment. Another kind of man might have turned his military service into another kind of success, becoming the great warrior hero, but not Chance. He chose the navy because he thought he looked good in that uniform, served less than honorably, was dismissed, and returned home in disgrace. He was no Sergeant York. Alexandra was right: no longer viable for even second-tier roles in films, his only path now is to serve as a lapdog for rich old ladies.

Over the years, Williams (like the Princess) had seen hundreds of such handsome young men and women, never talented enough or lucky enough to make it big, but still consumed with the need to become stars. Failures by age thirty, such pathetic figures would drift into the limbo of prostitution before disappearing from the celebrity orbit, opting for either ordinary life or early death. Alexandra Del Lago summarizes this cruelly realistic vision of the story in her memory of Franz Albertzart (*Theatre, Vol. 3*, 113). It is to be Chance's real story—at least for now and for her—as "a beach-boy I picked up for pleasure, distraction from panic" (119). He is not the hero of the tale, as told by Alexandra or the townspeople, but the sacrificial victim.

Each character creates a parallel story: Boss Finley's text is the newspapers and the other media. His dream of political dominance, a rise from his obscure roots to the role of power broker, draws on images he has seen on television and heard on the radio. With visions of Huey Long dancing in his head, he brings in Southern mythology for his climb up the ladder of power and is frustrated by Heavenly's irrational love of the wrong boy. He wants to be in the headlines, on the news programs, his words and works acclaimed by all. Instead, his mistress scribbles obscene messages about him in lipstick on restroom mirrors, and hecklers shout insulting remarks about his daughter.

Heavenly's fairy-tale dream of love and marriage is a traditional story for the American teenager. She wants the romance, the royal wedding, the simple home she has seen in all the movies. This dream, reinforced by stories in all the women's magazines, is blocked by her father's dominance and her own weakness. Chance could be her knight in shining armor if he were stronger and truer to their love. He does envision Heavenly as his ultimate goal—as her name signifies. The Princess could save them both but is too selfish to bother with this small-time hustler and his wimpy girl. They are not even footnotes on her story of triumphal return.

Moving from these in popular texts to his own controlling "metatext," the author shapes them into a timeless story. Williams ties this star-struck American imagery to ancient myth—the king that must die. Once again, to universalize his tale, he turns to the Greeks and the central fertility myth made famous in Eliot's *The Waste Land* as the Fisher King. The corn god is a glorious golden boy who emerges in the springtime, soaks up the adoration of the community, and is sacrificed to the goddess of fertility. Like the flowers that are his usual symbols, after a brief flourishing, he dies. Critics have discovered this "text" to be the source for much of Tennessee Williams' work, including this play, which is sometimes tied to Adonis and Aphrodite, sometimes to Narcissus. (See Hayes 1966.)

Again, as in *Cat on a Hot Tin Roof*, it is easy to see how each of these tales applies: Adonis was a handsome young man whom Aphrodite, the goddess of love, a kind of Earth Mother figure, discovered after being wounded by an arrow from Cupid's dangerous bow. The goddess enjoyed Adonis' favors for some time out of desire for his beauty. Knowing that he loved to run and hunt in the woods, this older huntress goddess warned him to keep clear of wolves and bears. She knew that these animals were too dangerous for this effeminate and gentle youth, but he mistakenly believed that his beauty would touch the hearts even of lions and bristly boars. A wild boar buried his tusks in the side of the handsome youth. (Freudians have enjoyed the possible meanings of this imagery!) Aphrodite (or Venus) was riding by on her swan-drawn chariot when she saw him bloody and dying. She lamented his death loudly but went on to take other lovers.

The parallels with *Sweet Bird of Youth* are obvious: the young man and older "goddess," the failure as a warrior, the warnings about the vicious animals, the taunting of the old brute, the eventual bloodletting that leads to the death of his sexuality and hopes. Her Cadillac convertible with the silver horn becomes a wonderful substitute for Aphrodite's swan-drawn chariot. The constant playing of the thematic music of the Lament reinforces the parallels. Although the "princess" is no goddess, her own triumph makes her version of the "bitch goddess Success" in Williams' mythology. (She is, of course, also a self-portrait.) Like Williams, she understands the rules of the game of King of the Mountain and knows that this no-longer-young gigolo is too naive to compete successfully. She finds his challenges to her so pitiful that they are "touching." This old warrior knows full well how to fight wolves and bears and old boars.

Williams seems to have another Greek myth in mind as well, the famous tale of the handsome Narcissus. He was a handsome but cruel youth, who had no feelings for those who lavished love upon him. The gods punished him by showing him his own reflection in a pool of water. He fell in love with that phantom youth, who rippled and disappeared when touched. Unable to draw himself away from this dazzling image, he wasted away and died. Narcissus thereby became the symbol of the beautiful and effeminate young egotist, who is pursued by eager and frustrated lovers. His death and transformation into a flower make him another variation of the sacrificial fertility god. He is also a symbol of the seasons, the evanescence of youth and beauty. (See Bullfinch 1990, 58.)

Narcissus, alias Chance, preens in the mirror, obsesses with his thinning hair, thinks only of himself. He rudely ignores Alexandra's pathetic efforts at friendship and affection, continuing his fixation on himself. He has clearly caused pain to both his mother and his lover. His callous lack of concern at his mother's death is a scandal in the community. His selfish use and casual infection of Heavenly bring universal hatred. He does not die the brutal death of Adonis but the wasting death of failure and emasculation. His humiliation in the power struggle with Alexandra, his failure to achieve selfless love of another, and his reduction to the role of gigolo all contribute to his emotional castration.

Tennessee Williams was never reluctant to provide his audience a dazzling overlay of multiple myths, including Christian ones. Easter bells are ringing in preparation for the ritual castration/crucifixion, as in the Orpheus/Christ passion play. Orthodox Christians would be offended by the implied identification of the mythic images, as Williams had discovered in his earlier use of them in *Battle of Angels/Orpheus Descending*. In his later plays, he buried the imagery deep enough to avoid such open controversy.

While the young man is the image of the seed that is buried, flourishes, and is cut down, the Princess (aka, the Great Mother or the devouring mother) is the image of the earth itself. In Greek myth, she is the ogre the hero must confront on his journey to find the Golden Fleece—the Medea or the Gorgon. Alexandra announces that she is a monster, which Williams had come to identify not only with fairy tale and myth but also with the process of art. The great artist, he came to believe, is a monster of selfishness. Like Daedalus, he is less concerned with the consequences of his acts—creating the means for making a monster or for housing him—than he is with the joy of creation. At the end, he can leave the others to their tragic consequences while he flies away to another world.

Each of Tennessee Williams' plays incorporates some reference to a poem that expresses the kernel of the idea. The actual poems are often presented as epigraphs introducing the plays (Ford, "If the Epigraph Fits . . . ," a speech at the New Orleans Tennessee Williams Festival, March 23, 2000) . In the case of *Sweet Bird of Youth*, the poem is by Hart Crane, one of Williams' favorite authors and a submerged text for much of his writing: "Relentless caper for all those who step/The legend of their youth into the noon." As mentioned earlier in the discussion of Brick Pollitt, this image of the hero who has outlived his golden youth, described so beautifully by A. E. Housman in "To an Athlete Dying Young," haunted Williams. In the case of the characters in *Sweet Bird*, he also seems to be moving to the potential solution of mortality in the portrayal of Alexandra's triumph through art. This appears to rely on another of his favorite poets, William Butler Yeats. In his poem "Sailing to Byzantium," Yeats noted that "This is no country for old men." Popular culture is obsessed with flesh. In contrast, Byzantium is the image of an immortal culture of Art, where things of value prove eternal. The Princess, in rising above the superficial delight of the fleshly beauty that was her original claim to fame, has found an art that will continue. She will die, but her films will live on.

Her Byzantine myth is quite different from Chance's Orphic one: She had had her time in the spotlight, celebrated for her beauty and talent, and now may either entertain herself with captive young men and exotic drugs until her days drag to an end or confront the truth, transform her understanding into something golden, and sail out on new voyages. She chooses to look steadily at that image in the mirror of the magnified screen, not in a flattering mirror that told her she is the fairest of them all. In the process she discovers that her art transcends time.

Each of the self-images—the dreams, the stories of the individuals—turns out to be partially right and at the same time sadly wrong. Each has some truth to tell to the other, some life-lie that he or she cherishes about self. Each image has roots in the past, in archetypes, and in American history. And each resonates with an audience attuned to films and contemporary myths. Williams confronts his audience with this conflicting set of "truths" that play against one another while we seek to decide on which we will accept and which we will reject. As Milton said, the Truth is like the body of Osiris, scattered about the countryside. We, like Osiris's sister Isis, must wander through life, picking up bits and pieces, trying to fit them together, seeking to reconstruct the lost body of Truth. Williams was, by nature, a postmodern writer who had no real faith in seeing the Truth and telling it clearly. He thought that we never quite know the Truth, because there is no ultimate Truth. We must, therefore, tell that part we know—and as Emily Dickinson said—"tell it slant."

8

The Night of the Iguana
(1963)

On September 2, 1959, Tennessee Williams wrote a sad letter to Brooks Atkinson, one of his favorite critics, from Hollywood. He told his friend that he found that "fame and money made it so much harder to go on working as purely" as he had done in the years before he had achieved them. Williams, who had tried to deal with the effects of fame and wealth in *Sweet Bird of Youth* and he had focused on the attrition caused by Time, explained to Atkinson that he was not the same author who wrote *A Streetcar Named Desire*.

Along the way, he discovered that Time was not the only enemy he faced. He grew increasingly aware of his moral slide. From time to time, he would proclaim, "I want my goodness back." This sense of depravity is particularly apparent in a series of confessional dramas and stories that he wrote in the latter part of his life. In its central self-portrait, *Sweet Bird of Youth* signals his own ironic sense of disorder. A year earlier, he had portrayed a gay poet as Saint Sebastian in *Suddenly Last Summer*, a shocking story that parallels his sister's descent into madness and his own descent into a kind of aesthetic cannibalism. That play contained a fearful picture of God as a predatory bird, waiting for signs of weakness in order to attack fragile creatures and destroy them. Like the biblical character Jacob, Williams was wrestling with angels. This match continued in *The Night of the Iguana*. a play that chronicled his descent into self, with its portrayal of a priest living beyond his faith. Other self-portraits were to follow in *In the Bar of a Tokyo Hotel* and *Small Craft Warnings*, originally named *Confessional*.

These are bleak plays, relieved by occasional flashes of humor and grace. The characters are frequently callous users of others. Sexuality has become a blood sport, leaving the victor dissatisfied and the victim humiliated. The search for a bond with another human leads to the disappointing discovery that the bed partners have nothing more than an animalistic urge. They seem to have lost their true path, taking instead a byway that is leading into chaos. Through it all, God is silent. As the Heckler told the barroom gathering in *Sweet Bird*, "I believe that the silence of God, the absolute speechlessness of Him is a long, long and awful thing that the whole world is lost because of" (*Theatre, Vol. 4, Sweet Bird*, 105).

Writing out of the anguish of his own inner life, Williams once again sought the key to putting together the Grand Puzzle he saw as life. This time, he turned to a painful memory of despair and discovery, his month on the beach in Acapulco in 1940, when he was 29 years old. Uncertain about his career, devastated by a failed love affair, and living from hand to mouth. Tennessee Williams had suddenly left New York for Mexico. Tormented by his perennial attacks of "blue devils," he followed his usual solution to such distress; he ran to a warm beach where he could swim and think and write. He retreated to one of his favorite places, Mexico.

He settled first at "Todd's Place" and then at Hotel Costa Verde. As he had discovered previously, he was delighted by the sexual license and carefree life of the region. He found the warm climate, the swimming, the natives, the simple life in Mexico precisely the tonic he needed to heal his overwrought nervous system. He realized that he could not return to his previous simpler, happier kind of faith and decency, but he could achieve a new depth of understanding of himself and his world. While in Acapulco, he wrote a series of long letters to his friend Joe Hazan describing days of writing, drinking, and talking. They are filled with bits of poetry, philosophical discourses, observations, and personal reflections. This idyllic and colorful sojourn in this primitive region, not yet discovered by tourists (other than some particularly obnoxious Nazis), remained in his memory for years, inspiring him to write a short story which he called "The Night of the Iguana," first published in 1948.

The deeper meaning of that September in Mexico became clearer in 1959, when he contemplated much of what he had learned in almost two decades of living. For some years, he had been comfortable with Frank Merlo, who was more than a beloved partner; he was in addition a perceptive critic, an emotional support, and a manager of his mundane affairs. At times, they had been joined by Williams' grandfather, the Reverend Walter E. Dakin, who died just before *Cat* opened, at the ripe old age of 97. Williams missed his grandfather desperately. He also found he was growing suspicious of everyone around him, including Frank, and was increasingly promiscuous. He was keeping bad company, experimenting with different drugs, and drinking far too much (Spoto 1985, 264–66). In spite of his wealth and success, his private life was beginning to break apart.

PLOT DEVELOPMENT

This brief tale, "The Night of the Iguana" (in *Tennessee Williams: Collected Stories* 1985, 229–45), was set in the Casa Verde, the same spot in Mexico where Williams had enjoyed his respite from the struggles of New York. Among the few guests are two homosexual lovers and a Southern spinster who is lonely at an out-of-season resort. She wants to strike up a friendship with the two men. Her clumsy artifices are at first comical, but they build to a moment of hysteria when she becomes distressed by the sounds of the iguana that is trapped under her window, and runs to the men to escape. She gushes out her fears and her own personal history, ignores their stony response, and then precipitously invites herself to move to their end of the hotel. They are fully aware that she is a snoop who is planning to eavesdrop on their conversations and activities, but they make no effort to alter them. They keep the light on in the room and speak openly and derisively of her, laughing at her silly efforts at subterfuge. She leaps up and goes to their door, accusing them of cruelty. One of the men leaves to deal with the iguana. The other grabs her in an attempted rape, which she fights off. Frustrated, he spills his semen on her clothing just as his friend returns, having freed the iguana. She returns to her old cubicle, curiously at peace.

Never one to waste any elements of a good story, Williams recycled the rich setting of the Costa Verde and the iguana image and some of the sexual bits into a short play based on the original story. The scene of the two men in a room, discovered by a Southern lady, became a key element in *A Streetcar Named Desire*, the brief flash of discovery that Blanche had of her young husband's hidden sex life. Years later, this cluster of images still lingered in his mind, finally shaping themselves into the expanded full-length play using the same name as the short story—*The Night of the Iguana*. The play is a remarkable elaboration of the earlier tale, with the central image of the iguana and elements of Williams' own life, particularly his long relationship with his grandfather.

He also drew on his own internal battle of angels for what has been called a morality play (Jackson 1965, 130). This description does work if we recall that the medieval morality play often portrayed Everyman torn between his good and bad angels. In this case, the "hero" of the play, the Reverend T. Lawrence Shannon, has been trying to act as the guide of tour groups, but he is unable to adhere to a schedule or keep his hands off the prettier and younger tourists. At this point, he is being fired by the tour company and abandoned by the furious ladies. These harpies are screaming at him because he has just seduced their favorite young girl and has also deviated from the published itinerary. They want their money back.

Shannon has brought his busload of screaming Texans to an old safe haven, a run-down hotel at the top of a hill in a rain forest adjacent to a saltwater beach near Acapulco. Maxine Faulk, the bawdy hotelkeeper of this dilapidated paradise, welcomes him. An old friend of Shannon's, accustomed to his regular breakdowns, she clearly wants him to settle in for the duration. Maxine has recently been widowed, is currently satisfying her appetites with nubile young natives, but eyes him as a prospective lover for the long term.

In this moment of his apparently inevitable capitulation to Maxine's generous but emasculating dotage, an alternative character trudges onto the scene: Hannah Jelkes, a sturdy New England spinster who has been touring the world with her 90-year-old grandfather. She has been earning her way as a quick-sketch artist and now, like Shannon, is at the end of her rope and also seeks to find a haven in this place. Maxine spots Hannah and her grandfather as penniless liabilities she is not willing to shoulder. She also calculates Hannah to be a potential competitor for Shannon's favors. It is no surprise that she tries to turn them away. Maxine has a soft spot—though not a very large one—that causes her to allow the odd couple to spend a single night in the hotel. This act of grace allows time for the play's action to unfold. The two women wage an undeclared war over Shannon.

The long evening moves from Shannon's confrontation with his female tormentors from the bus tour through his defeat and self-punishment to his confinement in a hammock and period of quiet communion with Hannah, who ministers to him and helps him back to the edge of sanity. He also comforts her, revealing vestiges of the old Shannon as a gentle pastor. She grows agitated at the sounds of the captive iguana scratching to escape. The natives have caught the ugly creature and plan to use it for a meal. At her bequest, Shannon "plays God" and cuts the rope holding the iguana, setting the creature free.

At the evening draws to a stormy conclusion, Nonno, Hannah's grandfather, completes his final poem and then dies. Hannah prepares to leave the next morning, facing new customers, new friends, new vistas. Although Shannon proposes to go with her, she tells him that they both know this is impossible. As the play ends, Shannon settles for Maxine's offer, agreeing tacitly with her that he could do worse.

If we view this as a morality play, the flesh has proven victorious over the spirit. The ending is wistfully comic in the mode of *The Rose Tattoo*—an affirmation of the healing power of sexuality. We know that for this tortured soul, the gross animalism offered by Maxine is not enough. Shannon is a man hungry for God. Curiously, as he tells Maxine that he will go downhill with her, she comforts him with the knowledge that she will help him back up. He has abandoned his temptation to take a "long swim to China." No longer suicidal, he has found a temporary safe haven—enough for a Williams hero.

The savvy Williams reader will quickly recognize the classic elements of the plot and setting: in a place filled with cubicles and walls, strangers come together briefly to talk about their solitude. After confessing their deepest fears and confronting one another with their terrible truths, they part, some of them two-by-two. The ending is the tentative promise of a brief time of comfort, not a lifetime of love. It is the reverse of the old romance with its obligatory blissful ending (Thompson 1987, 152). They find no final solution, no absolute Truth, no God, only one another—for the moment.

If we consider Shannon's plot as a parallel to the central image of the iguana, we realize that his psychological drama replicates the reptile's physical trauma: the chase, the capture, the torment, and the release. In both cases, the escape is only a temporary reprieve. As usual, Williams sees the conclusion as inconclusive. We live "between the times," and despite all our best efforts, we end in defeat. If we are very lucky, we are not left alone to face that inevitability .

The Night of the Iguana has a plot pattern similar to those in *Cat on a Hot Tin Roof* and *Sweet Bird of Youth*. In each case, the drama itself is almost static. The activity is emotional, with stage business sprightly enough to disguise the absence of larger action. Native swimmers scamper about, giggle at offstage obscenities; Nazis march about with radios and swimming gear, looking like something out of a nightmare, Shannon and Maxine have a slapstick tug-of-war over the drink cart; Shannon is tied up onstage after dancing drunkenly among bits of broken glass. Actually, the play does not move beyond Shannon's agonizing and inevitable decision. Williams is seeking to capture the dynamics of a relationship. The antihero at the center of this story, as in so many of his plays, is weak and self-destructive. A strong woman—older but loving—ensnares and cages the male for his own good, a salacious mother image. Many of his plays, bearing the unmistakable aroma of incest, conclude with the male offered a choice between self-destruction or claustrophobic "love." It is no wonder that we are uncomfortable with the "happy" ending of *Iguana*. Once again, it represents a dark vision of life's ultimate choices.

CHARACTER DEVELOPMENT

Tennessee Williams is never content to repeat himself; he always delights us with his variations on a theme. T. Lawrence Shannon, for example, is the oversexed idealist whom we have known since Valentine Xavier (of *Battle of Angels*) first wandered into Two Rivers County with his guitar (in some versions a slim book he is writing) and his oversized libido. He derives in turn from the old

D. H. Lawrence hero whom Williams admired so much as a youth. This drifter is invariably appealing to the women he meets because he is both attractive and free. As Williams sees women, they love to trap men. Shannon points this out to Hannah, when he is tied up in a hammock, "All women, whether they face it or not, want to see a man in a tied-up situation. . . . Their lives are fulfilled, they're satisfied at last, when they get a man, or as many men as they can, in the tied-up situation" (*Theatre, Vol. 4, Iguana,* 345). Women are by nature driven to domesticate the male. Men, by nature, want freedom.

Shannon is an aging idealist who despises himself as well as those he uses. His sexuality is as confused as Brick's. Apparently, since his mother stopped his infantile masturbation with the admonition that both she and God disapproved, Shannon has felt guilty about this sexuality and has harbored a grudge against both Mama and Jehovah. This dynamic of love and hate for central power figures in his life drives him to become a minister and then to betray his ministry. He refused to let even God capture him and imprison him. His open rebellion against God-the-repressor begins when he sympathizes with the grief and loneliness of a sweet young parishioner. It then moves to sexual expression and ends by his turning viciously against his partner in sin, blaming her for his fall. Like Old Adam, he strikes out at the woman rather than confessing his own violation of God's law. This becomes an obsessive-compulsive pattern for his life. Sexual indulgence is for him not a rich pleasure but a nervous tick. The subsequent episodes of self-flagellation are equally ritualistic and bereft of gratification. In productions of this play, a latent homosexuality helps to explain his "spook," that demon that blocks him from any happiness. It is particularly evident in his caricature of saintly suffering. There is a strong element of sado-masochism in his self-imposed "voluptuous crucifixion."

Just as he blames and attacks his partners in love, so he turns against God, whom he calls a "senile delinquent" for establishing laws that the weak man inevitably breaks. In some ways, God Himself is a character in this drama, the epic antagonist of Shannon, and his would-be lover. By setting himself up for a "voluptuous crucifixion," Shannon is able to ape Christ's passion without significant cost. He tears at the ornate cross hanging on a golden chain around his neck, mutilates his clerical collar, and taunts God by calling Him names as he has his painless moment of contrived agony. Golgotha, the bleak hill on which Chirst was crucified, was very different from the hammock on the patio of a hotel in a rainforest where Shannon suffers luxuriously.

This tormented character has clear ties to other modern literary figures, notably the whiskey priest in Graham Greene's *The Power and the Glory* and the defrocked Calvinist minister in William Faulkner's *Light in August.* These secular saints are men who cannot escape from the Hound of Heaven, even though they have betrayed their vocation.

Such a man, in an epic struggle for his soul, cannot find more than tempo-rary comfort in the arms of an earth mother such as Maxine Faulk. Though she is lusty and affectionate, she can offer only sensual gratification. Shannon's lust is far deeper than sexual hunger. While he contemplates the long swim to China, the ultimate union with the Oversoul, she offers him a midnight swim, an evening of indulgence. It was her late husband, Fred, that Shannon came to see, the priestly host, who is now dead, food for fish. Poor Shannon is left to the Mother Goddess instead, the patrona.

Maxine reminds the reader of the Princess. Even her name has the echo of "maxima," the powerful female victor. (Her last name, *Faulk*, is a not-so-subtle reference to her sexual prowess.) She will enfold, entrap, and feed on her vic-tim, like the black widow spider to which she is compared. She contemplates future uses to which Shannon may be put, not only for her own gratification, but also to jolly her female clientele—as a gigolo—while she caters to the men. In an explicit statement as to this grotesque scheme, she discusses setting up a motel in Texas where rooms are rented by the hour. Although apparently be-nign in her earlier relationship with Fred, Maxine-as-widow is now openly predatory. She hires young men to service her and aspires to the acquisition of Shannon. This is no more love than is the Princess's offer to Chance to take him along on a golden chain, domesticated and obedient, for her amusement at some future time.

Maxine is characterized as larger than life, overflowing her blouse and her slacks, loud, obscene, full of vigor. Life has toughened her, but she has some re-deeming qualities. She can assess situations realistically and shrewdly; she makes few moral judgments, even about Nazis. While she can understand what Hannah is going through and can project where Shannon will end with-out her help, she has no interest in generosity. She wants to be paid. For Wil-liams, she is the archetypal patrona. He had previously portrayed her as the lusty landlady in "The Mattress in the Tomato Patch," and the hard-bitten Mrs. Wire in the short stories that would eventually become *Vieux Carré*.

Some new characters also appear in this powerful play, Hannah and Nonno. At first, we may think of Hannah as the classic Williams Southern belle, like Miss Edith Jelkes in his original short story. Hannah, however, is a New Eng-land type, based on Tennessee Williams' Coffin relatives. She represents a dif-ferent brand of Calvinism from the perverse Southern type we see in Shannon. Hers has been tempered by life and travels, particularly her travels in the Ori-ent, where she has adopted some Buddhist practices. She is a virgin by choice, a companion to her old grandfather, a willing nurse for the dying. Nonjudgmental, she sounds like the angel in the alcove, a figure Williams had earlier used in a short story. In this play, she is characterized as a "standing-up Buddha," and an "emancipated Puritan" (*Theatre, Vol. 4*, 344). He also had the image of her as a medieval saint, the attenuated figure we see in Gothic cathedrals, stiff, thin, and ascetic. Her Biblical first name, Hannah, refers to the mother of the prophet Samuel. Her name means "grace," surely a signal to the core of Williams' character.

Hannah is also a quick-sketch artist of some talent. She has the ability to understand others and to capture their essence in pastels. Like Williams himself, a sometime artist as well as a sketcher of word-portraits, she is a perennial outsider. An observer rather than a participant in life's drama, she characterizes others while coolly seeking to avoid involvement. Her flat chest and androgynous nature are striking contrasts to Maxine, whose breasts burst out of her blouse and whose buttocks fill her slacks to overflowing. Hannah has no sexual interest in Shannon and no plans for marriage in the future. Her winsome narrative of sexual encounters describes sad little perverse acts, one of which frightened her, the other of which she tolerated out of pity. She seems to view sexual hunger as pitiable. At the end, when Shannon proposes teaming up with her, she gently rejects this notion as clearly impractical. Once her grandfather has died, she will travel alone.

Her Kabuki costume and her ritual tea ceremony mark her as a kind of priestess. She administers a mystic potion to Shannon, a drink of poppy seeds and honey, which will give him rest. It is an Oriental rather than an Occidental solution to his woes, not the communion that he no longer administers.

Her primary ministration is to her grandfather, Nonno, who is another new character for Williams. He is, of course, modeled on Williams' own grandfather, one of the playwright's favorite people, even as he grew both deaf and blind in later years. He had been the source of Tom's vast and eclectic literary taste from the early years in Clarksdale. Later, he was an advocate for the boy, always proud of him, eager to be with him. In his clerical collar and straw hat, the cadaverous old man was a colorful contrast to the Bohemian crowd that gathered around the Williams conclave in Key West. His grandson loved him for his dignity, his eccentricities, and his wisdom. This character was his tribute to the man.

The minor characters, the Mexican boys, the Texas teachers, and the Nazi honeymooners are all typecast. They point to his stereotypes of Mediterranean and Nordic cultures, as lusty Sun People and frigid Ice People. He had used warm-blooded Mexican or Mediterranean characters in a number of plays—as the tempting mistress for John Buchanan in *Summer and Smoke*, as the heroine of *The Rose Tattoo*. Some of the difference between these Latin characters and the Anglo-Saxons he attributed to the difference in religious heritage. He thought the Anglos were rooted in Puritanism, while the Latinos came from a Roman Catholic tradition. This became particularly significant in *The Rose Tattoo*, where the argument between veneration of the Virgin Mary or of Venus was central. In *The Night of the Iguana*, this contrast is apparent in the mock battle between the old-maid schoolteachers from Texas and the half-naked young natives from Mexico. They signify the exaggerated distinctions between body and soul that we see all through the play, a battle that clearly is fought daily inside of Shannon.

THEMATIC ISSUES

Williams designed the role of Hannah with Katharine Hepburn in mind. As a balance to Maxine-the-tramp, Hannah-the-lady is a witty and dignified image of the pilgrim searching for Truth and Beauty. Williams had prefaced the play by quoting from Emily Dickinson's poem about the conversation of the dead:

> I died for beauty, but was scarce
> Adjusted in the tomb,
> When one who died for truth was lain
> In an adjoining room.
>
> He questioned softly why I failed?
> "For beauty," I replied.
> "And I for truth,—the two are one;
> We brethren are," he said.
>
> And so, as kinsmen met a night,
> We talked between the rooms,
> Until the moss had reached our lips,
> And covered up our names.

This poem is an interesting choice: Dickinson was always one of Williams' favorites, but she also seems to have been a spiritual and physical model for Hannah Jelkes, another New England spinster. The poem also points to our final anonymity.

The poetry in the play, especially the central poem that Nonno completes just as he dies, explains some of the implied ideas of the story. Like Emily Dickinson, Nonno writes in rhymed quatrains, combining simple diction with complex and anguished ideas regarding the human condition. His poem also deserves to be reread and analyzed.

> How calmly does the orange branch
> Observe the sky begin to blanch
> Without a cry, without a prayer,
> With no betrayal of despair.

Sometime while night obscures the tree
The zenith of its life will be
Gone past forever, and from thence
A second history will commence.

A chronicle no longer gold,
A bargaining with mist and mold,
And finally the broken stem
The plummeting to earth; and then

An intercourse not well designed
For beings of a golden kind
Whose native green must arch above
The earth's obscene, corrupting love.

And still the ripe fruit and the branch
Observe the sky begin to blanch
Without a cry, without a prayer,
With no betrayal of despair.

O Courage, could you not as well
Select a second place to dwell,
Not only in that golden tree
But in the frightened heart of me? (*Iguana* 371–72)

In this poem, given particular significance by its climactic placement in the play, we see some of Williams' central themes: Using the Oriental image of the silhouetted branch against the pale sky, he transforms the tree (of life) into a symbol of nature facing death. The nonhuman world meets death simply—and he suggests, beautifully—because it is without rational thought. This stoicism, an acceptance of natural patterns that Hannah displays in the play, is beautiful compared with human fear. The beauty of nature is coupled with the need to "compromise" with the earth—for propagation of the species. This mingling with mist and mold, which produces the ripe fruit in its time creates no tension in nature, which also makes no distinction between the ideal and the physical. But in the human, a being of a different kind, who seeks the idealism of the sky rather than the corruption of the earth, the pull of the flesh is a source of anguish. The hunger for the green branch to arch above this gravitational pull is doomed. The approaching darkness, the broken branch, the inevitable death and decay are met with serenity by thoughtless nature. The final stanza is a prayer that the same courage may dwell in the heart of man. These are the lessons that Hannah preaches and Shannon learns: Nature presents us a picture of stoicism and beauty; man, self-aware and idealistic, resents the inevitable descent into decay; and the final hope is the grace that comes of courage. Williams simplifies it still further in the motto, "No sweat."

If we expand this poetic construct into a fuller exploration of the play, we see the problems facing the hero of the Williams universe: the natural world has no special concern for any of its creatures, including man. The rhythm of the sun's rising and setting, day and night, the seasons of fruitfulness and decay continue without meaning. This cycle of birth to maturity and back again to death and decay is an outrage to "beings of a golden kind."

The human, believing that he is only a little lower than the angels in his being, judges and laments the "obscene, corrupting love" of the earth but is nonetheless forced into its relentless cycle. The dream of perennial youth, the green arch of new growth above the earth, reaching into the sky, is doomed. Williams himself, in this ripe season of his own fruitfulness, realized that he was losing his idealistic reach. He felt instead the steady pull toward the earth, bending him toward decadence. Shannon clearly feels this same blighted dream of purity, despising himself for finally relaxing into the corrupting bosom of Maxine.

The tree, that lovely Oriental image of nature, has a grace in its quiet acceptance of the blanched sky, the approach of darkness. Hannah parallels this stoic imagery, a sentient creature in her case, able to mimic the golden tree that can observe the change in the sky "without a cry, without a prayer." Williams' plea for courage to accept the limits of life and the inevitability of death, resorting to neither the support of others nor intervention from God, strong and alone, is a sad acknowledgment of mortality, an acceptance of his solitary path. Big Daddy had proclaimed that man is an animal that must die. This is what Tennessee Williams calls "truth."

As the epigraph from Dickinson preaches, Beauty is the kinsman of Truth. The beauty of the tree against the sky, the glory of the arching stem, the richness of fruition—these are the delights of life. One who feels this deeply, who can burst the grape against his palate and relish the full glory of its taste, such a one will also lament the broken stem, the decay. (See Keats' "Ode on Melancholy.") This theme of the value of the passionate existence runs through much of Tennessee Williams' work.

Our comfort lies in the belief that new life invariably proceeds out of this decadence; the individual creature is lost, but life on earth continues. (The image of the sea as the womb and tomb of mankind, a kind of natural Oversoul, reinforces this cycle and this loss of individuality.) The one virtue for which the poet begs is courage, the courage to accept the pattern as beautiful, inevitable, and true. As Williams works through this meditation on the decline from the zenith of life, this hope for a second history, he acknowledges his fear.

In these six quatrains of rhymed tetrameter couplets, Tennessee Williams has encapsulated his naturalistic philosophy.

STYLISTIC AND LITERARY DEVICES

The Night of the Iguana is an extremely compact, meditative, poetic play. Starting late in the action, moving barely at all in the course of a day, it ends with many of the problems as yet unresolved. We meet most of the characters when their golden days are passed. Fred, the one man who might have solved Shannon's problems for him, is dead. Hannah, who is also at the end of her rope, finds here no permanent rest. Her grandfather, the oldest living, practicing poet, dies. These would appear to be the materials for a decidedly downbeat, depressing, and dry piece of theatre. Remarkably, the play is fast-paced and frequently funny.

The rapid changes in pace are marked partially by the clashing rhetorical styles: the harsh nationalistic marching songs of the Germans, the Führer's rage-filled voice over their radio, are quickly replaced by the nostalgic romanticism of Nonno's poetry, which in turn contrasts with the visual and aural violence of thunder and lightning in God's universe.

The characters race in and out, dancing, screaming, singing, taunting, fighting, comforting in turn, distracting us to the point where we barely notice that the characters themselves are static. This is not an drama of action, but a drama of discovery. The roles of the different characters are carefully balanced, as in a ritual, with modern adaptations to disguise the actual meaning of the saintly sinner at the core, the good and bad angels at either side, the replacement of the artist's smock with the Kabuki robe to signal Hannah's change from artist to priest. This is managed with a naturalness and ease. The play climbs toward awe at certain moments and tumbles toward laughter at others.

The humor is partially visual, with the contrasting physical types on stage and the references to them. Certainly the slapstick moments, provided in a grotesque manner by the Nazis and in a semi-serious way by Hannah and Shannon fighting over the cart of drinks, break the meditative tone. In addition, the characters tell jokes, either laugh at them or make fun of them, turn phrases in ironic ways, and snicker at one another. The combination of pain and pleasure, always a characteristic of a Williams play, is particularly obvious here. For example, when Nonno makes his anachronistic, well-rehearsed little jokes, anticipating delighted applause, Hannah shudders with embarrassment. Others laugh at him instead of laughing with him, revealing their cruelty. The Germans are particularly delighted by the suffering and humiliation of others, turning their observations into broad comedy. By contrast, Hannah, as she gently pokes fun at Shannon's pleasure in his own "voluptuous crucifixion," is sweetly ironic.

The poetic tone of the play is preserved primarily by sequestering the obscene activities off-stage. We know from her conversation that Hannah had a couple of shocking "sexual" episodes, but we do not see them. Nor do we see Shannon's passionate encounter with young Charlotte, the innocent on the tour who becomes the target of his attention. Actually, for all of the attacks on Williams as a pornographic playwright, his plays rarely display physical passion. These activities, like the violence, are primarily out of sight. Perhaps, like the Greek use of offstage violence, they become more vivid for being a part of our imagination.

The other obscenities are also left to our interpretation: we hear about the travels to countries where people dig through piles of excrement for bits of food, but we do not see this. Nor do we see Shannon urinating on the luggage of the Texas Baptist ladies. Instead we get a raucous account of the event by the delighted Germans. We suspect what Maxine does with her nubile young Mexican boys, but we are not burdened with the explicit presentation of those encounters.

This narrative rather than the dramatic quality of the play extends to its central image—the iguana. We hear him but do not see him. The characters describe his ugly appearance, his uses, his torment, and his release. The characters project their experience and reactions onto him, reminding us that his chase, capture, torment and release signal parallel activities onstage. We do not need to see the creature to believe in him any more than we needed, when watching *Suddenly Last Summer,* to see the turtles scurrying for the sea, being ripped apart by the great birds. Williams is able to maintain his lyrical tone primarily by playing with colorful words rather than crude portrayals.

This device, which creates a rich linguistic pattern for the play, would appear to make it talky and static. Williams overcomes this problem by filling the stage with "business." He is superb in the staging of activities to keep the audience amused and involved. Shannon changes from a fatigued tour guide to a prim priest to a saint dancing on broken glass to a twisted Christ figure in the hammock. His physical transformation is accomplished by his changes in clothing, tone of voice, level of action. We do not have the sense that we are passive eavesdroppers on a philosophical discourse. We are actively involved in his emotional transformations.

Each of the characters is a distinct type, with visual power, introducing dramatic shifts in the action. The American gothic types we have in Hannah and Nonno contrast with the lusty Mediterranean qualities of Maxine. The Germans are the very image of health, bursting with vigor. In contrast to their lavish display of flesh, loud songs, and slapstick behavior, we have the gentle tea ceremony of the Kabuki-costumed Hannah. A conversation grows serious, only to be interrupted by the crashing of bottles as the characters fight over a drink cart.

In addition, in the setting, the incidental references become natural, organic symbols as the play progresses. From the opening we are confronted with the cubicles of the casa, with a verandah as a general meeting place. The separation of the people into cubicles becomes for Shannon a symbol of the human condition, with moments of communication on the verandah. The hope to stay for the night, expressed by Hannah, is parallel to the need for a safe haven for the small ships we see in *Small Craft Warnings*. Each of us needs a sense of comfort from life's storms. Hannah adds to this imagery by discussing the "home" she has made with her grandfather over the years, a nest they have built in one another's hearts. We realize that this home that the odd couple built in their love is far more secure than the far more physical one Shannon and Maxine will build out of their shared needs.

Gestures become indicators of character: when Hannah offers Shannon her final cigarette, he sees it as an emblem of her grace. She in turn interprets his gracious offer of his ornate cross as a temporary loan, which he will later lament. In a gently ironic exchange, they speak of "redeeming" the cross, both aware at a deeper level that they are reversing the theological transaction of salvation. The play is replete with such fascinating turns of phrase, moments of insight, indicators of larger meanings. It is fair to say that this is Tennessee Williams' fullest theological statement.

ALTERNATE CRITICAL PERSPECTIVE: RELIGIOUS/THEOLOGICAL INTERPRETATION

From birth, Tom Williams had a special relationship with religion. His early life seemed to be framed by his relationship to his grandfather. Teachers called him a "preacher's kid." Not only was he saturated with the ceremonies and symbols of the Church of England, he was also convinced of the Christian vision of the world. He believed in God's existence, the afterlife, his particular role in human history, his obligations to use his gifts for a preordained vocation. Nor was this simply an intellectual construct. When he was seventeen, he had a mystical moment in the Cologne Cathedral: he said that he felt "the hand of our Lord Jesus" touch him with mercy and exorcise the phobia that was driving him "into madness" (*Memoirs* 1975, 21). Although he made fun of his innocent adolescent faith, he was always inclined toward some mysticism. He never lost his sense of transcendence, his belief in his own special calling. He said he knelt to pray before each new play opened.

Once away from the puritanical dominance of his mother, he gradually explored his own religious truth, moving away from the authoritarian structure of the Episcopal Church and the sharp edges of orthodoxy. Shifting toward the autonomy of self, shaping his ideas to match his feelings and his needs, he came to a much more heterodox religious view over time.

In the early days, Tennessee Williams was at war with the forces of established religion, with its law-giving God, its clear moral code, its harsh judgments. He separated the Old Testament Jehovah from the New Testament Christ, presenting them as opposing forces in his battle of angels. In Scripture, of course, it is Satan and his fallen angels who refuse to serve God and are cast into outer darkness. Williams was inclined to believe Christ was on Satan's side, a gentler, less legalistic, more humane kind of love than his law-giving Father.

His harsh Jehovah-God became increasingly ferocious in his imagination, climaxing in the memorable moment described in *Suddenly Last Summer*, when Sebastian's vision of God is described as a giant predatory bird attacking newborn, innocent sea turtles. The plays that followed, *Sweet Bird of Youth* and *The Night of the Iguana*, moved beyond this God of Judgment to an absent deity, or a Senile Delinquent. It is as if he thought that, by calling God names, he could force Him into direct communication once again. He was unwilling to believe simply, as did so many of his contemporaries, that God was dead.

By this time, Williams had become eclectic and amorphous in his religion. He rejected the scriptural basis for theology, the authority of the Church, and the careful distinctions of the traditional creeds. Unconcerned about his excursions into heresy, he challenged such old doctrinal views as the Trinity, the nature of Christ, the meaning of the Eucharist, etc. Instead of the established bases of authority, he wandered freely into Eastern thought, collected bits and pieces of faith that appealed to him, and morphed Christ into Buddha, Mary into Venus. When an orthodox voice, like the priest in *The Rose Tattoo*, complains, the play presents him as unfeeling, ignorant, or foolish. For Williams, human experience invariably outweighed theological constructs. This would explain why he has been called an Existentialist, albeit a religious one. He believed that God lived, but that—for the time being—He was silent.

Williams never shaped this set of beliefs into an explicit systematic statement. The ideas are apparent as the undergirding of his plays. Once recognized, they help the reader/viewer to interpret the imagery, to understand the plot, to recognize the setting, to see the full meaning of the characters. This is particularly true of *The Night of the Iguana*, a play that pictures a cluster of pilgrims at the end of their road.

The human life is often described as a path or a way. The seventeenth century novel *Pilgrim's Progress* left an indelible imprint on American literature, fixing firmly in our national psyche the concept of the journey of life. Even before that, it was already a solid part of Western thought, appearing frequently in Scripture, repeated in the classics, with their archetypal voyages out and voyages home, and in the medieval imagery of the religious pilgrimage. Thus, when Emily Dickinson speaks of setting out on a journey with Death, a gentleman who "kindly stopped" for her, we understand this in metaphysical terms. We also understand that Robert Frost was talking about more than just a fork in the road when he spoke of taking "the road less traveled." It is not surprising that someone as well versed in literature as Tennessee Williams would use the imagery of the journey to explain the plight of his characters.

The Reverend T. Lawrence Shannon, whose name reminds us of Lawrence of Arabia as well as that old seeker after truth, D. H. Lawrence, has exchanged his clerical leadership role in the Episcopal Church for a secular equivalent as the "conductor" of Blake's Tours. Stripped first of the keys to the church (and the keys of the Kingdom), he is now being stripped of the keys to the rickety bus. He is a minister who has been on sabbatical for most of the time since his ordination, continuing his pilgrimage of discovery among God's creatures. Having witnessed unspeakable human depravity along the way, he has now come to the end of the road, on a hill in a tropical rainforest near the sea. He now contemplates suicide—"a long swim to China."

For Hannah and Nonno, the pilgrimage has been less frenzied and more hopeful. Their discoveries along the way have been more benign, their love for one another has made for good fellowship and mutual support. Now, ready to part with her as he undertakes his solitary journey into death, Nonno seeks the path to the "cradle of life"—the sea. He is selecting a natural and appropriate way for one in his nineties, not the rushed and violent choice that Shannon, in the middle of his journey of life, only halfheartedly contemplates. Nonno dies echoing some of the first words spoken by God and the last words by Christ: "It is good," and "It is finished." Although his granddaughter has to push his wheelchair up the narrow path to the top of the mountain, signaling his entrance into a second childhood, he is content with his life and with his death.

Hannah, finally free of her beloved burden, must go on, following her own lonely path that will take her away from this "House of Dying" into new adventures. She and Shannon are both seekers, both Puritans working out their salvation in individual, existential ways. Hannah, the New England spinster, is a celibate with little real temptation from the flesh. In her journeys she had adopted the openness of Eastern mystics, who put tolerance before orthodoxy. She passes no judgment on Shannon's sins—does not even label them "sins." She comments mildly on his unkindness to others and to himself. The violation of another's humanity is her ultimate evil, not a transgression of God's law. As a sketch artist, she observes and records without rendering judgment.

Her dispassionate observations are tempered with a generosity of spirit that allows her to give her last cigarette to Shannon and a piece of her underwear to a pitiful Australian salesman. She enthusiastically bears the burden of her grandfather's care to the very end of his extended life. She may be a "female standing up Buddha," but she is also a "Christian saint." At times, she acts as a Kabuki dancer performing ritual actions. At others, she acts the role of the Christian priest hearing confession, giving absolution, and administering the sacraments.

Shannon, the actual, ordained priest in the story, is at first eager to dress in his clerical costume, but then is even more eager to tear the splendid gold and amethyst cross from around his neck. The gift to Hannah of this ornamental cross at the end of the play, to fund her continued pilgrimage, is reciprocated by her promise to return it—or the pawn ticket to redeem it at a later time. The very language of "redeeming" the cross, as was noted earlier, rather than being redeemed by the cross signals the reversal of values in Shannon's life. He has betrayed his faith in his mad pilgrimage of the flesh, yet he cannot rid himself of the vestiges of that faith. He advertises himself as a minister of God leading tours of God's world, yet he takes his customers through the most depraved sights possible. He wins their respect for his theological training, forces them to recognize human depravity, and then seduces the prettiest, youngest, most vulnerable of the flock. Filled with guilt and self-loathing, he subsequently punishes the partner of his lust. He remains a Puritan, ill at ease in the decadent tropics. He is both a Southern gentleman and a crude animal, who urinates on the luggage.

The key to this confusing blend of Freudian psychology, Eastern mysticism, and Christian tradition is found in the name of the tours that Shannon conducts—Blake's Tours. William Blake, Tennessee Williams' all-time favorite mystic poet, was an early English Romantic. He believed that the Christian life was almost the exact opposite of what proper people prescribed. For instance, he believed that God had created humans with good instincts that they should indulge in natural ways. God created and loved the tiger as well as the lamb, the passionate, dark mysteries of life as well as the simple, innocent beauties. Blake believed that the "dark satanic mills" of the industrial world were crippling and polluting God's good earth. He also believed that primly righteous people crippled and destroyed God's children.

The account of Shannon's childish practice of masturbation, which his mother interrupted and forbade, pronouncing that it made both her and God angry, had turned Shannon against all authority figures, who became symbols of sexual frustration. His image of God as a negative force, with the voice of thunder and lightning, grows out of a need to fight for his natural appetites. Blake, Williams appears to believe, would have approved of Shannon's judgments on the sick people and sick cities. He also would have sympathized with the tied-up iguana and applauded Shannon's freeing it as an act of grace.

The religious imagery that weaves through almost every speech in the play forces the audience to analyze the theological content and the author's implied message. Williams' religious message is invariably man-centered, with God a threatening background figure. His laws are perceived as arbitrary restrictions, not particularly helpful as guidelines for the good life. The plays almost always have a "fantastic" level that transcends reality, never settling for the flatly factual level of existence. Williams tends to focus on "big" questions—self-discovery, death, beauty, truth, love, etc. For example, in *The Night of the Iguana*, the concern is not whether Shannon can hold on to a job with Blake Tours, but whether he can retain his dignity, discover his true path, find meaning in his life. In spite of her poverty, Hannah has found an inner peace. She knows who she is, what she must do, how she must live.

In this play, we have already discussed a number of the Williams theological signatures: The setting indicates a transcendence. In this case, the sea is the Oversoul waiting at the end of the path. The heat of the locale adds to Shannon's sense of decadence. The rainforest, teeming with life, symbolizes the earthly existence, full of fertility and corruption. The hotel, our earthly dwelling, has its classic meeting place where the solitary lives mingle briefly. God strikes out in lightning and thunder, heals with rain. The wind is the Holy Spirit that brings healing and comfort.

The characters are pilgrims, fishermen, saints, sinners, and would-be saviors. They look on the surface like slightly peculiar contemporaries, but their peculiarities hint that they are archetypes (see discussion on archtetypes), the earth mother, the androgynous saint, the eternal wanderer, the outsider/stranger, or the suffering savior. The heroic figures are plagued with evil spirits—blue devils or doppelgangers or spooks. Although Williams never really explains these tormentors, they were quite literally a part of his life. His journals, and even his letters, make regular reference to his blue devils.

The characters' actions take on ceremonial qualities, reinforced by the costumes and lighting. Preparing a cup of tea becomes a Japanese tea ceremony, which in turn becomes a consecration of the elements of the mass. Binding a drunk in a hammock becomes the crucifixion of a would-be Christ. Writing a poem becomes a creative act akin to that performed by God Himself.

If we consider in depth the act of creation, for example, we see that Nonno's poem becomes the focal point of the final scene. Like Sebastian's poetry, long in the gestation process, perfect in the execution, Nonno's poem becomes a statement about life. Certainly for Tennessee Williams, writing was the process by which he overcame his "blue devils," creating a beauty out of the torment of his existence—like Alexandra Del Lago. Life itself, he says over and over, is a series of incomplete sentences. This poem, by contrast, like Nonno's life (and Christ's atonement) "is finished."

Hannah has accepted the message of the poem—"no sweat." Shannon also appears in the process of adopting that message of Oriental acceptance, as he goes for a swim that is not all the way to China. Hannah's search for Beauty and his for Truth have brought them together briefly—as in the Dickinson poem quoted earlier. They accept the creed of Keats's Grecian Urn: " 'Beauty is truth, truth beauty,'—that is all/ Ye know on earth, and all ye need to know" ("Ode on a Grecian Urn"). This is a religion of the aesthetes, not of the common folk. It is most specifically Williams' firmly held belief.

Williams had articulated this in his earlier statement of his "creed" as a playwright. Here are his words, quoted from Shaw's play, *The Doctor's Dilemma*: "I believe in Michelangelo, Velásquez and Rembrandt; in the might of design, the mystery of color, the redemption of all things by beauty everlasting and the message of art that has made these hands blessed. Amen" (*Where I Live* 1978, 69). He demonstrates no apparent concern that he is replacing the Apostles Creed with this aesthetic one.

Basically, Williams had an amateur's relationship with theology. He followed the popular trends of the day: at times, he was a dedicated Episcopalian, at others a member of the Roman Catholic Church, more frequently a vaguely pious nonconformist. He was attracted to the Roman Catholic ceremonies, delighted with the Greek "corn gods" and mystery religions, and tempted by the existentialists and Eastern mystics. If he were alive today, he would undoubtedly be involved in the "New Age" movement. His was a restless mind in lifelong rebellion against the settled theologies of the church of his grandfather and his mother.

Like most Americans, he was no philosopher or theologian. He made no effort to codify his evolving faith or match it against the ancient heresies it mirrored, yet his plays are often sermons aimed at the community he seeks to convert to his own personal vision of reality. He was like the roving evangelist who exploited the theatre as if it were a camp meeting, full of passion and conviction, not a carefully calibrated intellectual discourse.

While Tennessee Williams, like much of the intellectual community of the 1960s, was attuned to Eastern mysticism in an effort to reach out to other religions with a fresh openness, he never quite relinquished his Episcopalian roots. This tension created both colorful imagery and cloudy theology.

He loved to focus on individual experience and feeling, a sense of well-being that might be enhanced by the use of alcohol or drugs. He adopted the imagery—and perhaps the idea—of the Oversoul. He was comforted by the Eastern absence of sexual regulation or Puritan morality, leaving the ethical decisions to be determined on a case-by-case basis—a moral suasion called "situational ethics."

Williams was to repeat some of this half-formulated religious philosophy in his later plays—notably *Small Craft Warnings, Slapstick Tragedy,* and *In the Bar of a Tokyo Hotel.* The pattern of a predatory, merciless deity, clarified in the image of the turtles racing for the sea and the malevolent circling birds, was already frighteningly apparent in *Suddenly Last Summer.* To this he added the "circle of light," as the image of the brief, intense and heroic moment of the human struggle—as man fights furiously to be a hero, swaggering in the spotlight, only to disappear into the darkness. The human inability to communicate becomes a series of "unfinished sentences," his solitude mirrored in the cells that he and his fellow humans inhabit, knocking on walls in an effort to reach fellow creatures. In the midst of this terrifyingly lonely existence, filled with cruelty and brutality, where man dashes madly hither and yon pursuing his meaningless freedom, there are small moments of grace—when "There's God, so quickly."

Williams wants us to see all of this: the beauty, the degradation; the courage, the fear; the rebellion and the surrender of the wayfaring pilgrim. Unlike Eastern mystics, this old Romantic believed that the salvation lay in the struggle of the hero, not in his success. He assumed for himself the role of Christ, nailed to his own cross, refusing the substitutionary sacrifice. Shannon wants to redeem rather than to be redeemed, He does not choose to *serve* God, but prefers to *be* God.

Finally, it is perhaps wrong to place Williams in any neat categories. For most of his life, he was like Shannon, a man of God on a prolonged sabbatical.

9

The Two-Character Play or Out Cry (1967–1979)

The Night of the Iguana (1961) was Tennessee Williams' last real success. He continued to write, to experiment, to give talks and readings, to appear at revivals until his death in 1983, but he was never again a genuine success. The playwright seemed able to work at a good pace, almost as he had earlier, but the plays he produced were increasingly confessional and embarrassing. They continued to reveal flashes of insight and imagination, but audiences rarely understood them or responded to them with any enthusiasm. Critics, who had a fixed definition of a Williams play, seemed intent on forcing him to recreate his old stories and theatrical patterns. Tennessee Williams, ironically, had become his own toughest competition. This fierce old warrior, like Don Quixote, refused to bend to such pressures. He continued to write from his heart—an "out cry" of the human spirit.

The plays he wrote during the final two decades of his life often dealt with isolation, aging, and death. *Small Craft Warnings* (1972), earlier entitled *Confessional*, contained three versions of Williams himself separated into different characters, representing different stages of his life—a young lad on his way to California, a somewhat older writer settled into the gay lifestyle, and an alcoholic old abortionist. Even the setting, a bar on the California coast, echoes Williams' memories of his first trip West. When Williams himself appeared on stage in the role of the drunken doctor who bungles the birth of a baby, he advertised his own creative problems. (He often compared the genesis of a work of art to the birth of a child.) The appearances did little to help his reputation:

he was often drunk. He would stagger on stage, ad lib lines and confuse the rest of the cast.

Fully aware of his self-destructiveness, Williams seemed unable to control his need to play the fool. Tributes flooded his way, including a celebrated evening at the White House and the Kennedy Center, honorary degrees, and invitations to speak and read at colleges and universities. His spotty responses delighted some, disappointed others. He might oversleep and miss the appointment entirely, appear unsteady on his legs and confused, or act so outrageously that he embarrassed his hosts. He proudly insisted that he accepted the engagements simply for the money, though he was by this time wealthy beyond his wildest dreams.

In these final decades, he spent much of his time contemplating the approach of death, an obsession mirrored in his writing. One of his late plays deals explicitly with the death of the artist—a man who is brilliant and self-destructive. *In the Bar of a Tokyo Hotel* (which opened the same year as his near-death experience at Barnes, 1969) pictures a painter who sounds like a combination of Williams and his early acquaintance, artist Jackson Pollock, as he throws himself into his work, moving into such a mad frenzy that he drives everyone away from him, leaving him to die alone. In this play, his wife and his agent find the artist so mad that they can't even take him home on a plane: no airline would accept him. The solution for him and for them is his death, or as his wife says, his stepping out of the "circle of light." This protective circle allows us to live; the artist must break boundaries, step outside, violate the rules. If he goes too far, he loses his audience, his ability, and his life. The image is a wonderful blend of the theatrical spotlight and the older Anglo-Saxon image of the lighted room as life, the encircling darkness as death. Williams, like Mark (the artist in the play), had so identified with his work that he himself appeared as the walking wounded.

This sense of crippling had been developed even more fully in a pair of late plays that Williams wrote even earlier under the wonderful title of *Slapstick Tragedy* (1966). Both deal with mutilation, but it is the first that is the richer of the self-portraits. The pecking by critics was wounding him but not keeping him from his enduring quest. The dark meaning behind this slapstick play sharpens the anguish that it encapsulates.

By the early seventies, Williams had found himself alone: he had alienated not only Frank Merlo, who had subsequently died of lung cancer in 1963, but also Audrey Wood, his faithful agent. In 1971, after a number of misunderstandings, he changed handlers. Other agents tried to manage his affairs, but they soon found him impossible to deal with. His paranoia led him into outbursts filled with accusations and attacks that few professional people could bear. His old directors and producers were wary of him, realizing that he might well hand them chaotic bits of obscenity rather than a well-crafted play. He could still find some producers and some audiences, but they were people who cherished their memories of his earlier greatness—not the man he had become. In a kind of fierce truthfulness, Williams recognized his own failures as a person, characterizing himself as an old alligator. Amazingly, he could still use this self-knowledge for drama—although now for black comedy.

PLOT DEVELOPMENT

From 1967 until his death in 1983, Williems produced a succession of versions of the play he sometimes called *The Two-Character Play*, sometimes *Out Cry*. Lanelle Daniel notes that there were references to the play as early as 1959 (Kolin 1998, 177). None of his late works so richly summarizes his final decades of creative effort. It was one of the most remarkable creations to come out of this private voyage into Dragon Country and the final great play of his long career. He worked on many different versions of it the final decades of his life and never stopped hoping that this would win him the final honors for fresh creativity that he so desired. It is an intensely self-revelatory play, in which the structure itself is a mirror of his mind.

Williams always believed that writing should be "organic," that the form of a work should grow naturally out of the idea and emotional content of the inspiration. In a skewed world, he felt he must use a twisted, fragmented form to present his nightmarish vision. He had found early on that he could not follow a straight-line narrative in a play or story. He simply didn't see life or truth as linear or logical. Instead, he found that time often bends back on itself, that thoughts circle round and round certain events and ideas. Even the reading of his journals or letters reveals this insistent circular pattern, returning again and again to his home, which he loved and hated, reading and annotating his own life experiences, trying to understand them in reviewing them. When he wrote his *Memoirs* (1975), he reread his journals and letters, reliving his experiences and his reactions to those experiences. In *Memoirs*, he intermingles different periods of his life, layering memories with current events in a chaotic pattern of stream-of-consciousness narrative. *Moise and the World of Reason* (also published in 1975) is an even more revelatory self-loathing self-portrait, again involving this obsessive circling around his earlier experiences. He found that there was no escape from this circle, that in order to move at all, he was forced to press deeper into self, toward the center. Surely the meaning of it all must lie there—if anywhere.

Added to this organic form, he designed *The Two-Character Play* as a play about writing and producing a play—a play-within-a-play. He was trying to capture on stage the complicated process of creating a play. The main character is both author and actor in a play, who is describing his own life in the piece he is drafting. He and his sister—who often refuses to follow the script, forgets it, or argues with the facts on which he bases it—are the two characters. The play is being presented in an anonymous country, with no one else on stage to provide a yardstick for measuring reality. The play becomes a playwright's nightmare: the director and stagehands have all abandoned the brother-sister acting combination, leaving a message that they are mad. An audience seems to have gathered to see the play, but the actors have no one to dim the lights or open and close the curtains. The stage properties are not in place. The sister, Clare, has no clarity in her memories of events or lines; she appears to be on pills that help her to overcome her terror at acting but also confuse her. The brother, Felice, is clearly in charge as the playwright and the lead actor, but he too suffers some problems with reality. The pair undertake the play, changing lines as they go, and losing the audience along the way. By the time they finish the play, called *The Two-Character Play*, they are alone in a cold, dark theatre. They soon discover that there is no exit, nor would they be wise to try to escape since they have no money and no place to stay the night. As they shiver with cold and fear, they decide to return to the play-within-the-play. Through their willing suspension of disbelief, they can keep warm, by believing themselves to be once again in the summertime, in the deep South.

The brother and sister have sequestered themselves in their house since the murder-suicide of their father and mother. They are immured in that horrific memory by their own frozen wills, too frightened to venture out of the house into sunflower country. Like the closed circle of *The Glass Menagerie*, these loving siblings share the memories of their tormented parents. They cannot agree on the actual facts of their parents' violent deaths. They believe that the father murdered the mother and then killed himself. To get the insurance money, however, they must insist that their mother was the one who performed the murder and then the suicide. Apparently, the insurance company refuses to accept their story and will not pay an award from the father's life insurance in the case of his suicide.

As they try to remember, they also try to reach outside of the house. They consider going to the store for groceries, to telephone from a neighbor's house, to seek consideration from the insurance company. Each effort proves futile, as they are frozen into inactivity. Even a double-suicide effort, suggested by the revolver on the table, is not a real option. This paralysis of will fixes them in the circular pattern, allowing them to recapitulate events of the past but not to break out of their self-imposed prison. The play ends with the fantastic return to the acting of the play-within-the-play, circling once again into the cavern of their tormented family and their own love for one another. They take off their coats, warmed by the imagination, and the play commences once again.

Williams had worked before with indeterminate endings, allowing us to decide whether Brick would actually change or Maggie have a child. He had left us to wonder what would happen to the fragile Laura and her heroic mother. This, nonetheless, is far more stark in its insistence that nothing will change. This time, Williams lays bare his mode of creation as the structure of the play, from the idea, through the conversation with the actors to the details of production, to the audience and critics' response. He also shows that for those in the theatre, the process never stops: it is invariably another opening, another show.

CHARACTER DEVELOPMENT

Two characters carry this whole play. Williams had used the two-character format frequently in his short plays, but this is his only long work reduced to such bare bones. Felice and Clare, a brother and sister, both have long hair and androgynous characteristics. Felice, the brother, seems to be a bit more forceful and creative, somewhat more masculine. Clare, the sister, is the more passive, more frightened, and more feminine. She has her moments of rebellion but for the most part follows her brother's lead. They appear to have lived a single life and be destined to a single fate.

The deep love that binds these misfits to one another is a clear reflection of the near incestuous love Williams and his sister shared. Rose's letters to Tom and his to her in their teen years were surprisingly flirtatious. None of their romantic interests seemed to match the close camaraderie that they shared, although Williams explicitly denied any actual incestuous activity between the two of them. This play is not about their sexuality in any open way. Only the symbol of the gun, which they cannot use, suggests that sexual feelings hover over their tormented closeness. Their repression blocks them from enjoying the splendor of the enormous sunflowers of sexual delight that grow just outside their windows.

The play presents this pair as penniless paranoiacs, trying to come to grips with their past and find a way to live through another day. Their isolation from the rest of the world has become their destiny. They find that they have the imagination to escape but not the will. Williams had spoken of this failure of will in his notes on *Cat on a Hot Tin Roof*, in which he insisted that Brick's "paralysis of will" was at the root of his tragedy (*Theatre, Vol. 3*, 168). In 1970, in a one-act play he called "The Frosted Glass Coffin" (*Theatre, Vol. 7*, 197–214), Williams presented the same paradigm, including the house/prison, with characters reduced to the names "One" and "Two." This explains in part the absence of individualizing traits and personal histories that we see in *The Two-Character Play*. Felice and Clare are intended to be types of misfits, prisoners of their own fear. When confronted with a challenge, Clare pops another pill into her mouth, rendering her somewhat more vague. Escape is possible only through mental, not through physical action.

Williams insists that day-to-day life under these circumstances is heroic. It takes more courage for a frightened person to survive with such fear than for the strong person to undertake great voyages. Once again, the author employs the imagery of the old nursery tale "Jack and the Beanstalk." Like Chance in *Sweet Bird of Youth*, these two are like Jack climbing out of the world of cows and beans into Beanstalk Country, facing giants who threaten children with ovens. For them, the ogres are both the parents and the neighbors. Like *The Glass Menagerie*, this play is clearly based on the Williams family's life in St. Louis, where neither of the Williams children felt comfortable with their parents or with the community. Turning to one another for creature comfort, they huddled together against the outside world, unnaturally close in their powerful love, which became for both their emotional core of being.

The violence of these parents, remembered by Felice and Clare, is pictured here as a murder and suicide. It was actually sexual in the real life of the Williams marriage. The mother was so puritanical and frigid that she screamed during the act of sex. The father, a robust masculine man, found himself despised and excluded. He would break out in rage, frustrated and humiliated, disappearing for nights of poker and drinking. In this late companion play, *The Two-Character Play*, the father is presented in dim recollections of happy times at the seashore, but this background is clouded by images of rage and violence. The mother thwarts the father's delight in the water and the children by carping about the cost of the vacation. The mother and father, though central to the story, are present only in the warped memories of their offspring. Their story is reduced to the house, a prison, the furnishings, an old shirt, and a revolver hidden under the papers on the stage.

Other characters are hinted at: we know there is a grocery man, who poses a threat to them because of their debt; there are neighbors, who might inquire into their affairs; and there are social workers, who want to intrude on their privacy. A whole system that includes insurance men, ministers, and other outsiders lurks outside of their claustrophobic setting. None of them is allowed to step through the door.

This reductive pattern produces a minimalist drama—not simple, but intensely simplified. The subtle differences between the characters, their inability to display emotions beyond fear and love, their narrow circumstances and frozen attitudes make these roles a challenge to all but the most talented actors. Williams himself finally came to realize that only remarkably talented and well-seasoned actors could perform these roles satisfactorily. Young actors could look right for the parts, but they could not bring out the full range of intensity banked up in these radically flattened figures.

THEMATIC ISSUES

The Two-Character Play sums up several of Tennessee Williams' recurrent themes, which derive primarily from his experience as a son, brother, artist, and seeker. They include the view that marriage is a form of warfare, the close encounter in the eternal battle of the sexes; that "homes" are built too often on the shaky foundation of materialism; that the individual must excape from the prison of family love in order to beome a creative artist; that the demand for such freedom is necessarily cruel; and that the result of winning is painful loneliness.

As the son of incredibly destructive parents, he spent his lifetime studying the scars of old household wounds. His mother's and father's continuing marital battle convinced him that love between a man and a woman was impossible, that sexuality was essentially a form of deadly conflict. His mother's revulsion at sex convinced him that the phallus was a weapon used to inflict pain in the guise of love. From her manipulation of others to achieve her inflexible will, he came to believe that the female only appeared to be weaker than the man but was actually the stronger, the more practical, and by far the more subtle. In explaining this torturous dynamic of heterosexual relationships, he insisted that—as playwright Strindberg said—"They call it love-hatred, and it hails from the pit" (*Where I Live* 1978, 73).

In *The Two-Character Play*, this dynamic is summarized in the children's shared memory of the seashore vacation, where the father joins the children in a time of freedom and fun, while the mother poisons the atmosphere. The children recall that the mother refused to stay at the Lorelei on the beach, but insisted that they stay at the Hotel Commerce instead. She would hover over the happy father until he would shout, "Go back to the Hotel Commerce, continue your mathematical talk with the cashier, subtract, divide if you can, but don't multiply, and don't stay here in the sun, it disagrees with you" (*Theatre, Vol. 5,* 333–34). The happy memories of racing down the beach in the sun, tearing off their suits, being carried into the water on the father's golden shoulders, learning to swim are suddenly interrupted. The recollection of freedom shifts to an awareness of others, a self-conscious concern with proper behavior, ending with the settling back into the prison of self. From the preceding dialogue, we assume that this obsessive concern with propriety derives from the dead hand of the mother.

For Williams, this cruel calculation and restriction of the mother are by-products of puritanical hatred of the flesh. For her, niceness was more important than pleasure; appearance took precedence over joy. The metaphor of commercial calculations—not including multiplication, which would be enriching—encapsulates her mind-set. The contrary generous nature of the flesh-loving husband becomes fearful to the growing children, who are tormented by the sunflowers growing outside the window. They study the worn figure of the rose on the carpet, but cannot bear to gaze on the dazzling gold of the sunflower.

Williams referred to himself as a "rebellious Puritan." In his painfully different parents, he experienced the conflict between the flesh and the spirit, the body and the soul. In *Summer and Smoke*, he demonstrated this conflict in the lesson of the anatomy chart. He spoke of it as the duality between Cavalier and Puritan within his own heritage. From beginning to end, it was his central theme. (For a book-length study of this idea, see Tishchler 1961).

For such a battle between the sexes, the ultimate conclusion must be violent. In *Cat on a Hot Tin Roof,* the ending could be gentle because one of the armies refused to fight. Brick chose to capitulate to Maggie's continued storming of his will. As Williams says of Brick, "Of course, now that he has really resigned from life, retired from competition, her anxious voice, strident with the heat of combat, is unpleasantly, sometimes even odiously, disturbing to him." Even so, he will return to her as a "devoted slave" (*Where I Live*, 73). A similar surrender by the male marks the "happy" ending of *The Night of the Iguana*, when Shannon is overpowered by Maxine's smothering love, but such a reconciliation is not always possible. As we saw in *Sweet Bird of Youth*, a male may be willing to resist the predatory female to his death.

The violent ending of the marriage is inevitable. The brother's and sister's confusion about the murder-suicide is their means of participating in and trying to comprehend this violence. The female both invites and endures the violence, in which the male expresses his anger and frustration. The mutually assured destruction of this marital warfare is neatly summarized in the confused act of murder and suicide that leaves the children as the final victims.

The play also lays bare the tormented theme of sibling love. Williams loved his sister Rose more fiercely and tenderly than he ever loved any other human being. As in his quote from the Song of Solomon, he saw her as a "garden enclosed," not only because of her forbidden sexuality but also because the petals of her mind closed during the early years of her adolescence, leaving her permanently cut off from him. He came to see this sibling relationship as both love and imprisonment. The incest taboo restricted any sexual expression, yet the intense closeness of the pair was akin to the "one flesh" paradigm of marriage. Their beautiful and fragile shared memories are transformed over time into a nightmare. So also is their exclusive love turning into a grotesque "home" that blocks both their escape from one another's love and walls them away from other relationships.

In the play, brother and sister can neither leave the house nor open the door to others. They can finish one another's sentences, but they cannot move outside of this circular pattern of thought, operating as a closed loop in their brains. The monster sunflowers are constantly a part of their awareness. They speak of the flowers that glisten in the sunlight, growing ever larger.

Far gentler by nature than their parents, mirror images of one another, they cannot approach or attack one another in the destructive way their parents did. Although they are aware of the phallic gun that their parents used, they continue to hide it. Williams noted in *Memoirs* that he and Rose were quite shy with one another physically. This reticence is reflected in *The Two-Character Play*. They will never be able to approach the other in the violence of sexuality, nor will they be able to attack one another. The gun, though always present, will never be an instrument they can use on one another.

Even more than a twisted member of a tormented family, Williams was also an essential and exclusive artist. The play speaks eloquently of this lifelong obsession with art and life. From his early youth, he saw himself as basically different from other people. Like Shelley, he believed that the artist was more sensitive, more delicately attuned to the world. Although a reader who relished the creativity of others, he invariably found his true subject of art to be his own experience. *The Two-Character Play* lays bare the process of rethinking relationships and events in a quest for truth. At the same time, the characters are trying to shape those memories into art. They find that facts break through the imaginary dialogue, leading them off into real-life interruptions, reevaluations of the experiences, forcing them to reconsiderations of the expression of those memories. This circular recapitulation of words and ideas is an effort to find the precise means of reflecting the truth and determining that truth. As always, Williams is determined to capture in the "net of words" his individual experience of life. His theme is that truth is chameleon, not easily identified or put neatly into words.

He knows that the transformation of life into words is itself a distortion and a distillation. He knew that a cold objectivity crept into the artist as he fixed the past into an artistic shape. Trying to get Clare to memorize lines that are based on her own life, Felice recognizes the artificiality of the situation. He invites her to improvise but really wants to control the shaping of the play. He also realizes that they do not see or hear the same things, even though they share the same tiny world. In the end, one of their visions must dominate in order to produce an artifact, a play. This subtle discourse on shaping life experiences into art forms mirrors his lifelong concern.

Williams was also mesmerized by the performance aspect of play production. When he had come to the realization that his vocation lay in the theatre, he realized that his life's work finally depended on other people. It was they who would publish, produce, interpret, act, hear, and criticize his art. His words lay lifeless on the page until they were given vitality by a whole community of other people, most of whom would warp the meaning and change the tone. Yet the thrill of seeing audiences respond to his characters and his phrases compelled him to remain hard at work in the theatre. Although late in his life he saw audiences and critics abandon him, proclaiming him mad, he could not reciprocate by abandoning them. Instead he found he could not escape from his life sentence to imprisonment in the theatre, without parole. He could not stop writing without stopping living. Every morning, he sat down at his typewriter and tried once again to put the words on the page that would explain to himself and to the world the nature of his own experience. As he proclaimed, *work* was always his favorite "four letter word" (*Memoirs*, 241).

At the center of the stage in *The Two-Character Play*, as at the center of Tennessee Williams' life, was the dark specter of fear—a haunting, ever present fear. He was uttering an outcry from his heart when he revealed the madness that he and his sister shared and the fear that they overcame daily. Their courage was their most heroic quality. For Williams, the playwright must be a kind of Sisyphus, the existential hero, who can't die, can't escape, can't succeed for long, but also can't stop trying. Reality itself becomes a terrifying circle of effort to understand in the midst of madness.

STYLISTIC AND LITERARY DEVICES

Much has been made by critics of the parallels between *The Glass Menagerie* and *The Two-Character Play*, which sometimes have been played in tandem. (Lyle Leverich's troupe was working on the two productions when he first met Tennessee Williams.) Certainly the plays share the brother-sister love, the love-hate relationship to the parents, the home-as-prison, and the haunting specter of madness.

A number of critics have also noticed Williams' reference to the playwright Pirandello in the opening comments, pointing us to the parallels between this play and *Six Characters in Search of an Author*. In both cases, the play is being written as it is being played, emphasizing the process of creativity. In the "Production Notes" to *The Glass Menagerie*, Williams had told us that he had no interest in the nineteenth-century fourth-wall convention. He was eager to discover a deeper reality by destroying this artificial pretense of reality: "Everyone should know nowadays the unimportance of the photographic in art: that truth, life, or reality is an organic thing which the poetic imagination can represent or suggest, in essence, only through transformation, through changing into other forms than those which were merely present in appearance" (*Theatre, Vol. 1*, 131).

Truth, for the expressionist, lies within the mind not in the outside world with its real refrigerator with its actual ice cubes, "the exhausted theatre of realistic conventions" that Williams dubbed it (131). Pirandello had made a similar point in his plays, forcing people to go beyond the futile search for truth in the facts, discovering it instead in lived situations, actual experiences. We never really know what happened to the parents in *The Two-Character Play* (the facts), but we can learn something of the dynamics of their love/hate relationship, the impact of their pitched battles on these perennial children, and the symbolic deaths they inflicted on one another and on themselves (the truth). It is not clear whether the father was, as a matter of fact, an astrologer. We know that he lives in the minds of his children in this role.

For the purpose of forcing the audience to acknowledge the artificiality of the scene before them, to recognize from the beginning of the play that they are witnessing a play, rather than true life, Williams presents us with a disordered stage. Most educated audiences, studying the stage not yet ready for performance, cluttered with the accidental props, would think of the very theatrical devices of such authors as Thornton Wilder and Bertold Brecht, who also insisted on denying the material level of reality. These are antinaturalistic techniques designed to force the audience to study the play's meaning by entering into the artist's mind.

In this case, Williams is providing us the experience of deconstructed experience, rather like his own excursions into himself through psychotherapy. By tearing apart the play and putting it back together again, he reveals something of his own creative process. Williams was a writer who constantly rewrote his plays, not simply revising, but redrafting whole sections. He admitted that it was a wasteful process; but when he had an idea, he was forced to take it through a complete cycle. Most of his more powerful stories appear in a variety of forms (as poems, essays, one-act sketches, and full-length plays), and they all exist in numerous draft forms. This play, for example, has at least three distinct scripts, with at least two different names. Even after a play was on the stage, Williams continued to revise and rewrite it—to the distress of actors and directors.

Because his plays were so intensely personal, and because he was striving so frantically to describe his inner reality to an audience that might well prove as unsympathetic as the one characterized in *The Two-Character Play*, he tried every possible strategy to communicate. Painfully aware that art is a collaboration, he knew that stagehands might misplace props, that designers might botch the lighting or costumes or sets, that actors might muff lines, emphasize the wrong points, or improvise. The whole process of communicating through this temporary collaboration of strangers is fragile at best.

This play, then, may be seen as a playwright's nightmare. Nothing is as it should be: not the sets, the curtains, the lights, the props, the actors, nor the audience. Since this is a nightmare scenario, almost everything may serve as a symbol. The putting on and taking off of coats signals the changing of persona, the entry into the play, and the exit from it. The name of the Southern scene, "New Bethesda," is an ironic place without healing. The sunflower, the Blakean symbol of sexuality, becomes a comic block shutting out the sunlight, its stems prison bars. The gun is a phallic, Freudian symbol of sexuality. Such flat symbolism is unusual for Williams, who tends to develop his symbols naturally out of the action. The comic-strip quality of these images, suitable for dreams, is part of the reductionist methodology of the play. (It reminds us of his other, more romantic dream-play, *Camino Real*.) Any student of Williams will easily discover the host of images that he has used in various of his other plays, and can easily see how much more flattened they have become in *The Two-Character Play*.

For example, his favorite and most frequently used symbol is the rose. Because of the two beloved Roses in his life, his sister and his grandmother, the name and the flower took on special significance for him. He had made so much of the variations on roses in *The Rose Tattoo* that he drove critics to distraction. We know from that play that he had derived the iconography of the rose from the medieval symbolism of the Rose of the Blessed and rose windows in cathedrals. He undoubtedly knew of the sexual symbolism of the *Roman de la Rose*, a famous medieval dream allegory that drew its references from the lavish sexual imagery of the Song of Solomon, a part of scripture that embarrasses many prim Christians. As previously noted, in *The Two-Character Play*, Williams quotes the key verse from this epithalamion, or wedding song—"my sister a garden enclosed is." This reference equates virginity with a walled garden. The rose becomes a female sex symbol, while remaining a religious symbol. This curious blending of religion and sexuality is typical of medieval chivalric literature and continued into the seventeenth-century Metaphysicals. Without seeking to sound like a scholar or to make a big display of his rich literary background, Williams simply touches on the imagery from this tradition. Those who can resonate to it do, those who can't may yet understand that the sister's problem is her frustrating and culturally-determined virginity. In *The Two-Character Play*, the rose design is in the carpet, a focus for the eyes of the actors, though probably not visible to the audience. If we notice their reference to the design on which they are fixated, we respond only to their awareness of the rose symbolism, seeing it as a gentle symbol of the frustrated love of these siblings, who pant for one another.

The astrological signs all through the play remind us that they are star-crossed lovers, doomed to be separated because they are brother and sister. As far back as *Streetcar*, Williams had displayed some interest in the influence of the stars on human character and conduct. Blanche asks Stanley his sign of the zodiac and then comments on his being born under the sign of the Goat. He of course responds by demanding to know hers and snorts in laughter when she asserts she was born under the sign of the Virgin (*Theatre, Vol. 1, Streetcar*, 328–29). In *The Two-Character Play*, the zodiac shirt and the references to the zodiac in connection with the father, who was an accomplished reader of astrological signs, lead us to believe that Williams is commenting on fate. As T. S. Eliot had slyly noted in *The Waste Land*, the psychic has replaced the priest for many moderns. We are inclined to consult Madam Sosistrotis and her deck of tarot cards rather than go to church, preferring the daily horoscope to the Bible. These poor superannuated children that haunt Tennessee Williams belong to no community of faith. They are doomed by their birth in this tragic family to be what they are, to do what they do. They ritually act out their assigned roles in a universe they don't understand.

Complementing this sense of isolation and meaninglessness is the telephone, which brings enigmatic messages and may even be disconnected. This echoes Kafka's *Castle*, in which the phones are not used for communication but as sources of frustration and confusion. Doors, windows, mailmen, telephones are all indicators that man is not alone, that he is part of a larger community. Yet for Felice and Clare, none of these really invites escape from the confinement of the haunted home.

Mr. Grossman, the grocer, serves a purpose much like the grocer in *The Glass Menagerie*—a frightening outsider who is necessary for survival, but who demands payment or at least communication. Just as Laura was terrified then, so her is Clare frozen in the face of such a challenge. He is an emissary of that world beyond the house that involves lawyers, neighbors, social workers, and ministers, none of whom the siblings trust. His name, like theirs, is symbolic of his nature. His "grossness" is balanced with their "de voto"—votive quality. While he counts money in his office, they blow soap bubbles out the windows into the sunflowers, like Laura's glass menagerie, an image of beauty and evanescence.

Taking this symbol as an example, we may judge the radically simplified mode of Williams' expression in this late play. For Laura's menagerie, the delicacy was balanced by its naturalness as an expression of her. It was her image, but it also constituted her obsessive activity, the center of her days. The unicorn, her favorite, is doomed to be broken. Yet we know that the broken unicorn is only a crippled anachronism, not a freshly created horse. The symbolism is complex and organic to the dramatic action and characterization.

In the case of the soap bubbles, they are introduced with little explanation. The props are mentioned early in the play; they provide a moment of activity in a basically static play, and they are handy symbols of childhood. Yet they have no deep dramatic rooting in the drama. They are useful images, but not fully developed or richly evocative. If we miss them in our concern for the painful blockage of these characters, we have missed little. In *The Two-Character Play*, the symbols lack the natural quality of his earlier works; they are not fully explored or exploited; they also seem to lack his old affection for his own lyrical bits of stage business. Williams' stage has now grown bleak and chill.

The language is as circular as the plot, with the siblings reciting a script and studying it for errors at the same time. As they return again and again to the phrases, they struggle to get them right. Working together as two parts of a single mind, they find it essential to complete one another's thoughts. Rather than using the Renaissance device of stichomythia, in which characters indulge in line-for-line verbal fencing, Williams breaks lines and thoughts in half, allowing one character to start a line and the other to finish it. This use of "unfinished sentences" reflects the increasing sense that words do not fully express thoughts or experience. They are as clumsy as the stage props and as fragile as the soap bubbles. For genuine communication, words are both necessary and useless, inadequate tools for breaking through to one another.

Over and over Williams had puzzled over the need to cast a "net of words" to capture a moment of truth. For him, human experience was far too much of a mystery to be reduced to the ink on the printed page. Pauses in the midst of sentences can convey something of the inability of the speaker to communicate, repeated phrases with slight changes can mirror the mind's wrestling with the objective means for expressing the inexpressible. This play lays bare the playwright's perennial struggle.

The Two-Character Play was a labor of love. For years he fretted over this final "out cry" to the audiences who had deserted him. For one last time, he wanted to show something of his life to the audience that was deserting him. He kept returning to it, while writing other plays of varying length, hoping that the stars and the planets would finally prove favorable to one final moment of communication and love.

ALTERNATE CRITICAL PERSPECTIVE: PSYCHOLOGICAL CRITICISM

In their impressive survey of critical approaches, *Theory of Literature*, René Welleck and Austin Warren said that the term "psychology of literature" might mean any one of a number of things—the psychology of the writer, a study of the creative process, a study of the psychological types and laws in works, or the effect of literature upon readers (1956, 81). Any of these approaches might well work with Tennessee Williams, but the one that is probably most useful for *The Two-Character Play* is the study of the writer himself and his relationship to the psychological types he presents in this particular play.

At the time he was working on *The Two-Character Play*, Williams was recovering from the series of personal tragedies and problems mentioned earlier. His world was now sadly depleted. His mother, that old beloved irritant, gradually lost her mind long before she died in 1980 , reminding him during these final tormented years of the recurring madness that he claimed to exist on both sides of his family. (He was known to insist that he was the only sane one of the bunch.) Of course, Rose, though still alive (even outliving him by some years), was dead to him as the lively playmate who had enriched his childhood. This painful loss of Frank Merlo and Audrey Wood had left him the troubled center of a lonely crowd.

In 1969, when he had became increasingly self-destructive, his brother had him committed to the psychiatric ward at Barnes Hospital in St. Louis, where he was unceremoniously deprived of his stockpile of pills and alcohol. By this time, he was addicted to a host of uppers and downers, was on amphetamines, and other medications, which apparently had an appalling synergistic effect. The radical "drying out" of his system brought on a seizure he thought to be a heart attack. In the recovery period that followed, he lashed out at his brother for forcing this on him. He also began to understand the dangers of his various addictions, which had cost him a "lost" decade. Looking back at the 1960s, he called them his "stoned age."

In the final years after this near-death experience, he turned against his brother and wrote him out of his will. He still had people around him but no one that he believed loved him for himself. The last years of his life, until his death in 1983, saw a less violent Williams. He continued to drink, to wander from place to place, to forget appointments and disappoint hosts, but he was more meditative. A kind of senile paranoia set in, making him lash out occasionally at one person after another, alienating his few remaining friends and business associates. He was rich and famous enough to coast through these final years, but not content to sit in a corner and snarl. He was determined to produce some kind of final masterwork—and he was certain this would be *Out Cry*.

The Two-Character Play or *Out Cry* was Williams' final consummate effort. He did work on other plays, poems, and stories during the last two decades of his life, but he placed his hopes on this creation. Given the loving attention he lavished on the multiple drafts of the several scripts for different productions, we can use the play as a mirror of his mind during this period. It is an ideal document for summing up the artist-as-an-old-man, perfectly suited for psychological criticism.

This form of literary criticism has always proven a tempting approach to Williams' works, in spite of obvious problems in the adequacy of the literary critic untrained in psychological methodology and the limitations in our ability to know the author, who hides as much as he reveals. After all, the psychology under consideration here is that of a man no longer available to us, approachable only through his works, which themselves have been shaped and filtered to produce certain deliberate results. Furthermore, this is an author who had read a great deal about psychology, who deliberately included symbols and dreams in his writing, who spent time in analysis himself. It is unlikely that he included many inadvertent elements in these carefully scripted versions of the play. Not specialists in analysis, we must acknowledge from the outset that this is a flawed and clumsy critical approach, but tempting nonetheless.

Tennessee Williams invites our invasion of his privacy though his obsession with his own mental processes, his explorations of his own experience. He said a number of times that he considered his work a kind of psychotherapy. In *Memoirs*, he spoke openly of his time in analysis with Dr. Kubie (173), the troubling advice he received from him, and his concerns that his art might indeed have grown out of his "madness." From Plato to the present, many philosophers, artists, and psychologists have connected art with madness, some even believing that when inspired, the artist was in the throes of a kind of divine madness. As early as 1957, Williams had identified a developing tension inside him that was "verging on the psychotic" (*Where I Live,* 89). He came to believe that, at least for him, art and madness were inextricably united. Especially after watching the "cure" for his sister Rose, he knew that the peacefulness of a lobotomy was also a kind of hell-on-earth. His torment was an essential part of his creativity.

In *The Two-Character Play*, Williams carefully delineated two central characters who appear to be the two sides of his own psyche, his *animus* and *anima*. They are also images of Tom and Rose as younger people, with their shared terror of their parents' violent history and their timidity in the face of the outside world. Their bonds were so close that they could complete one another's thoughts, read one another's minds.

As Rose had slipped into madness, Tom often feared for his own sanity. He tried to imagine what she was going through, looking at the world through her eyes. Tom in *The Glass Menagerie* could not escape Laura. Tennessee could certainly not escape Rose, whose tragedy became the source of his success. This hideous guilt trailed behind him throughout his successful years, haunting him, forcing him to take her into himself, to experience her tragedy for himself.

This stretch to feel the pain of another increased his sensitivity to women. Williams spoke of the value of having the female within him, allowing him to understand the feminine point of view, to create living female characters. He attributed his sensitivity in part to his sexuality. As Coleridge had noted, the creative mind is itself androgynous, allowing the artist to explore a wider range of human experience than most people can.

Felice is easy to identify with Tennessee Williams. Like Williams, Felice is writing an autobiographical play, in which he is also playing a part, as Williams himself had done in *Small Craft Warnings*. This process of transforming memory into art and understanding becomes the main action line of the play. Although the Romantic is forced to discover his subject matter in his own experience, his objectification of the people in his life must perforce create considerable ambivalence within him. This is contradictory to the image of the sensitive artist. In Williams' case, basing his first real success on his sister's failure was the constant source of pain. In this story, the characters are seeking to profit from the violent end of their parents, shaping the truth to meet their own purposes. They know they cannot receive the life insurance money if their father killed himself, suicides being excluded from most policies. Thus, they are striving to shape their reality to their needs—an exigency for survival.

The play is a genuine effort to picture his own psyche with all its furniture. He had said that the real need in the world is self-knowledge. Although accused of "solipsism," he believed that this must start with each individual artist. He knew that this kind of brutal self-analysis was not the stuff of happy Broadway plays, but he could not cater to an audience that denied his vision of reality. He saw his as a "desperate vocation," one that required him to write his individual truth. He did not exaggerate his importance, he considered himself a "minor artist who has happened to write one or two major works" (92).

In *Out Cry*, the "home"—which is quite obviously also a theatre—is for Felice a haven and a prison. This home, also called a "house not meant to stand" in one of his late plays, was the construct of the family. The father and mother, their heritage of madness and violence, tradition and faith, their continuing war with one another, their destructive impact on their doomed children are at the center of this home. Their furious love-hate relationship permeates the walls, turning this cursed House of Williams into a kind of Greek myth. (The famous Hellenistic statue of Laocoon comes to mind, a baroque twisting of struggling, intertwined bodies, being punished by a cruel god for disobeying his arbitrary rules.)

The windows provide a view of an enclosed garden, with gigantic sunflowers that symbolize the sexuality that is in view but not in reach—a tantalizing image for these sibling lovers. Blocked from expression of their incestuous urges, the characters turn inward. Rather than breaking out the doors, running to neighbors and others for companionship and community, they make a world of two. The androgynous quality of the two siblings and their mirror identities lead to a path of narcissism; they find themselves in one another.

At the center of their world is the powerful, formless image of Fear. For Williams, it was the objective correlative of his blue devils, his spook. For Rose, it was her shadow. She wanted terribly to reach out to other people, to have boyfriends, to marry, but she was frozen in a kind of permanent infantilism. Young Tom had watched this hideous transformation from an imaginative child to a disfigured adult and feared for himself. She became the living image of what he would become without his art to save him.

Compared with this interior landscape, the furnishings of the outside world appear random and meaningless. Felice and Clare understand telephones and pianos, but they cannot use them effectively. The telephone is probably disconnected, the newspaper does not seem to have this day's news. Their clothing makes no sense—the father's shirt, a twisted tiara. Just as Williams himself was prone to use clothing as costume, sometimes appearing in white linen suits, sometimes in moth-eaten fur coats, sometimes in riding britches, so these figures use clothing in individualistic ways, expressions of their internal disorder, their lack of social awareness.

The dialogue is both real and constructed, just as his own language was. Williams would return again and again to conversations and letters and diary entries with the same compulsive need he displayed in his plays and poetry. He needed to get the phrasing right, to retrieve the idea for future use, to remember and polish the memory. It is fascinating to trace an image through all of Williams' work, to see the consistency of his usage. For example, in the reference to the rose that was explored earlier, we can also find it in an essay on the god of the theatre, Dionysus. His essay on "The Meaning of *The Rose Tattoo*" points to the "*rosa mystica*, the light on the bare golden flesh of a god whose back is turned to us or whose face is covered" (*Where I Live*, 56). In this quotation, it becomes clear that even the lighting is tied to a larger vision of the meaning of color that relates it to sexuality and mysticism. This is a man who explores all of human expression in an endless attempt to understand and express himself. His plays and his life were largely concerned with this effort to comprehend the mysteries of the self and the others who touch that self.

The Two-Character Play is a perfect work to sum up Williams because it reflects perfectly his vision of the world. In "The World I Live In," an interview between Williams and Williams, he insists that his plays mirror the world. He never finished his plays because to put the period to them was to destroy their life; they were alive for him, and he lived his most vibrant life in them. They were the finest part of him, the only way he could stay alive.

"Home" for him was the theatre. He was nothing if he was not a playwright. His subject was always himself and his family—the dynamics of those tortured relationships.

Bibliographical Essay

The Lively World of Williams Scholarship

Tennessee Williams has become an American classic. Even during his lifetime, he found that theatregoers were recalling the early days when he and Arthur Miller shared the laurels of Broadway as the golden age of American theatre. On November 7, 1999, Ben Brantley wrote a summary of the century of American theatre, which he called "Broadway Doesn't Live There Anymore," (in the *New York Times* Arts and Leisure section). He noted that by the mid-1950s, "the burden of American drama rested mostly on the shoulders of two men, Tennessee Williams and Arthur Miller." In the remaining years of the century, many of the successful plays have been derivative of Williams' work.

Since his death in 1983, there has been a blossoming of scholarship regarding Tennessee Williams' life and his works. In addition to a newsletter, a journal, and more recently a review that are all dedicated to the study of Williams, we also have Williams festivals quite regularly in New Orleans; Clarksdale, Mississippi; Williamstown, Massachusetts; and Hartford, Connecticut. Each of these festivals and the numerous special meetings that occur sporadically contribute still more articles and insights to the body of Williams scholarship.

In the bibliography that follows, I have included all editions of the plays published by New Directions, most of which were overseen by Williams himself in *The Theatre of Tennessee Williams* and in the separate volumes that have been produced recently. The page references in the text are all keyed to these volumes. I have not included the many variations and manuscripts that provide alternate phrasing, and sometimes alternate plots for the plays. At present, several scholars are studying the variant texts, the most impressive of them being Brian Parker, who has turned his attention to one after another of the major works. Within a few years, we will also have available even more editions of the early works, most of which have never before been published. All of these are new to most of the theatre public, and will probably be compiled in another volume in *The Theatre of Tennessee Williams* series. New Directions is also planning to publish a collection of his poetry, including numerous poems previously unpublished, which have been available heretofore only in obscure or out-of-print journals.

We are also in the process of discovering more accurate details about Williams' life. Lyle Leverich, who died at the end of 1999, was at work on volume 2 of his biography, which was planned to follow the highly acclaimed first volume, *Tom: The Unknown Tennessee Williams*. Leverich drew much of his material from correspondence and journals, which are also being edited and published in full. I am working with my coeditor Albert Devlin on the *Collected Letters of Tennessee Williams*, the first volume of which is to be published in the fall of 2000.[1] Margaret Thornton is currently editing the journals. These resources will make the study of Williams' life and works even more lively in the future—and more accurate.

Each year, we also see the publication of new collections of essays. Greenwood has recently published *Tennessee Williams: A Guide to Research and Performance*; Cambridge Press published *The Cambridge Companion to Tennessee Williams*. Others are currently at press. There are also studies of individual plays, of the reviews, and of course bibliographies of Williams scholarship and works.

The large collections at Columbia University, Harvard, and the Harry Ransom Humanities Research Center at the University of Texas, Austin, are rich repositories of scholarly and artistic opportunities. Recently, the discovery of the manuscript of *Not About Nightingales* was the beginning of a theatrical adventure that ended with a Tony award for its Broadway production.

In the near future, Richard Leavitt plans to publish another pictorial study of Williams' world, supplementing his earlier collection. We have recently seen two television programs on Williams; though they plowed no new ground, their very creation is testimony to his continuing popularity. Thousands of pictures lie in files, waiting to be discovered and used by imaginative historians of film and theatre.

I see no evidence that this interest in Tennessee Williams will diminish. From the time, as a young graduate student, I undertook to write the first Williams dissertation, *Patterns of Imagery in the Major Plays of Tennessee Williams* in 1957, to this work, which will be my last scholarly activity of one century and my first of another, I have found something new with each reading. To my everlasting delight, I have also discovered that my favorite playwright continues to resonate with others, both scholars and theatre lovers. He deserves to be called the greatest American playwright.

NOTE

1. Manuscripts of Williams' letters reside in a variety of places, including The Billy Rose Theatre Collection, The New York Public Library, at Lincoln Center; Columbia University Rare Books, Butler Library, New York City; Harvard Theatre Collection, Cambridge, Massachusetts; and The Harry Ransom Humanities Research Center, The University of Texas at Austin.

Bibliography

WORKS BY TENNESSEE WILLIAMS

PLAYS

The Theatre of Tennessee Williams, Vol. 1: Battle of Angels, A Streetcar Named Desire, The Glass Menagerie. New York: New Directions, 1971.

The Theatre of Tennessee Williams, Vol. 2: The Eccentricities of a Nightingale, Summer and Smoke, The Rose Tattoo, Camino Real. New York: New Directions, 1971.

The Theatre of Tennessee Williams, Vol. 3: Cat on a Hot Tin Roof, Orpheus Descending, Suddenly Last Summer. New York: New Directions, 1971.

The Theatre of Tennessee Williams, Vol. 4: Sweet Bird of Youth, Period of Adjustment, The Night of the Iguana. New York: New Directions, 1971.

The Theatre of Tennessee Williams, Vol. 5: The Milk Train Doesn't Stop Here Anymore, Kingdom of Earth, Small Craft Warnings, The Two-Character Play. New York: New Directions, 1976.

The Theatre of Tennessee Williams, Vol. 6: Twenty-Seven Wagons Full of Cotton and Other Short Plays. New York: New Directions, 1981.

The Theatre of Tennessee Williams, Vol. 7: In The Bar of a Tokyo Hotel and Other Stories. New York: New Directions, 1981.

The Theatre of Tennessee Williams, Vol. 8: Vieux Carré, A Lovely Sunday for Creve Coeur, Clothes for a Summer Hotel, The Red Devil Battery Sign. New York: New Directions, 1992.

Not About Nightingales, ed. Allean Hale. New York: New Directions, 1998.

The Notebook of Trigorin: A Free Adaptation of Anton Chekhov's "The Sea Gull," ed. Allean Hale. New York: New Directions, 1997.
Something Cloudy, Something Clear. New York: New Directions, 1995.
Spring Storm, ed. Dan Isaac. New York: New Directions, 1999.

POETRY

Androgyne, Mon Amour. New York: New Directions, 1977.
In the Winter of Cities: Poems by Tennessee Williams. New York: New Directions, 1956.

PROSE

Memoirs. Garden City, New York: Doubleday and Company, 1975.
Moise and the World of Reason. New York: New Directions, 1975.
The Roman Spring of Mrs. Stone. New York: New Directions, 1950.
Tennessee Williams: Collected Stories. New York: New Directions, 1985.
Where I Live: Selected Essays, ed., Christine R. Day and Bob Woods. New York: New Directions, 1978.

INTERVIEWS AND LETTERS

Devlin, Albert J. *Conversations with Tennessee Williams.* Jackson: University Press of Mississippi, 1986.
Five O'Clock Angel: Letters of Tennessee Williams to Maria St. Just, 1948–1982. New York: Alfred A. Knopf, 1990.
Letter to Audrey Wood, 12/43. In *Selected Letters of Tennessee Williams,* vol. 1 (1920–1945), ed. Albert J. Devlin and Nancy M. Tischler. New York: New Directions, 2000.
Letter to Audrey Wood, 2/23/45, from Chicago. In *Selected Letters of Tennessee Williams,* vol. (1920–1945), ed. Albert J. Devlin and Nancy M. Tischler. New York: New Directions, 2000.
Letter to Audrey Wood, 2/18/46. Unpublished. Harry Ransom Humanities Research Center, Austin, TX.
Letter to Cheryl Crawford, 2/10/52. Unpublished. The Billy Rose Theatre Collection, Lincoln Center, New York Public Library.
Selected Letters of Tennessee Williams, Vol. 1 (1920–1945), ed. Albert J. Devlin and Nancy M. Tischler. New York: New Directions, 2000.
Tennessee Williams' Letters to Donald Windham, 1940–1965, ed. Donald Windham. Athens: University of Georgia Press, 1996.

BIOGRAPHIES

Hayman, Ronald. *Tennessee Williams: Everyone Else Is an Audience*. New Haven: Yale University Press, 1993.

Leavitt, Richard. *The World of Tennessee Williams*. New York: Putnam's, 1978.

Leverich, Lyle. *Tom: The Unknown Tennessee Williams*, Vol. 1. New York: Crown, 1995.

Spoto, Donald. *The Kindness of Strangers: The Life of Tennessee Williams*. Boston: Little, Brown, 1985.

Williams, Dakin, and Shepherd Mead. *Tennessee Williams: An Intimate Biography*. New York: Arbor House, 1983.

Williams, Edwina Dakin, and Lucy Freeman. *Remember Me to Tom*. New York: Putnam's, 1963.

THE GLASS MENAGERIE

REVIEWS

Cassidy, Claudia, "Fragile Drama Holds Theater in Tight Spell." *Chicago Tribune*, 27 December 1944: 11.

Hewes, Henry. "Helen of Sparta." *Saturday Review*, 8 December 1956: 29. (Review of revival).

Krutch, Joseph Wood. Review in Drama Section. *Nation*, 14 April 1945: 424–25.

CRITICISM

Bloom, Harold, ed. *Modern Critical Interpretations: Tennessee Williams's* The Glass Menagerie. New York: Chelsea House Publishers, 1988.

Hale, Allean. "Tennessee Williams's St. Louis Blues." *Mississippi Quarterly* 48:4 (Fall 1995): 609–25.

Mielziner, Jo. *Designing for the Theatre: A Memoir and a Portfolio*. New York: Bramhall, 1965.

Parker, R. B., ed. *Twentieth Century Interpretations of* The Glass Managerie. Englewood Cliffs, N.J.: Prentice-Hall, 1983.

A STREETCAR NAMED DESIRE

REVIEWS

Atkinson, Brooks. "*Streetcar* Tragedy: Mr. Williams' Report on Life in New Orleans." *New York Times*, 14 December 1947, sec. 2:3.

Brustein, Robert. "Williams's Nebulous Nightmare." *Hudson Review* 12 (Summer 1959): 155–160.

Gibbs, Wolcott. "Two Views of the South." *New Yorker*, 25 February 1956: 90, 92–93.

Krutch, Joseph Wood. Drama Review. *Nation*, 20 December 1947: 686–687.

Watts, Richard, Jr. "*Streetcar Named Desire* Is Striking Drama." *New York Times*, 4 December 1947: 43.

CRITICISM

Adler, Thomas P. A Streetcar Named Desire: *The Moth and the Lantern*. Boston: Twayne, 1990.

Bloom, Harold, ed. *Tennessee Williams's* A Streetcar Named Desire. New York: Chelsea, 1988.

Chesler, S. Alan. "*A Streetcar Named Desire*: Twenty-Five Years of Criticism." *Notes on Mississippi Writers* 7 (1974): 44–53.

Holditch, W. Kenneth. "The Last Frontier of Bohemia: Tennessee Williams in New Orleans, 1938–83." *Southern Quarterly* 23 (Winter 1985): 1—37.

Hurrell, John D., ed. *Two Modern American Tragedies: Reviews and Criticism of* Death of a Salesman *and* A Streetcar Named Desire. New York: Scribner's, 1961.

Kazan, Elia. "Notebook for *A Streetcar Named Desire*," in *Directors on Directing: A Sourcebook of Modern Theatre*, ed. Toby Cole and Helen Krich Chinoy. Indianapolis: Bobbs Merrill, 1976.

Kolin, Philip C., ed. *Confronting Tennessee Williams'* A Streetcar Named Desire: *Essays in Critical Pluralism*. Westport, Conn.: Greenwood Press, 1993.

Miller, Jordan Y., ed. *Twentieth Century Interpretations of* A Streetcar Named Desire: *A Collection of Critical Essays*. Englewood Cliffs, N.J.: Prentice-Hall, 1971.

CAMINO REAL

REVIEWS

Clurman, Harold. Theatre Review. *Nation*, 4 April 1953: 293–294.

Crist, Judith. "Revival of *Camino Real* at St. Marks Playhouse." *New York Herald Tribune*, 17 May 1960: 22.

Gibbs, Wolcott. "Erewhon." *New Yorker*, March 28 1953: 69–70.

Hawkins, William. "Camino Real?—Just Enjoy It!" *New York World-Telegram*, 20 March 1953. 28.

Hewes, Henry. "Tennessee Williams–Last of Our Solid Gold Bohemians." *Saturday Review*, 28 March. 1953: 25–27.

Kerr, Walter F. "*Camino Real*." *New York Herald Tribune*, 20 March 1953: 12.

Nathan, George Jean. "Theatre." *Theatre Arts* 37 (June 1953): 88–89.

CRITICISM

Parker, Brian. "A Developmental Stemma for Drafts and Revisions of Tennessee Williams's *Camino Real.*" *Modern Drama* 39 (Summer 1996): 331–41.
———. "Documentary Sources for *Camino Real.*" *The Tennessee Williams Annual Review* 1 (1998): 41–51.

CAT ON A HOT TIN ROOF

REVIEWS

Atkinson, Brooks. "Tragedy to Scale." *New York Times,* 1 September. 1957, 2:1.
Kerr, Walter F. "A Secret Is Half-Told in Fountain of Words." *New York Herald Tribune,* 3 April 1955, 4:1.
Simon, John. "A Cat of Many Colors." *New York,* 12 August 1974: 48–49. (Revival).
Zolotow, Maurice. "The Season on and off Broadway." *Theatre Arts* 39.6 (1955): 22–23.

CRITICISM

Ganz, Arthur. "The Desperate Morality of the Plays of Tennessee Williams." *American Scholar* 31 (1962): 278–94.
Hale, Allean. "How a Tiger Became the Cat." *Tennessee Williams Literary Journal* 2.1 (1990–1991): 33–36.
Shackelford, Dean. "The Truth That Must Be Told: Gay Subjectivity, Homophobia, and Social History in *Cat on a Hot Tin Roof.*" *Tennessee Williams Annual Review* 1 (1998): 103–18.
Tischler, Nancy M. "On Creating *Cat.*" *Tennessee Williams Literary Journal* 2.2 (1991–92): 9–16.
Wilson, Edwin. "American Classics." *Wall Street Journal,* 26 March 1990: A6.
Winchell, Mark Royden. "Come Back to the Locker Room Ag'in, Brick Honey!" *Mississippi Quarterly* 48 (Fall 1995): 701–12.

SWEET BIRD OF YOUTH

REVIEWS

Aston, Frank. Review of *Sweet Bird of Youth. New York World-Telegram,* 11 March 1959: 30.
Atkinson, Brooks. Review of *Sweet Bird of Youth. New York Times,* 11 March 1959: 39.
Brustein, Robert. "Sweet Bird of Sucess." *Encounter* 12 (June 1959): 59–60.

Gassner, John. Review of *Sweet Bird of Youth*. *Educational Theatre Journal* 11 (May 1959): 122–24.

Hays, Peter. "Tennessee Williams's Use of Myth in *Sweet Bird of Youth*." *Educational Theatre Journal* 18 (October 1966): 255–258.

Kerr, Walter. Review of *Sweet Bird of Youth*. *New York Times*, 21 December 1975: 2.5. (Revival).

CRITICISM

Debusscher, Gilbert. "And the Sailor Turned into a Princess: New light on the Genesis of *Sweet Bird of Youth*." *Studies in American Drama, 1945–Present* 1 (1986): 25–31.

Gunn, Drewey Wayne. "The Troubled Flight of Tennessee Williams' *Sweet Bird*: From Manuscript through Published Texts." *Modern Drama*, 24 March 1981: 26–35.

Hays, Peter. "Tennessee Williams' Use of Myth in *Sweet Bird of Youth*." *Educational Theatre Journal* 18 (October 1966): 255–258.

THE NIGHT OF THE IGUANA

REVIEWS

Adler, Jacob H. "*Night of the Iguana*: A New Tennessee Williams?" *Ramparts* 1:3 (1962): 59–68.

Barnes, Clive. "God, Man & the Lizard." *New York Post*, 27 June 1988: 29.

Brustein, Robert. "A Little Night Music." *The New Republic*, 22 January 1962: 20, 22, 23.

Chapman, John. "Williams Is at His Poetic, Moving Best with *Night of the Iguana*." *New York Daily News*, 29 December 1961: 44.

McCarten, John. "Lonely, Loquacious, and Doomed." *New Yorker*, 13 January 1962: 61–62.

Simon, John. "*The Night of the Iguana*." *Theatre Arts* 46 (1962): 57.

CRITICISM

Adler, Thomas P. "The Search for God in the Plays of Tennessee Williams." *Renascence* 26 (1973): 48–56.

Matthews, Kevin. "The Evolution of *The Night of the Iguana*: Three Symbols in the Manuscript Record." *Library Chronicle of the University of Texas* 25:2 (1994): 67–89.

THE TWO-CHARACTER PLAY OR OUT CRY

REVIEWS

Clurman, Harold. "Theatre." *Nation* 216 (19 March 1973): 380.
Funke, Lewis. "Tennessee's 'Cry.' " *New York Times,* 3 December 1972, 2:1, 27.
Van Gelder, Lawrence. "Stage: Williams' '2 Character Play.' " *New York Times,* 22 August 1975: 16.

CRITICISM

Adler, Thomas P. "The Dialogue of Incompletion: Language in Tennessee Williams's Later Plays." *Quarterly Journal of Speech* 61 (February 1975): 48–58.
Devlin, Albert J. "The Later Career of Tennessee Williams." *Tennessee Williams Literary Journal* 1.2 (Winter 1989–90): 7–17.
Novick, Julius. "*Out Cry (Two-Character Play).*" *Village Voice,* 8 March 1973: 58.
Pagan, Nicholas O. "Tennessee Williams' Out Cry in the *Two-Character Play.*" *Notes on Mississippi Writers* 24.2 (1992): 67–79.

RELATED SECONDARY SOURCES

Arnott, Catherine M. *Tennessee Williams on File.* London: Methuen, 1985.
Bixby, C.W.E. *A Critical Introduction to Twentieth-Century American Drama.* Vol. 2. Cambridge: Cambridge University Press, 1984.
Boxill, Roger. *Tennessee Williams.* London: Macmillan, 1987.
Campbell, Joseph. *Hero with a Thousand Faces.* Cleveland: The World Publishing Company, 1956.
Cash, W. J. *The Mind of the South.* New York: Vintage Books, 1960.
Clum, John. *Acting Gay: Male Homosexuality in American Drama.* New York: Columbia University, 1992.
Crandell, George W. *The Critical Response to Tennessee Williams.* Westport, Conn.: Greenwood, 1996.
———. *Tennessee Williams: A Descriptive Bibliography.* Pittsburgh: University of Pittsburgh Press, 1995.
Dumas, Alexandre. *La Dame aux Camelias.* London: Oxford University Press, 1972.
Dollard, John. *Caste and Class in a Southern Town.* Garden City, New York: Doubleday & Co., Inc., 1949.
Falk, Signi Lenea. *Tennessee Williams.* 2d edition. Twayne's United States Author Series, 10. Boston: Twayne, 1978.
Ford, Christine. "If the Epigraph Fits. . . ." Unpublished paper. Scholars Panel, New Orleans Tennessee Williams Festival, March 24, 2000.
Frazer, James George, Sir. *The Golden Bough: A Study in Magic and Religion.* New York: The Macmillan Company, 1922.

Gunn, Drewey Wayne. *Tennessee Williams: A Bibliography.* 2d ed. Metuchen, N.J.: Scarecrow, 1991.

Hirsch, Foster. *A Portrait of the Artist: The Plays of Tennessee Williams.* Port Washington: Kennikat, 1979.

Hoffman, Frederick J. *Freudianism and the Literary Mind.* New York: Grove Press, Inc. 1945.

Jackson, Esther Merle. *The Broken World of Tennessee Williams.* Madison: University of Wisconsin Press, 1965.

Keats, John. *Poetical Works.* Oxford Standard Authors Series. London: Oxford University Press, 1960.

Kolin, Phillip C., ed. *Tennessee Williams: A Guide to Research and Performance.* Westport, Conn.: Greenwood Press, 1998.

———. *Confronting Tennessee Williams's* A Streetcar Named Desire: *Essays in Cultural Pluralism.* Westport, Conn.: Greenwood, 1993.

Leavitt, Richard F., ed. *The World of Tennessee Williams.* New York: Putnam's, 1978.

Martin, Robert, ed. *Critical Essays on Tennessee Williams.* New York: G. K. Hall, 1997.

Murphy, Brenda. *Tennessee Williams and Elia Kazan: A Collaboration in the Theatre.* Cambridge: Cambridge University Press, 1992.

Nelson, Benjamin, *Tennessee Williams: The Man and His Work.* New York: Oblensky, 1961.

O' Connor, Jacqueline. *Dramatizing Dementia: Madness in the Plays of Tennessee Williams.* Bowling Green, Ohio: Bowling Green State University Popular Press, 1997.

Pagan, Nicholas. *Rethinking Literary Biography: A Postmodern Approach to Tennessee Williams.* Rutherford, N.J.: Fairleigh Dickinson University Press, 1993.

Phillips, Gene D. *The Films of Tennessee Williams.* Philadelphia: Art Alliance, 1980.

Rose, H. J. *A Handbook of Greek Mythology.* New York: E. P. Dutton & Co., Inc., 1959.

Roudané, Matthew C. *The Cambridge Companion to Tennessee Williams.* Cambridge: Cambridge University Press, 1997.

Savran, David. *Communists, Cowboys, and Queers: The Politics of Masculinity in the Works of Arthur Miller and Tennessee Williams.* Minneapolis: University of Minnesota Press, 1992.

Schumach, Murray. *The Face on the Cutting Room Floor: The Story of Movie and Television Censorship.* New York: Morrow, 1964.

Stanton, Stephen S. *Tennessee Williams: A Collection of Critical Essays.* Twentieth Century Views. Englewood Cliffs: Prentice-Hall, 1977.

Tharpe, Jac, ed. *Tennessee Williams: A Tribute.* Jackson: University of Mississippi Press, 1977.

Thompson, Judith. *Tennessee Williams's Plays: Memory, Myth, and Symbol.* New York: Peter Lang, 1987.

Tischler, Nancy M. *Tennessee Williams: Rebellious Puritan.* New York: Citadel, 1961.

Welleck, Rene, and Austin Warren. *Theory of Literature*. New York: Harcourt, Brace & World, 1956.

Yacowar, Maurice. *Tennessee Williams and Film*. New York: Frederick Ungar Publishing Co., 1977.

Index

About the Author

NANCY M. TISCHLER wrote the first book-length study of Williams and his work, *Tennessee Williams: Rebellious Puritan*. Since then, while teaching at the George Washington University, Susquehanna University, and Pennsylvania State University, she has continued to write books and articles on this amazing playwright. Now retired from Penn State, Tischler continues her work on Williams, editing his letters for New Directions, and serving on boards of journals that focus on Williams. In addition, she has also written on other literary topics including modern drama, Black literature, the American South, Dorothy L. Sayers, and women and Scripture.